P9-DDM-096

Life Is Too Short

Life Is Too Short

MICKEY ROONEY

 VILLARD BOOKS NEW YORK 1991

Villard Books is a registered trademark of Random House, Inc.

Grateful acknowledgment is made to the following for
permission to reprint previously published material: THE NEW
YORK TIMES COMPANY: Excerpts from: Andre Sennwald's review
of *A Midsummer Night's Dream;* B. R. Crisler's review of
Stablemates; Walter Kerr's review of *Sugar Babies;* Vincent
Canby's comments on *The Black Stallion.* Copyright 1935, 1938
© 1979 by The New York Times Company. Reprinted by
permission. CPP/BELWIN, INC., AND INTERNATIONAL MUSIC
PUBLICATIONS: Excerpts from the lyrics of "Pal of My Cradle
Days" by Al Piantadosi and Marshall Montgomery. Copyright
1925 (renewed 1953) by Leo Feist, Inc. Rights assigned to EMI
Catalogue Partnership. All rights controlled and administered by
EMI Feist Catalog Inc. and EMI United Partnership Limited,
London WC2 HOEA. International copyright secured. Made in
U.S.A. All rights reserved. Reprinted by permission of
CPP/Belwin, Inc., and International Music Publications. RANDOM
HOUSE, INC.: Excerpt from "Under Which Lyre" from *W. H.
Auden: Collected Poems* by W. H. Auden. Copyright © 1976 by
Edward Mendelson, William Meredith and Monroe K. Spears,
Executors of the Estate of W. H. Auden. Reprinted by
permission of Random House, Inc. FILMS IN REVIEW: Filmography
of Mickey Rooney from June-July 1982 issue. Reprinted by
permission of *Films in Review,* New York.

Library of Congress Cataloging-in-Publication Data

Rooney, Mickey.
Life Is Too Short
p. cm.
ISBN 0-679-40195-4
1. Rooney, Mickey. 2. Actors—United States—Biography.
I. Title.
PN2287.R75A3 1991
791.43′028′092—dc20
[B]   90-50665

Manufactured in the United States of America
9 8 7 6 5 4 3 2
First Edition

To my God, my wife, and the world

Acknowledgments

I'd like to express my thanks to all who have helped me pull together the up-to-now scattered pieces of my story. To Robert Blair Kaiser, the friend and Rooney fan who pushed me to write, and to my oldest friends, Dick Paxton, Dick Winslow, Sig Frolich, Sidney Miller, Dr. Robert Buckley and his wife, Barbara, Bill Gardner, and Kevin Pawley, for helping me remember some things I had long forgotten. I thank Sterling Lord, the veteran literary agent, and his assistants Mark Melickian and Vikki Kriete, who shepherded this project through New York's literary canyons. I thank Peter Gethers, publisher and editorial director of Villard Books, for his faith in me and in my way of writing my story, and to his associate Stephanie Long, who helped keep me organized. I should also thank Gethers, Mitchell Ivers, Amy Edelman, and Jeff Smith for their deft editing (God knows how much I've needed editing), and to Heather Kilpatrick of Villard's legal department for performing what she called "a mild legal review." I must thank my do-everything office manager, Cindy Smith, and my lawyer, Richard Hoefflin, and his associate Elise Marylander, for seeing all the contracts through to a happy conclusion. My final thanks to my wife, Jan Chamberlin, whom I love with all my life and who spurred me to keep writing. "Millions of people," she said, "will love this story." Millions? I hope she is right. But that will be up to the people, won't it?

Contents

Life Is Too Short

☆ *1* ☆

Joe Yule, Jr.

I *was born on* September 23, 1920, on a dining-room table in a rooming house at 57 Willoughy Avenue in Brooklyn. I'm told I was delivered by a Chinese doctor, who patted me on the bottom and said, "Okay, kid, you've been resting for nine months. Now get to work."

Two weeks later, my mother, Nell Carter, bundled me up and followed my father, Joe Yule, out on the Columbia vaudeville circuit. They were both performing with Pat White's Gaiety Girls, my father a comic, my mother a chorus girl.

In the burlesque of those days, twelve tall girls danced in the back row, and twelve short girls danced in the front row. The tall girls were show girls. The short girls were ponies. Nell worked the end position, front row—end pony.

I know I have good genes—I've always had the energy level of an Olympic athlete—but I can't say I had much of what the gentler folk call "background."

My father, Joseph Ninian Yule, was born in Edinburgh, Scotland, came to this country when he was six with his mother and his younger brother, Jim, and grew up in a section of Brooklyn called Greenpoint (pronounced Greenpernt, which is slightly north of Williamsboig). His mother died shortly after they arrived in this land, so Joe and Jim took care of each other for most of their childhood.

In 1917, Joseph enlisted in the U.S. Army and did his duty during the war. When he came back from France, he haunted a New York stage door until he was hired on as a prop man for a touring vaudeville troupe called Jack Reid's Record Breakers.

My mother was born somewhere in Arkansas, orphaned at an early age along with her sister, Edna, and two brothers, Charlie and Harry. She left home at the age of fourteen to join a traveling show called "Miller's Maidens." The show was a combination of loud singing, minimal movement, bad costumes, one-night stands, and filthy living conditions. Nell earned a dollar a week.

She moved up in class (very slightly) by catching on with a vaudeville group called "Bobby Barkers," rambling along the dirt roads of Oklahoma and Kansas and Missouri, playing the smallest of small towns for several more years. She danced her way out of the sticks when she landed a job with—you guessed it—a burlesque troupe called Jack Reid's Record Breakers.

By then, she was making fourteen dollars a week, which wasn't bad money at the time. Shopgirls at S.S. Kresge's (now K mart) made about two dollars a week. But it was a lot less than top comics might be getting, even in the smaller towns, and it was hardly enough, considering that she'd been dancing professionally for almost nine years. But vaudevillians didn't have a union. They took what they got.

One story tells it. It's about Barney Ferguson, who had taken a lot of falls during his slapstick routines in the comedy team of Ferguson and Mack. He had grown quite deaf because of the ax-in-his-head routine that ended every show. Now, here was Barney, come to Chicago in 1912 and asking an agent named Doyle if he had any work. Doyle said, "I can send you to Cedar Rapids, Barney, but all I can give you is sixty dollars."

"Well," Barney said, "fifty dollars is better than nothing."

He went for fifty dollars.

On the other hand, the really big vaudeville stars made thousands because vaudeville was just about the only entertainment there was in the country then. Lillie Langtry, a singer who had been the mistress of King Edward VII, made her American debut in 1906 for one thousand dollars a week.

The people supported vaudeville (the word comes from the French *voix de ville*, meaning songs of the streets) because vaudeville was the theater of the masses, who couldn't seem to get enough of what vaudeville had: acrobats, tumblers and clowns, singers, dancers, comic storytellers, knockabouts, tramps, jugglers, mimes, blackface, hoboes, magic acts, tightwire acts, slackwire acts, mind readers, trick dogs and dancing chickens, bears who rode bicycles, contortionists, monologists, midgets, conjurers, female impersonators, harmonica boys, xylophonists, tank divers, weight lifters, sharpshooters, rope skippers, female boxers, fencers, ventriloquists, freaks, educated geese, female baritones, barbershop quartets, quick-change artists, talking birds, dancing monkeys, and boxing cats.

People would pay for this kind of entertainment, and so there was no shortage of men and women who were ready to provide it—entrepreneurs at one end and working stiffs at the other. My mother and father were at the working end. It was not love at first sight when they met. Father was still a prop man, in charge of the clothing trunk. Mother needed a dancing costume. He handed her an evening gown.

"I don't want an evening gown," she said. "I have to go onstage. I need a costume."

"All I can find," he said, playing dumb and being a tease, "is an evening gown."

Nell huffed off in a fury and found her own costume, and after that they feuded for several months. Finally, my father had to admit he liked this gal's spirit. Furthermore, he thought she was pretty darned cute—and shorter than he was, too. He was five-five, so most of the chorines towered over him. One night, the whole cast was dancing together behind the curtain during the orchestra's overture and Red—my father had light red hair—came up to Nell, cut in, twirled her around once or twice, and announced, "Nellie! You're never going to be out of my sight again."

"Why?"

"I'm going to marry you."

In those days, every girl wanted to get married, sooner rather than later, and Nell had already been fending for herself, alone, for eight years. She was a twenty-one-year-old spinster. Three days later, they were playing Niagara Falls when Joe made a serious proposal. Nell didn't hesitate. Sure, this guy hadn't made it big yet, but he was funny and full of life. She was ready to go over the falls and she said yes. As soon as they could get a day off—it was in Rochester—they found a judge willing to tie the knot for Mr. and Mrs. Joseph Ninian Yule.

Nell soon found a new job, with Pat White's Gaiety Girls, and she negotiated a spot for a new prop man, too. And then, when one of Pat's comedians up and died, Pat walked up to that prop man and said, "How'd you like to become a comic?"

"Wonderful," said Joe Yule, dropping three props.

"We'll give it a try, Joe. We'll see how you work out." He paused. "And by the way, pick up those props. You don't start as a comic until tomorrow."

Nell worked in the chorus until August, six weeks before I was born. For the final days, she stayed in the rooming house in Brooklyn, a crumbling old brownstone. She had the normal expectant mother's craving, a yen for watermelon and chop suey, usually in the middle of the night. And when Joe went out to get it, he usually succumbed to the normal expectant father's cravings: Scotch whisky. I weighed in at five pounds, seven ounces, and my father weighed in at two fifths, one pint. The night I was born, they found Red Yule singing Scottish ditties in a heap of laundry at the bottom of the clothes chute.

The day after I was born, Pat White's show finished its run

in Brooklyn and moved on to Newark, New Jersey. Joe joined the company in Newark, leaving Nell to cope with the kid. Two weeks later, Nell had me baptized in a Catholic church, then put me, my bottles, and my diapers on a train to Newark to take her place in the chorus.

In the beginning, God said, "Let there be light." And in my own beginning, He saw to it that I was bathed in light. My close-in world was the warmth of my mother's breast. But the world outside was a kaleidoscopic glow, the glow of the theater. I was only four weeks old when mother went back to work, still an end pony, still, I am told, petite and blond and lovely. There were no nannies for me; Joe and Nell couldn't afford them. Where they went, I went.

I spent a good deal of time backstage, sleeping in a tray in a baggage trunk and waking when the spotlights flashed around me. According to my mother, the lights didn't make me cry. They made me curious. I followed their fits and starts and gurgled with joy at their different shades—reds, blues, pinks. I blinked at them and squinted against the glare of the bulb in the dressing room shared by Nell and Joe, and I was fascinated by the lights of the theater marquee. It's no wonder, then, that I've always enjoyed the lights of the theater, no wonder that even now, when I open a refrigerator door, I feel like performing.

My other senses were assailed by the theater, too—the sounds, smells, touches and tastes. I loved the smell of greasepaint, resin, smoke pots, and face powder. My ears perked up at the sounds of the chorus girls' coos—and they thrilled with the crash of the tympani and the blare of the horns in the orchestra.

A little later, I learned to distinguish other, less pleasant sounds: my father's curses as he and my mother argued into the night and her deep sobs in the dark. My first recollection of my father—I know I wasn't even two years old—was drunken and ugly. My parents were checking into a strange new hotel, and I scrambled up the spiral wooden staircase overlooking the lobby, then put my head through the banister and looked down at them. All of a sudden, it gave way and I tumbled through with a yelp. Luckily, my shoestring had caught on a nail; it held me just long enough for my mother to see what had happened and come running. My mother broke my fall, and we both went sprawling. She was only shaken and bruised. But I had broken my leg. My father, who had already had a few, screamed and cursed all the way to the hospital. "You and that goddamn kid," he said over and over in the taxi, pausing every now and then to quench his thirst with a swig from a flask he carried in the pocket of his overcoat.

A short time after that, I caught diphtheria. My father knew what to do: curse his luck. "You, Nellie, you and this goddamn kid. You and this goddamn kid."

I loved my father, but I never knew what to expect from him so that I wondered what was wrong with me. I would have given anything to please my dad. But I wasn't at all sure how to do that. Sometimes, I couldn't do anything wrong. No matter what I did, or what I said, we'd end up laughing and rolling around together on the floor. Other times, all I'd have to do was ask him if we could play together and he'd get mad and turn on Nell with his whisky breath and say, "You and this goddamn kid, Nellie. You and this goddamn kid."

Some people get discovered waiting or sitting at a soda fountain. I got my first break because I sneezed. You see, it was a sneeze that revealed my hiding place underneath the shoeshine stand—a piece of scenery on the stage of the Haymarket Theatre in Chicago—where, at the ripe old age of seventeen months, I was watching the show.

Even then, I was fascinated with the stage. I'd stand and gaze at the footlights. I'd marvel at the make-believe scenery, the bright costumes, the clownlike makeup my dad wore, the long legs of the lovely girls.

The theater was an unusual nursery. Instead of blocks, I played with props, and my favorite toy was a mouth organ, which my mom tied around my neck with a stout cord, so I'd never be without it. And now here I was, under the shoeshine stand in the middle of the show, giving away my position by sneezing.

A large hand reached into my secret spot and pulled me into the glare of the spotlight.

"What are you doing back there, Sonny?" said the voice.

"I play."

"You play? You play what?"

"Play iss, *iss.*" I held up my mouth organ.

"Well," he said, "go ahead and play it, Sonny."

It was then that I noticed my father in one of the wings, shaking a finger at me. I glanced to the other side of the stage and saw my mother doing exactly the same thing. I was trapped. I knew I'd get a whipping for sure. There was no way out. So I put the tiny mouth organ up to my lips and blew.

The audience erupted in laughter.

Suddenly, it was all too much for me—the laughter, the spotlight, and my parents scolding me silently from the wings. I bolted for my mother—toward the lesser of the two punishments that I knew were waiting for me—and cried.

Then something marvelous happened. After the curtain came down on the first act, the manager of the show appeared at my mother's side as I still clung to her knee. "Let's keep this kid in the show, Nellie. He was terrific."

My father frowned.

"What do you think, Red? I tell you, he's terrific."

My father hesitated.

The manager persisted. "He can talk, he can walk, and, what's more, with that body and that face, the kid looks like a midget. Let's keep him in, Red."

My father shook his head.

"We'll add another three bucks a week." He paused. And so did my father. He was figuring: that meant that he and Nellie would be knocking down a total of twenty-five dollars a week.

That did it. I was in the show.

They chose a gentleman by the name of Sid Gold, the show's song and quick-patter man, to work up something with me. It wasn't going to be easy working with a kid who wasn't even two yet, but to Sid it was a challenge. He decided to try me on a song, "Sweet Rosie O'Grady."

In three short weeks, I had the song down pat; my memory was good even then. They made a tuxedo for me, so I'd look like a midget. And then a strange thing happened. When I put on the tuxedo, I became a little adult. I started talking like an adult. Talk, talk, talk. I didn't know what the hell I was saying. I was just ad-libbing. But it sounded good. This was a new game for me, the talk game. Other kids played grown-up by dressing up. I did so by talking up. So I jabbered on—as if I knew what I was jabbering about—and strutted around—as if I knew what I was strutting about. Then, the big night came. I was eighteen months old, and I was making my first professional appearance on the stage.

Sonny Yule didn't let anybody down. I began a little patter with Sid Gold. He fed me some straight lines and I responded. It was a joke that was old even then. "Why does a fireman wear red suspenders?" Sid asked.

And I piped up with a wink, "To hold up his pants up." Believe it or not, the audience roared. Maybe it was the cute fumbling way I said it. Then Sid asked me to sing a song. I took a big breath and started to squeak out my little ballad.

Sweet Rosie O'Grady,
My sweet little rose.

I paused, looking up nervously at Sid. He made a circular motion with his right hand. I stumbled through the rest of it, running my words together, then finished strongly with:

I love Rosie O'Grady,
And Rosie O'Grady loves me!

The house exploded with applause. There were cries of more, more, more. I bowed with my left hand holding my cummerbund. I bowed to the right. I bowed to the left. Sonny—that is, Joe Yule, Jr.—was a hit. Sonny was in show business to stay.

☆ 2 ☆
A Childhood That Ended Too Soon

As an infant actor, I traveled the circuit with my parents, playing the East and the Midwest and sometimes looping up to Canada. When we were flush, we stayed at hotels. When we weren't, we rented in a rooming house.

Now, there were rules against cooking in the rooms, but that didn't stop us. On her Sterno stove, mother learned how to whip up everything from boiled eggs to Irish stew. She did the washing in the room, too. She'd rig some sort of clothesline, then open the window to whatever zephyrs blew. I almost always woke to see my father's long johns and my mother's bloomers billowing in the breeze.

I loved staying in hotels because I soon learned I could order room service on my own, or, better, march down to the dining room at lunchtime and order what I wanted, steak or scallops or a fudge sundae, by conning the waiter into thinking I was a midget. But, of course, I wasn't a midget, as my angry father tried to explain to the management when he saw the check.

I think I knew, if only intuitively, that I was paying more of my own way than most two-year-olds. In addition to my regular performances, Pat White had me stand in front of the theater in my tuxedo and talk to every passerby. "You, sir! Have you seen our show? Twelve beautiful dolls, the notorious Red Yule, Sid Gold and Sonny Yule, *and* the music of Harry Humphrey's orchestra. Yes, sir, step right up! Only a few seats left . . . down front."

Naturally enough, some do-gooders didn't think it was too cute to see a two-year-old working on the stage—or the sidewalk. Had the authorities forgotten about the child labor laws? Wasn't it terrible how Pat White was exploiting this child? Mother, father, and I soon ended up in the office of the governor of the state of New York, Al Smith. I sang for him and did a little clowning and sat on his lap. Fortunately for me, Governor Alfred E. Smith always liked show business. And so he himself gave me a special work permit. Sure, he was against child labor. But singing and dancing—that wasn't really work now, was it?

To thank the governor, Pat White took the whole troupe into the New York State Penitentiary at Ossining—Sing Sing for short—to entertain the inmates. When the warden asked me if I'd like to sit in his nice electric chair, I did so in the absolute confidence that no one would throw the switch while I sat there. After all, everyone loved me, right? Except maybe my father when he was drinking.

I was aware, even at age three, that my father had a penchant for going off by himself after a show, then returning at dawn with a nervous grin on his face. I could only guess, from my mother's angry reactions, that he was doing something that hurt her very much. She kept talking about my dad's "floozies"— which I took to be another name for "bartender." You see, I thought my dad had a problem with Punch, not with Judy.

I finally realized what the trouble was when, after a show one night, Mom caught Dad backstage in a compromising position with one of the other girls from the chorus. I was with her when she saw him and the girl together. Mom gave a little squeak, no more, then turned away and yanked me off with her to our dressing room. She locked the door and wouldn't come out or let Dad in. Finally, he went stumbling off into the night.

Soon, my mother and I were off to Kansas City to live with her sister, Edna, and Edna's husband, Wade Pruitt, a steamfitter with a good job in the local high school. Gosh, I thought, how marvelous for my uncle to be connected with higher education.

My mother and father hadn't divorced, only separated, and so, like a lot of separated couples with kids, before and since, they had a number of reconciliations. We took some trips to Chicago, where Joe Yule was doing his shtick. But things didn't seem to work out. I was about four when my mother and I were in one of the two Chicago train stations heading back to KC. My father was seeing us off. Suddenly, my mother turned to him and said, "Joe, we can't go on."

"What?" he said.

She opened her crocheted boodle bag and counted out the family savings. Slowly and carefully. Ten. Twenty. Thirty. Forty dollars. "We can't go on, Joe. Here's half the boodle bag. Twenty dollars. Good luck."

I wasn't sorry we split. I didn't enjoy being "that goddamn kid." I didn't like watching him growl at my mom or hearing her shouting back at him. I didn't want to spend half my life crawling under beds and behind sofas and cupping my palms over my ears so as not to hear the drunken brawls. On the train back to KC, my mom bought me a bag of popcorn. Maybe she thought the popcorn would be some kind of consolation prize for what she had to tell me: I wouldn't be seeing my dad anymore.

She could have saved herself the price of the popcorn. I said, "Good."

Her eyes widened at that. She said, "But he'll always be your father, Sonny. You know that, don't you?"

I nodded and tossed back a handful of popcorn. But it would be a long time before I ever saw my father again.

Mother went right to work, but not in show business. She started her own chicken shack in Kansas City, where chickens were cheap. She took in a partner named Myrtle Sutherland, and they did a fair business, serving a whole chicken dinner, including biscuits and gravy *and* a glass of beer for twenty-five cents.

I loved Kansas City back in 1924. It was my first (and all too short) taste of what most folks might call a normal childhood. I loved having dinner with the family at the same time every night. I loved having a dog, a big police dog named Ziggy, to play with. I loved digging worms in the backyard with Uncle Wade and catfishing with him along the banks of the Missouri River. I loved the smell of catfish frying in Aunt Edna's big black skillet while I gobbled the first course, Cream of Wheat with lots of salt and pepper and butter on it. I loved going to the Circle Theater, about four miles away on the streetcar, seeing the silent movies there and eating the hot, buttered popcorn, and, then, the ride back home on the streetcar.

I loved the summer evenings, when we'd sit in the living room and wait with the front door wide open for the tamale man to come by on a bicycle, singing, "Hot tamales, two for a nickel, four for a dime. Two for a nickel, four for a dime."

It all seems so idyllic now. But if it was so idyllic, why were my mother and I eager to leave? We were eager, both of us, whenever we heard the cry of a train whistle in the night— which was to say, every night. There must have been a lot of boring days and nights in between the catfish expeditions and the streetcar trips to the movie house.

Mother was still reading *Variety*, the show-business paper, and she was smart enough to figure out that if someone could make it in the movies, they'd be sittin' pretty. One day, she read that a producer named Hal Roach was looking for child actors.

"Myrtle," she said to her partner. "What do you say we go to California?"

"Where?" said Myrtle. She was tired. She had just finished cleaning a batch of chickens.

"California. I have a feeling about Sonny and the movies."

For just a moment, Myrtle paused and looked around her and adjusted her apron, flecked with blood and stinking of chicken livers and gizzards. Then she said, "When do we leave?"

In a few days, we were ready. My mother sold the business, then bought a Model T Ford, and a pup tent. She and Myrtle strapped their baggage down and hung some canvas water bags on the side of the car and turned the crank on the front end. We were off.

☆ 3 ☆
Hollywood or Bust

Our trip to California took the better part of four weeks, with a lot of hard driving, over roads that were nothing more than ruts. We usually slept in the pup tent, but, if it was raining, we spent the night in the car or in a roadside cabin that charged fifty cents a night. In 1924, we had no highways, much less a great transcontinental highway, no Holiday Inns, no Ramada chain, no AAA guides—and darn few gas stations either. In those days, people didn't go cross-country by car for fun.

Nell and Myrtle bought food and cooked it over an open fire alongside the road. This was only a slight variation on cooking with Sterno inside a rooming house, and Mother did just fine. Near El Paso, she even snared a rabbit and broiled it over glowing coals of mesquite.

We took a southern route, through Texas and New Mexico and Arizona. In Yuma, I wandered away, curious as always, and when my mother found me on a little sand dune playing with a large rattlesnake, she almost had a heart attack. The snake didn't bite me, but I soon made up for that. I fell off a teeter-totter on a nearby playground and broke my left arm. In case you haven't guessed it already, I was accident-prone.

I knew we were in California when I started smelling the orange blossoms. Broke and hungry, we stopped near an orange grove and helped ourselves to some oranges and ate them right there on the spot. It seems appropriate that my first recollections of California were the aroma of orange blossoms and the taste of stolen fruit.

Hal Roach didn't seem to notice that we'd come to town. And when his assistant director took my mom aside and said he could probably get her kid on the payroll for five dollars a day, she turned him down on the grounds that other kids were earning five times that amount. By Christmas, we were all but penniless, with not even enough money to buy a Christmas tree. But Mother, ever resourceful, found a good-sized pine branch at a neighborhood lot and set it up in the living room with a popcorn string to go around it.

On Christmas Eve, Mother left me with Myrtle while she went off on a mysterious little shopping trip (I later learned that she'd gone to S.S. Kresge's and bought fifty cents' worth of little toys for me), and on Christmas morning, I woke up happy, filled with a hope that all would be right with our world. Sure, we were broke and lonely and without a glimmer of a job in Hollywood, but we had a gloriously decorated tree, and I had some toys from Santa Claus.

Eventually, Nell found a job in a chorus line in Oakland, for twenty-five dollars a week—a big comedown from the five dollars a day I could have gotten with Hal Roach. Oh well, we'd gambled—and ended up in Oakland. But even that didn't last. We were soon on our way back to Kansas City, by train, minus Myrtle (who had stayed in LA with the Model T). But within the year, we were on the road to Hollywood again, this time to stay.

Back in Kansas City, one of my mother's friends, Dorothy Ferguson, a chorus girl, introduced her to George Christman, a man who managed a failing theater at Twelfth and Walnut. He was putting together a company to take Hollywood by storm. Maybe Nell could give it another try? Dorothy said she was going. There was room for Nell.

"And Sonny, too? I gotta take Sonny," Nell said.

"Well, sure," Dorothy said. "He won't take up much space. Long as you chip in a little extra on the expenses."

And so, it was California Here We Come—again. There were eleven of us in two cars. We slept out of doors, not in a tent this time, but right out there under the stars. Now, with navigator George Christman charting the course, we got there in ten days.

As it turned out, Christman and company might have been ready to take Hollywood, but Hollywood wasn't quite ready to take them. Mother soon realized that her earlier instincts were right: if anyone in the family had a future in show business, it was going to be Sonny.

Nell and I struck out on our own, making the rounds of all the studios. Each of us was carefully groomed, and as charming as a geisha girl. But it seemed the hills were full of well-groomed, charming kids and their well-groomed, charming mothers, all out there looking for the pot of gold at the end of the rainbow. These aspiring young actors and actresses knew that Jackie Coogan and Rin Tin Tin had made millions. Why couldn't they?

Some kids got jobs, of course. But nobody seemed to want *this* yellow-haired, freckle-faced moppet. Gradually, Nell's funds dwindled, and soon she was looking for a job. She ended up with two jobs—one as manager of a bungalow court in Hollywood, which paid no money but gave us a free roof over our heads, and the other as a telephone operator.

Since Nell was working every day and couldn't make the daily casting calls at the studios, she had to figure out another way to get me in pictures. For starters, she enrolled me at Daddy Mack's Dance Studio, a little place on Melrose, jammed to the rafters with kids of all shapes and sizes, every last one of them eager as hell to please Daddy Mack. The first time I saw Daddy Mack, I thought he looked ridiculous: slightly under five feet tall, overweight, with a cigarette always hanging from his lower lip. His voice was strange, too; he'd bark out the commands in a guttural kind of soprano voice. But then, I watched him move, as light on his feet as Tinker Bell, and I didn't think he was ridiculous anymore. I learned a new, important lesson then, that "ridiculous" is in the eyes of the beholder, and I also learned to dance—*one, two, slap, slap, three, four, pat, slap, pat.*

Daddy Mack not only taught us how to dance, he also got us some exposure. One day he took us all to do a show in a town that was out in the sticks, a place called Whittier, California. (Richard Nixon was probably in elementary school out there at the time.) It was a long, hot drive, and we left early in the morning to make the Saturday matinee. When we got there, we saw a big paper sign tacked onto the front of the showhouse: DADDY MACK'S REVIEW HERE TODAY. I did my part real good. I came out, smiled, did a few steps, and bounced off the stage. Then somebody told me my fly was open.

Will Morrissey also made a living in Hollywood by showcasing young talent. Since he also had a kind of school for young actors and actresses, he made out on both ends. First, parents would pay him tuition for their kids. Then theater owners paid him to put on shows with that talent.

It was only a matter of time before my mother hooked up with Will Morrissey. He was casting a small musical revue at the Orange Grove Theater on Hope Square in downtown Los Angeles. So he put out a casting call, and we answered.

At the tryout, my mother had me dressed in a white sailor suit with blue and red stripes on the collar and I sang a ballad of the day called "Pal o' My Cradle Days" (the song would win an Academy Award for Al Piantadosi and Marshall Montgomery in 1925) and delivered a recitation that would tear the heart out of an ax murderer. I sang:

> *Pal o' my cradle days,*
> *I needed you always*
> *Since I was a baby upon your knee,*
> *You sacrificed everything for me . . .*

Morrissey had a little orchestra there and an orchestra leader who was pretty savvy. With his violin tucked under his chin, he was watching me closely and directing the musicians to follow my tempo.

> *Pal o' my cradle days,*
> *I needed you always.*
> *I stole the gold from your hair, and*
> *I put the silver threads there.*
> *I don't know any way I can ever repay*
> *Pal o' my cradle days . . .*

The orchestra now played pianissimo, soft and low. I stopped singing and began my recitation:

> *Now what would I give if I could erase*
> *each little wrinkle on your darling face,*
> *put there through sorry and worry and care?*
> *And sometimes I think it was I who had put them there.*

I thought I could see Morrissey weeping as I continued the recitation and then picked up and continued with the last four bars of the song, arms wide open, blond hair glistening, squeaking the refrain once more:

> *I don't know any way*
> *I can ever repay*
> *Pal o' my cradle days.*

I was right: Morrissey liked what he saw. He signed me for a featured spot in the revue—for fifty dollars a week. Wow! Now that was more like it.

On opening night I went around and assured all the others, all of them older than I and some of them much older, that they'd be just great. They must have wondered at my self-assurance, especially since I was all of five and a half years old. But why shouldn't I feel that way? I was a veteran. I'd been in show business since I was eighteen months old. I'd played the Roxy, I'd played the Orpheum, I'd played the Palace. Why couldn't I play the Orange Grove?

As it turned out, I could. Edwin Schallert of the *Los Angeles Times* was in the audience, and he singled me out for special mention in his review of the show. Mother knew this was the break we'd been looking for. Soon, she thought, every movie producer in town would be after me. The fifty clams a week also meant she could quit the phone company and become my full-time representative again. She also quit her job managing the bungalow court we were living in and found us a place in a small U-shaped complex, nine cottages on Burns Avenue, just above Hollywood Boulevard. They called the place The Bugs Ears.

My job in Morrissey's revue only lasted a few weeks. The State of California had people who kept a close eye on kiddies who were being employed in Hollywood, and they took a non-negotiable position on my working every night—"Imagine, he isn't even six years old!" This time, there was no climbing up on the lap of the governor and charming him into giving me a special permit. So once again we were in the soup. Either Nell had to find me another job or she'd have to go back to work with Ma Bell. Over the next few weeks, we made all the casting calls we could.

In those days, Los Angeles was just about as big as it is now, a modern Nineveh, the kind of place it took several days for a prophet to walk across. Our casting calls were as likely to be in Burbank as in Beverly Hills. We traveled by rail when we could—on the big red cars run by Pacific Electric—or by bus when we couldn't. Either way, it was a hassle. And tiring, too.

It was about the same time that I lost my innocence. When the money stopped coming in, my mother got desperate. I wasn't even six years old, but I knew something had changed. Mother was starting to see a lot of different men, entertaining them in our little apartment. I'd wake up in the middle of the night and hear the tinkling of glasses in the front room. Next night I'd hear whispers and sometimes squeals and moans. Once, I got up and peeked from around a hallway corner into the dimly lit living room to see some money changing hands. Carefully, quietly, I tiptoed back to my room and threw myself on my bed and covered my head with my pillow.

I know, my dear mother, you did it for me.

☆ 4 ☆
Survival of the Misfits

M*y first break* in pictures came when a talent scout from Fox Studios phoned my mother one day in 1926 and told her Fox might have something for me, in a movie called *Not To Be Trusted,* with Matt Moore and Bud Jamison. The scout had been at the Orange Grove Theater on my opening night, and he had remembered Edwin Schallert's nice comments about me. Could she bring young Master Yule over to Fox? "Could I? Could I?" she said, trying, but not succeeding, to control her excitement. "Is there a Republican in the White House?"

Things had been rough for us. We'd been reduced to eating boiled rutabagas for dinner. If I didn't land something soon, we'd be eating dandelions.

Nell found me in the playground at the Logan Street School, a little bit dirty and scuffed up (I was playing football with my classmates during lunch hour). Without telling the principal or anything, she yanked me home, cleaned me up, and dressed me in my best suit. Nobody my age seemed to have a wardrobe like mine, tailor-made suits and all. But that was show biz. We set out, by bus, for the Fox Studios, which were way the heck out on Pico Boulevard, many miles and several bus transfers away.

"Yes, sir!" I said to the director. "I can talk and I can do what you tell me to do. I can do everything."

The director appraised me like a newfound wart, then said to Nell, "I don't believe it, I don't believe this kid." He turned to me. "How old are you, kid?"

"Two," I said. I was really five, but I was small enough to pass for two.

That's the way Mom had coached me. "The younger they think you are, Sonny," she'd said, "the better they'll remember you."

He shook his head in disbelief. He said to my mom, "He talks so well. He looks like a midget who could also pass for a kid. He's just what we need. He's got the job. We can pay him five bucks."

At that, Nell gave me a sly wink, then nodded at the guy. Five bucks, now, was just fine. To break me into pictures, my mother would have had me work for nothing. I couldn't quite figure out what my perfect diction had to do with anything. Nobody would hear me anyway; this was going to be a silent picture. But we didn't think of it as a silent. Talkies were a few years into the future; *everything* then was silent.

An alert assistant director hustled over, a skinny guy with a large cap, who handed Nell a piece of paper and said, "Seven o'clock on the set, ready to go tomorrow morning. We'll tell the kid what to do when he gets here. Remember seven sharp."

Mother and I got up at three-thirty and were there at six A.M. There were a lot of others milling around, too. A movie job was a good one—even the carpenters earned a lot more than union scale—and studio people made a point of being early. They took me right over to wardrobe and fitted me into a velvet, Little Lord Fauntleroy suit. A stitch here, a rolled-up sleeve there, a few pins. Yes, it would do. They finished me off with a lace collar. Then I went to makeup, where they slapped on some greasepaint and eye shadow and fitted me with a blond wig, with curls.

According to the story line, I was a midget and a con man,

working with a crack burglar played by Bud Jamison. I would pretend to be a kid, an orphan up for adoption to a rich couple. Once I got established in their mansion, I'd help Jamison steal their diamonds and sapphires and rubies. I had some good scenes with Jamison, going into a tirade with him, complaining (with my wig off and smoking a cigar) that I was already sick of being pawed over by these doting foster parents. "Let's get the job done quick," I said, "just get it done quick and over with." Those were the words, at least, that appeared on the movie's titles.

Jamison had to warn me to be careful and not blow my disguise. "If you're caught . . ."

Of course, at the end of the picture, we *were* caught, as they say, red-handed, I with some of the jewels in my arms, no curls on my head, and a cigar in my mouth—much to the shock of my parents, as Jamison and I were led off to jail. The director and the cameraman and the other members of the cast treated me like a midget, not like a kid.

"Get the midget over here," they'd say. Or, "We're ready for the midget now." As for the cigar, no one thought much about giving a stogie to a half-pint kid. They just lit it, and I puffed away. I did what I was told to do. The cigar made me a little sick, but I couldn't afford to get sick. So I suppressed my nausea and told myself to get sick later, when I was off the set.

On the set of *Not To Be Trusted,* Mother met a beautiful young woman named June LaVere, who was playing the part of the maid in my foster parents' mansion. In real life, Ms. LaVere was—how should I put this?—well, a lady who knew her way around the hills of Hollywood. She was currently having an affair with a Southern California oilman who also owned a radio station and a Cadillac dealership. June and Nell became friends and would talk on the phone for hours. June was a wonderful source of news and juicy Hollywood gossip.

In Hollywood then, as now, knowledge is power. It certainly was for us, at least, when June told Nell that a friend of hers, a director named Al Santell, out at Vitaphone Studios, a subsidiary of Warner Brothers in Burbank, was casting a picture, another silent called *Orchids and Ermine*, starring Colleen Moore. He needed a midget.

"I hope I haven't insulted you by referring to Sonny as a midget," June said.

"It's all right," said Nell. "It's normal." Nell had been pushing me for more midget roles.

The next morning, we were off to Burbank. The casting office at Vitaphone was jammed with hundreds of people, people dressed in Indian feathers, cowboy suits, Eskimo furs, Chinese pajamas. It looked like one big Halloween party. I was wearing one of my tailor-made suits. I carried a cane and wore a straw hat.

Over the din, a voice of authority bawled out through a megaphone, "Joe Yule. Joe Yule, Junior. Step through this door, please."

I raised my cane, and a hand grabbed it and pulled me through the crowd, with my mother hanging onto my coat behind me. With the roar of the crowd diminishing behind us, we were led down a long, dingy hallway and into a small room, where a balding fellow with a slimy cigar that kept traveling back and forth across his mouth ordered my escort to close the door.

"Siddown, kid," he said. Without looking at my mother, he grabbed her proffered envelope, one that contained some eight by ten glossies of me that Mother had picked up during the making of *Not To Be Trusted*. He opened the envelope, started shuffling the shots, and commanded me to get up and walk. "Go ahead, kid, lemme see you walk aroun'."

I got up and strutted across the room, swung my cane, and tipped my straw hat. "Like this, Mister?" I said with a wink. "Like this, Mister?" I smiled.

For a moment, his cigar paused in its journey. "My God, kid, you're just what we want, just what the doctor ordered." Then he asked the question that always brought forth the answer that startled. "How old'r you, kid?"

I raised two fingers. "Two and a half," I said, and I strutted across the floor again. I stopped and took my cane and tipped up the back of my straw hat so it covered one eye at a jaunty angle. "Two and a half, Mister." I grinned.

His grin was bigger than the room. "Don't move, kid, don't move. I want someone to see you. Wait right here." He disappeared out the door.

Mother looked at me with a mixture of pleasure and surprise. I was pretty proud of myself. Soon, we heard laughing, happy voices coming down the hall. It was the casting director and two other guys, who turned out to be Al Santell, the director himself, and his gagman, Mervyn LeRoy. Every silent comedy had a gagman, someone who could make up spontaneous sight gags on the spot as they were shooting scene after scene. LeRoy, I later found out, was one of the better gagmen in Hollywood. The three of them sized me up and told me I had the part.

The casting director adjusted his cigar and said, "Kid, you start in two days, six-thirty in the morning, in makeup, dressed. Wear what you have on now. I don't think we got anything can fit you."

Perc Westmore was my makeup man. He did my face, pasted a small mustache on my upper lip, and then covered it with glue. I can still smell that glue. It must have had ether in it, or something like that. It made my nose twitch and I reached up.

"No," said Westmore, "don't touch it. Don't touch it with your hands." Percy Westmore was a very nice man who became one of Hollywood's legends. He headed the Warner Brothers makeup department for more than thirty years, doing his magic on all the greats who performed on the Warner lot—Paul Muni, Bette Davis, Errol Flynn, Edward G. Robinson, Jimmy Cagney. He held a towel against my lip for quite a while. "Don't move," he said soothingly. "Don't move." I looked wide-eyed at him over the towel and smiled.

I looked at myself in the mirror when we were done. I had greasepaint on my face, eye shadow and some eyebrow pencil, and a little mascara, too, because Westmore wanted to highlight my light-blond brows and eyelashes. I looked like a wax figurine. I hopped off the chair and, with my mother in tow, ran off to Stage 2 to rehearse with Colleen Moore.

She was a doll. As I was admiring her beauty, the director interrupted my contemplation to give me my marching orders. I was to get off an elevator, light up my cigar (my goodness, another cigar!), then walk over to a busy telephone operator's desk at this make-believe hotel. Miss Moore, who played the operator, was supposed to hear me and get all confused because she couldn't see me. Then I was to take off my straw hat, put it on my cane, and raise it up—her signal to rise off her chair and peer down at me.

"Gee, baby," I was to say, taking the cigar out of my mouth and giving her a wink, "you'd look great in an ermine coat." Then I was supposed to tap my cigar.

She was supposed to give me a dirty look and say, "Gee, but you're a fresh little thing." Then she'd smile and I'd wink and the camera would fade.

We rehearsed the scene six or seven times because they wanted to do a dolly shot, moving the camera along with me as I walked from the elevator door to my mark, which was a piece of tape stuck to the floor. This was a very daring shot back in 1926, having the camera move along with the actor, and we had to keep doing it to get it just right. On about the seventh take, I lit my cigar and proceeded to break off one of my front teeth. Everyone howled with laughter. Everyone, that is, except me.

"Cut!" said Santell. He looked with some exasperation at my mother and wondered what he was going to do now.

"No problem," said my mom. She extracted the piece of gum

she was chewing, picked my tooth off the floor, stuck it into the wad of gum, and fitted it back into the hole in my smile.

When we'd finally finished the last take, Santell shouted out, "Print it!" Then he picked me up in his arms and said, "Kid, you were great. We'll be seeing a lot of you."

LeRoy echoed his sentiments. "I'm going to write a lot of gags for you, kid, just you wait and see." As it turned out, he would do a lot more than that for me.

Next thing Mother and I knew, we were all alone on the set. Nell was clutching a yellow voucher for seven dollars, for one day's shooting. It wasn't much, but it was a 40 percent increase over my last picture. I may not have had all my teeth, but I was moving in the right direction.

☆ 5 ☆
Mickey (Himself) McGuire

W*ith only two* pictures under my belt, I already had a problem: I was "typecast." Anybody need a midget? Get little Joe Yule, Jr. Trouble was, there weren't that many midget roles being written. I went on a lot of calls, but I was always too young or too old or too blond or too short or . . . whatever. My mother got her job back at the telephone company, and I tried to enjoy the first grade at Logan Street School. In the early morning, I would walk to school down Hollywood Boulevard, clutching my lunch in a brown paper bag, a bologna sandwich and a hard-boiled egg, with a nickel wrapped in my handkerchief to buy a bottle of milk. I still remember the name of my teacher, Miss Dishaslo, and one fat little Japanese kid named Aichi Komasaki. Who could forget names like that? And who could forget the smells of that first-grade classroom? It smelled like damp bread, and bologna, and boiled eggs. (I guess we all brought the same basic lunch to school.) It smelled like chalk and ink. It smelled like Miss Dishaslo's perfume.

When *Orchids and Ermine* was released, an agent named John Michaeljohn, a tall, handsome banker-type guy, called on my mother and persuaded her to sign him on as my agent. He didn't get me any movies, but he did get me some club dates and some vaudeville stuff. I did my old routines—"Pal O' My Cradle Days," which was starting to bore me, and my Daddy Mack dance number. Eventually Michaeljohn decided that I wasn't going anywhere and, in a nice way, told my mother that he couldn't represent me anymore.

He did me a favor. If he couldn't help me, at least he got out of the way so somebody else could. The somebody turned out to be Harry Weber, an agent who looked more like an ex-boxer, stocky, balding, with a crooked nose, with posh offices on the fourth floor of a building on Wilshire Boulevard, not far from what are now the headquarters of the Motion Picture Academy of Arts and Sciences. Harry took me on and I began what I now think of as the "the hurry-up years."

"Hurry, Nell," said the voice on the phone, "get the kid over to Universal right away. Hurry, Nell, and get the kid over to Metro. Hurry, Nell, and grab the streetcar. Hurry, hurry, hurry." We moved to a place on Hoover Street so we could be closer to the bus and streetcar lines. I missed a lot of school.

Then, one day, I went on a call to the FBO Studios in Hollywood, which later became RKO. I was going on seven, and it was a turning point for me. A producer there named Larry Darmour had come up with a way of competing with Hal Roach, who was cranking out a very successful series of kid comedies called *Our Gang*. Roach had a fat child named Joe Cobb, a black kid called Farina, Spanky McFarland, Alfalfa Switzer. And there was a youngster named Jackie Cooper.

Now Darmour had made a movie deal with Fontaine Fox, a cartoonist who had scored big with a newspaper syndicate doing a feature called "Toonerville Trolley." Darmour was casting, looking for a muscular little lady to play Katinka, a handsome kid to play Stinky Davis, and a black youngster to play Hambone, Darmour's answer to Farina. He also needed a tough, little guy to play Mickey (Himself) McGuire. That's where I came in.

"Come on, Sonny," my mother said the night before the casting call for Mickey McGuire. "We've got some studying to do." She had gathered some of the Toonerville comic strips, back numbers from the *Hollywood Citizen-News,* and we sat down together to study the character of Mickey McGuire. By the end of the evening, I had a pretty good idea who I was supposed to be this time. Mickey was a very self-assured kid who went around with a stick in his mouth, cocked at a confident angle. (No, not another cigar role!) No one could tell him much, and he instigated a lot of trouble in Toonerville.

I was ready. I knew Mickey McGuire. I was ready to *be* Mickey McGuire—except for one thing: his hair was black, and mine was blond. But not for long. That night, mother bought some Anecto hair dye, not shoe polish, as an MGM publicist later reported it, and the next morning dyed my hair a jet black.

When we got to FBO, it seemed as if fifty other boys were there, too. One by one, each of them, accompanied by his mother, filed alphabetically into the offices of Darmour and his director, Al Herman, to audition for the part of Mickey McGuire. We watched them go in, and, as they did, my mother would say a silent prayer for them, a prayer that they would *not* get the role. Late in the afternoon, they called for Joe Yule, Jr.

Al Herman seemed to like me. He took me off to a nearby stage, a brightly lit barnyard setting, and told me he wanted to see what I looked like on film. He primed me, then called, "Camera!" I peeked around the corner of the barn, my face wrinkled in a tough scowl. Then I sat down on a box, crossed my legs, pulled a stick out of my pocket, and started to chew on it like an inveterate smoker.

Herman said he liked what I'd done.

Three long days passed, with no word from Herman or Darmour. Mother called the studio and said she had to have a decision. "We've got five other offers," she said. It was a slight exaggeration; we had no other offers.

"Have him back at the studio tomorrow morning," someone told her. "We want to do another test, this time in costume." Out came the dye again. The next morning they gave me a derby, a checkered shirt, some ragged pants, and a pair of shoes that were four or five sizes too big. With the camera rolling, I went through the same act, this time with just a bit more swagger.

Next day, when Darmour and Herman looked at the screen test, they knew they had their Mickey McGuire. When we went back to talk contract, Darmour offered fifteen dollars a week. My mother sensed that this was a bit low. She knew the "Our Gang" comedies were making a mint for Hal Roach. And she knew these Mickey McGuires would be hard work for me; they were going to try to shoot each two-reeler in three days. She sent for Harry Weber. He hustled over, went into executive session with Darmour, and emerged with a contract for five dollars a day.

That was more like it, especially since this wasn't going to be a one- or two-day shoot but an ongoing series. How long, nobody could say. But we ended up making maybe sixty-three of these "Mickey McGuires," sometimes as many as a dozen a year, from late 1926 until the Depression flattened everyone. Mother was finally able to afford a car, a Model A Ford.

I worked hard and hardly went to school at all. This was before the Los Angeles Board of Education started insisting that teachers be present on the set for a stated number of class hours each day. Our days were long, and mostly burning hot ones out in the sandy, deserted riverbed of the Los Angeles River or in the sagebrush of the San Fernando Valley. My costars included a menagerie of dogs, cats, and birds of all shapes and colors, and the props seemed designed as instruments of torture.

It was all part of slapstick comedy, which is what the series was all about. We depended on stinky smoke pots (the Toonerville kids always seemed to be brewing something or other) and big sponges that they dipped into a brown gook, a mixture of water, artificial coloring, and mud, then hit us in the face with. Once, the bunch of us almost drowned in a mudhole that was about eight feet deep. We were being pulled along in a wagon by a pair of feisty goats when the goats decided to take a mud bath—though this wasn't in the script. We all tumbled in, goats, wagon, me, Hambone, Katinka, the whole gang. The cameras kept grinding. I guess they got some pretty good footage before they hauled us out. Another time, I can remember hanging out the window of a high building in downtown Los Angeles, suspended by a slim length of whipcord. We had no stunt doubles. I think the producers' attitude was, "If you can make it, fine. If you don't, we'll get another kid."

We shot some stuff on the lot, of course. Studio carpenters built sets in an old warehouse kind of building with wooden floors all rotten and splintered. One day, I picked up a splinter about the size of a wooden match and ran it into my fifth metatarsal along the side of my foot. They took me to Hollywood Emergency Hospital and a doctor in the emergency room started cutting my skin like it was a piece of cloth.

"You're cutting my skin, you son of a bitch," I yelled at him. He cocked his head at that. But he had his own way of dealing with this cocky little actor with the smart mouth. He got a great big swab and stuck it in a jar of iodine, with big black XXXs on it and a death's head, and jammed it into the incision all the way to the bone. I whooped like I was shot, and I went straight up in the air, up seventeen floors right through the roof of Hollywood Emergency. When I came down, the doctor was smiling. I learned something: never smart off to a doctor who has a scalpel in his hand and a bottle of iodine nearby. I would later have a chance to transfer that bit of wisdom to other situations—to cops with guns, casting directors with clipboards, producers with fountain pens, all deadly weapons if they wanted to use them.

The Mickey McGuire comedies were immensely successful at the box office, and I was becoming a kind of household word in

America. As I played him, Mickey (Himself) McGuire came to mean "brash, wise beyond his years, smart-alecky, stubborn." And my character gave a young artist who had some space at the Darmour Studios an inspiration. One day, I passed a half-open door in the dirty old studio and peeked in. A slightly built man with a thin mustache who was bent over a drawing board glanced at me as I walked in, made a couple more marks with his pencil, then looked up and smiled. "What's your name, son?"

"Mickey. My name is Mickey McGuire." It really was. Mom had had it legally changed.

"Oh," he said, "you make those comedies with those kids?"

"I sure do, sir." I came closer to see what he was drawing. I was almost in his lap now. "What are you drawing?"

"I'm drawing a mouse, son." He finished an ear, then he drew a smile on the mouse's face. Suddenly, he stopped drawing, took me by the shoulders, and looked me square in the eye. "Did you say your name was Mickey?"

"Yes, sir."

"You know what I'm going to do?"

"No, sir."

"I'm going to call this mouse 'Mickey'—after you."

I smiled. I laughed. "Sounds great to me, Mister, uh, Mister—"

"Disney," he said. "My name's Walt Disney."

Becoming moderately famous as Mickey McGuire didn't do much for my attitude at school. I was becoming something of a discipline problem. Well, to be blunt, the principal was telling my mother I was a profane little hoodlum. My mother solved the school problem by taking me out of public school and enrolling me in Ma Lawlor's Professional School, a private academy for kids in the business, grades one through twelve. Ma Lawlor was a tall, lean, no-nonsense schoolmarm, who tried to look the part by wearing her hair in a tight little bun. She ignored my colorful vocabulary.

And she knew how to play the game with the LA Board of Education, which had, by now, started to catch up with movie producers. She kept the curriculum light and manageable for a grand lineup of kids who would pass through her halls: Deanna Durbin, Frances Gumm (who would later change her name to Judy Garland), Jean Darling (who played in the "Our Gang" comedies), Tom Brown, Anita Louise, Dawn O'Day (later Ann Shirley), Frankie Darrow, and Nancy Mars (who became the novelist Nancy Freedman), and two young contemporaries who would go on to work with me and become long-standing friends. One was Dick Quine, a slim young man from Detroit, and the other Sidney Miller, a hawk-faced kid from Brooklyn, whom Warner Brothers brought out to the Coast in 1931 to play in Booth Tarkington's *Penrod and Sam.*

The school wasn't like any other school. For one thing, the smell of adolescence was missing. The not yet sweet smell of success was mixed with an odor of hopefulness, and though we were learning something, I think we were playing at education. We had forty-five-minute classes in history, arithmetic, social studies, French, and Spanish. They should have called every class "looking." Everyone was always looking at everyone else. And everyone, and I mean *everyone* in the school, spent most of the time writing love notes. It was a time of life when every one of us, it seemed, was falling in love with someone new every day. Maybe it was there that I picked up this habit of mine: if I can't be near the girl I love, I love the girl I'm near.

If the truth be known, Ma Lawlor's school was a dodge, a way of pacifying the LA Board of Education. If I had to be gone for days at a time, Ma Lawlor would cover for me, and tell the board whatever the board needed to hear. Why not? Why should she piss on her own parade?

Is that what I said, at age ten? "Piss on her parade?" Probably. You see, I bought the idea that I was Mickey McGuire. The tough language was part of my identity. My mother went along with some of that identity stuff, too. She called me Mickey instead of Sonny, and so completely was she submerged in my identity that she started calling herself Nell McGuire.

Every once in a while, though, things got a little carried away. One day, when my mom put a plate of rutabagas in front of me, I told her I wasn't eating any more rutabagas. "Enough, already, with the damned rutabagas," I said. "Are we so fuckin' poor we have to eat rutabagas?"

Mom backhanded me across the mouth. Then, when I yelped, she sobbed so hard I had to comfort her. It was the first time she'd hit me in a long time. And the last.

"There, there, Mom," I lied, "it's okay. I was just kidding about the rutabagas. I love rutabagas."

"It isn't the rutabagas," she said. "It's your language. I haven't been a good mother."

"You've been a great mom."

"No," she said, dabbing at her tears with a dish towel. "I haven't been. You're playing a tough kid on film. Now, you're becoming one in real life. And saying words no little boy should be saying."

I had no answer to that. She pondered a moment, then announced her decision. "I think," she said, "you could use a little religion."

She ended up driving me every Sunday to a church in the Wilshire District. She'd take me, pick me up, but she never went inside the church herself. I haven't the slightest idea how it was that she selected a Christian Science congregation.

But I'm glad she did because those Sundays in church were just what I needed then. Mary Baker Eddy, the founder of Christian Science, had some mighty insights about Christ and Christianity. She said that Jesus Christ was the first true Christian Scientist, and that He had the confidence of the faith, the consciousness that, with faith, everything is possible.

I know that people make jokes about Christian Scientists, warn them not to stand in a draft and things like that, because, if they get sick, they can't go to a doctor. But Mrs. Eddy never insisted on that. She'd say, "If you don't have enough faith, go see a doctor." And she'd say, "Use whatever of this teaching that you can." But I know now that Christian Science was a very American approach to religion, American in its utter optimism about life, and I think that, deep down and as a little boy, I absorbed some of this optimism. I will never forget the bedtime prayer I learned at Sunday School: "Father and Mother God, Guide my little feet up to Thee."

I said it then, and I'm still saying it today. In a sense, my feet are still little. And I still need guidance.

☆ 6 ☆
Introducing
Mickey Rooney

T *he first* twenty-one Mickey McGuire movies were silents, and the rest were talkies. Making the transition to sound was no problem for me. My voice (like Mickey Mouse's) was a little squeaky, but that was okay. After all, I was going to play kid parts for the next twenty years. Still, everyone knew that Mickey McGuire couldn't go on forever. Darmour's writers ran out of new ideas, and the audiences grew tired of the same old gags. If he couldn't have figured that out for himself, Darmour got the message from the exhibitors.

And so it came to pass that my mother got a letter one day from Darmour's attorneys, Loeb and Loeb, which said that my services as Mickey McGuire would no longer be needed. The series was over. I accepted the end of the series, but I had some trouble with the idea of going back to being a guy named Joe. I'd gotten used to the name Mickey and I decided to keep it, as a nickname, at least.

With my movie career on hold, Harry Weber got me some vaudeville bookings in LA and environs, but the audiences weren't satisfied with my singing, my dancing, my jokes, or my imitations. They'd become used to me as Mickey McGuire. They wanted Mickey McGuire or nothing.

It was just about this time that Wynn Brown came into our lives. He was a used car salesman in downtown Los Angeles, and he liked my mother and he liked me. He didn't seem to mind when Nell came down to see him with me in tow, and many a night, before they closed the lot at ten P.M., I would fall asleep in the backseat of her car as they talked. Before too long, Nell and Wynn Brown were married.

Wynn Brown and I became good friends. He had a son about my age from a prior marriage, but since he was back in Indiana, Wynn and I palled around together. He took me fishing, to baseball games, to football games, prizefights, and wrestling matches—just about what the doctor ordered for a ten-year-old boy.

Slowly but surely, I came to love Wynn Brown, and one day I asked him if I could call him Dad. He held me close and said, "Your real daddy wouldn't like that." He paused. I said nothing. I hardly ever *thought* about my real daddy. I didn't remember much about him. Then he said, "But if you want to call me Dad, I don't think anyone will tell him." So Wynn Brown became my dad.

My life was beginning to seem "normal" again. My hair was its natural color, and I was going to a public school, Vine Street Elementary. Then, to complete the picture, I met a pretty little girl named Ann (she was eleven and I was ten) who introduced me to prepubescent sex.

One warm, lazy afternoon when her folks were out, she took me into her bedroom and lay back on her bed and slipped off her little cotton panties and guided my hand to her soft, smooth little bud. "Now, you just do this. And this. And this." She showed me some things, and then she invited me to lie down with her. "Get your knees between mine," she said. "Yes. Like that. Oh, yes."

I understand now that this kind of thing goes on in all cultures and climes and among all peoples, but I didn't know that at the time and I felt terribly guilty. None of my friends ever talked about it. My mom sure didn't tell me anything. No, I thought this was our own discovery.

Somehow—my memory is a little hazy on this—I started playing midget football on the grounds of a horseback-riding academy out in the Valley toward Glendale. The place was owned by Victor McLaglen, a rugged Irish actor whose Gypo Nolan in *The Informer* will always stand up as one of the classic movie performances of all time. I remember McLaglen dropping by one day and watching us play. He had a kind of rolling walk, like a sailor, and I can still remember him coming up to me and asking me if our team would like to sign up in a sandlot league that played on some Los Angeles playgrounds. I called the guys together to talk it over, with McLaglen hovering a few feet away.

Somebody wondered when we'd be playing. "When?" repeated McLaglen. He wrinkled his Irish face and he twinkled his blue Irish eyes. "Mostly Saturdays," he replied. "Maybe, sometimes, Sundays at Gilmore Field."

"Gilmore?" I said. "On Sundays? But that's where the pros play on Sunday. The Los Angeles Bulldogs. The Los Angeles Bears."

"Right!" he said. "I know the promoters. They're looking for some kid teams to play at halftime."

Gee. Halftime at Gilmore Field! That did it. Soon, we were regulars there. We never made any money, of course. But McLaglen got us uniforms with red and white jerseys (I wore number seven) and pads and helmets. The helmets were leather and pretty heavy, and they didn't have face bars in those days. I'm lucky, I think, being accident-prone and all, that I didn't get kicked in the face, break my nose, or lose some teeth. But if football had rearranged my face, it would have been okay with me. I loved football, a game that is a little bit like war but played for lesser stakes.

For two of the three summers after Mother married Wynn, I joined a troupe that played from five to eight shows a day, all across the country. My salary was fifty dollars a week. Among my fellow troupers—these are names that will mean nothing to most of my readers under the age of seventy—were Nick Lucas, Buster Shaver, Olive and George, and Chaz Chase, a guy who would eat everything but the folks in the audience. You name it, he ate it: cigarettes, matches, his underwear, the scenery.

I did my usual: a song called "Down by the Vinegar Works," a tap dance from my Daddy Mack repertoire, and, of course, "Pal o' My Cradle Days." Wynn, mother, and I would stay in nice hotels if we could find one (for two or three dollars a night) or in tourist cabins for one dollar a night.

In Chicago, Al Capone became one of my fans. I was playing a club date—I think it was at a place called Chez Paris—when, all of a sudden in came Capone, a light topcoat over his shoulders that he didn't bother to stick his arms in and a bunch of bodyguards wearing black shirts and black ties.

I went right on with my act. I did some of the Mickey McGuire shtick. And I ended with "Pal o' My Cradle Days." Heck, it had worked in Newark, it had worked in Sing Sing, it had worked in West LA. Why wouldn't Capone like it, too? He had a mother, too, didn't he?

I was right. He did like it. I think I even saw a single tear run down his cheek. At least, I saw him brush his face with the back of his hand toward the end of my song. Everybody, I guess, needs to laugh sometimes—and cry.

When we got back to LA, Harry Weber had found me some work. He had a part for me in something called *Emma,* with Marie Dressler, and another bit in *High Speed,* a Columbia picture that got cowboy star Buck Jones out of the saddle and into a race car. I was the orphaned kid of a dead driver who was there to applaud as Jones stepped out of his policeman's duds, won the race, showed up the mob, won the boss's daughter, and saved the life of the boss. The screen credits had me down as Mickey McGuire.

And I was still Mickey McGuire in my next picture, a real stinker called *Sin's Pay Day*. For me, the most notable thing about the movie was the presence of a director named George Seitz. In a few years, he would be directing me as Andy Hardy.

Then Weber told me that the people at Universal wanted me for a part in a movie called *The Information Kid*, but they didn't want me to be identified in any way with Mickey McGuire. "Mickey McGuire" was the wrong image: two-reelers that had worn out their welcome. So the name Mickey McGuire was also out. So what were they going to call me now—Joe Yule, Jr?

I couldn't buy it. How could I be a junior when I didn't even know the senior? I'd never even received a card from him on my birthday.

"Well," said Kenneth Wilson, one of the publicity men at Universal, "how about 'Mickey Yule'?" He savored it for a moment. "Nah. It doesn't sound right. The rhythm is wrong. I like Mickey. But Yule? No. We need another last name. Something with a 'y' in it. That would sound better. Mickey Maloney? Mickey Downey? Mickey Looney?"

"Yeah, sure," I said, crossing my eyes and doing a riff on my lips. "Bibbety, bibbety, bibbety. Yeah! Looney!"

"How about Rooney?" asked my mother. "I knew a guy in vaudeville, Pat Rooney."

"Not bad," said Wilson. "Mickey Rooney. I'll run it by my boss and see what he says." He never bothered to ask me whether *I* liked it. This is the kind of world I was born in, one in which I had only one reason for existence: pleasing others. This was very clear, now, with a second legal name change: even my name, even that, was designed to please others.

Wilson returned a few minutes later with a smile on his face. "Well, kid, that's your new name—Mickey Rooney."

☆ 7 ☆
My First Starring Role

I n 1932, my mother's dreams started to come true. And I was meeting a better class of people. The stars I played with that year have become Hollywood legends. O'Sullivan, Gleason, Devine, Huston, Harlow, Mix.

I must have done all right in *The Information Kid.* I won fifth billing, behind Tom Brown, Maureen O'Sullivan, James Gleason, and Andy Devine, who would do his gravel-throated roles for several decades to come. In the movie, Brown and Gleason are con men who build up a horse by having it win some minor races, then hold it back in some big races for a price. But then, a sincere, innocent orphan stable boy (guess who) comes along and helps them straighten out and fly right.

We made the picture at the Agua Caliente racetrack in Tijuana, and I was glad we did. In those days, Caliente was a mecca for Hollywood's sporting crowd, an open city where they not only had horse racing but gambling of all kinds and some of the best whorehouses in the world. My keepers kept me out of the whorehouses, but they didn't see any harm in taking me up to Caliente's Turf Club every afternoon and placing a small wager or two on my behalf. Sticking to two-dollar bets, I won a few and lost more than a few. That first afternoon I lost sixteen dollars.

I've spent the rest of my life (and millions of dollars) trying to win that sixteen dollars back. End of joke. To this day, a lot of people believe (because they want to) that I've lost millions at the track. Millions of dollars? Hah! How can you lose millions when you're earning (as you will soon see) peanuts? Get off my back.

Then I did my first picture at MGM, *Beast of the City*, with Walter Huston and Jean Harlow. This was in 1932, the year when J. Edgar Hoover started making big headlines with his Federal Bureau of Investigation and *Scarface* was making big money for Warner Brothers. Everybody in the nation was talking about cops and robbers, and the action seemed right for pictures with sound: lots of roaring cars, machine guns chattering in the streets, villains and heroes coughing out their last dying words.

So Hollywood made dozens of gangster films; the moviegoing public couldn't get enough of the catharsis that comes from watching cops kill crooks (and the perverse thrill that comes from watching crooks kill cops). As studio chief at MGM, Louis B. Mayer knew he'd have to climb on the crime bandwagon, but Mr. Mayer was a guy who was always interested in social uplift. So, as he climbed aboard, he would also try to change its course. *Beast of the City* was the result, a high-minded crime story. *Variety*'s reviewer said it was "a gang story for rural and home circle consumption, preaching the gospel of civic righteousness. They even make Harlow keep her skirts down."

In my next flick I won my first starring role—costarring, actually—with Tom Mix and his horse, Tony. *My Pal the King* was a fantasy Western in which I played the seven-year-old King of Alvania, saved by Mix from the clutches of an evil count. The movie got me my first mention in *The New York*

Times, whose reviewer spelled my name right and said I did "quite well." Universal also paid me $250—for ten days of shooting. I was coming up in the movie world.

I made six movies in 1933. I was happy to have the work, but none of them advanced my career very much. One of them, *The Big Chance,* tried to ride a popular trend: fight movies. This one had all the clichés: the crooked fight gang, the softhearted trainer, the beautiful young girl, the worldly-wise rival, even the kid (me), who hero-worshipped the boxer.

The World Changes was a kind of American pioneer epic, starring Paul Muni and Mary Astor, both standbys at Warner Brothers. Mervyn LeRoy directed.

The Life of Jimmy Dolan was another fight-and-crime flick, courtesy of Warner Brothers, starring two very good Hollywood pros, Douglas Fairbanks, Jr., and Loretta Young. I got ten days' work on this one and made six hundred dollars. By Depression standards, this was very good, about ten times what a worker was making on the production line at the Ford Motor Company.

I don't exactly remember where I first met Frank Orsatti, but I do know that he changed my life. Orsatti looked like a hood—overweight, undergroomed, and rough around the edges. (I heard later that he'd been a bootlegger during Prohibition.) I was impressed when he told me, "Ya got talent, kid, real talent." And I was doubly impressed when he started getting me parts at MGM. He had some close ties to Louis B. Mayer, but it wasn't until later that I learned what they were. I didn't need to know. He had the ties. And he got me the parts. That was enough.

(Orsatti, as it turned out, had run some speakeasies in San Francisco during Prohibition. When the authorities in northern California put the heat on him, he landed in Los Angeles, where he started supplying the movie colony with booze that he smuggled in from Mexico on his sailboat. He had a winning personality and a raffishness that was more charm than menace. He walked like McLaglen, with a kind of rolling gait that suggested piracy and romance on the high seas. Orsatti not only supplied Mayer with good champagne, he always had a line on the biggest poker games in Hollywood, where gambling was prohibited. And the most beautiful, available broads.)

And, eventually, Mayer encouraged Orsatti to start his own talent agency, with his three brothers as assistants. Orsatti asked my mother if she wanted to change agents. After some discussion with me, she decided to stick with Harry Weber. That didn't seem to make a difference to Orsatti. He still went on putting in good words for me with Mayer. And that is how I got my foot in the door at MGM.

MGM put me in *Broadway to Hollywood,* a rags-to-riches saga with songs, starring Frank Morgan, Alice Brady, and Jackie Cooper. I played the grandson of two old vaudeville troupers, a plot that would have moviegoers believe that a mere dancer in a vaudeville troup could end up with a mansion in Beverly Hills. But then, what else did anyone expect from MGM? Reality? Hey, this was Hollywood. More important, this was Louis B. Mayer's Hollywood, MGM, which he used as a pulpit to establish values for the whole nation. He did this by telling stories, not about the way the world was but about the way it *could* be.

I was doing a lot of work in 1932 and 1933, but I wasn't making that much money, and what little I made went to help with the household expenses and my professional expenses, like my wardrobe. I needed to look good in interviews, and unless I was in a costume picture, I usually had to supply my own duds in the films I was in.

If I wanted some spending money of my own, I had to figure out my own ways of getting it, such as collecting scrap paper and old bottles or selling newspapers.

Why did I need my own spending money?

Tennis.

I'd become a tennis nut. I played on some cracked old public courts on Melrose, with its torn nets and balls that were anything but white and a racket that always seemed to have a broken string or two. But my friends and I knew there was another, posh world of tennis, where the nets were never torn and the balls were always white. And that world was just a lob away, right behind a high green fence that bordered the public courts on Melrose. It was the Los Angeles Tennis Club.

I was told that only rich folks could play there, but when I checked things out with one of the playground directors, he said, "Yes, a lot of rich people do play at the LA Tennis Club. You can tell just by watching the Rolls-Royces and the Duesenbergs coming and going. But you don't have to be rich." He thought I could get a junior membership for $27.50. "Of course, they've got a dress code, too." He looked at my tennis outfit, a T-shirt and a bathing suit. "You have to wear tennis whites." He looked at my torn sneakers. "And white tennis shoes, too."

I got a good corner selling newspapers at Melrose and Vermont. It took me awhile, but the day finally came when I was able to go to my mother and tell her that I'd saved $27.50—for my junior membership in the LA Tennis Club. She blubbered a bit and hugged me and went out and bought me some real tennis shorts and two tennis shirts. She also brought home a bottle of whitener and sopped my tennis shoes with it. At least they'd *look* new.

Next afternoon, with my hair nicely combed and wearing my new tennis whites, I took my $27.50—in cash—to the front desk of the club. The woman behind the desk found it hard to smile. Very severely, she said, "Yes, what can I do for you?"

I said, "Let me be a member."

"What?"

Unflinching, I looked her straight in the eye and said, as earnestly as I could, "I want to become a member of the club."

She smiled at my manner, a genuine warmth came over her face, and she gave me a pen and an application form and said,

"Sign right here." As I signed, she said, "What did you say your name was?"

"Mickey Rooney."

"How old are you, Mickey?"

"I'm thirteen, uh, thirteen this September."

I shoved the paper across the desk, along with my $27.50.

She deposited my money in a green box, filed my application, and returned with a small card. As she wrote my name on it, she said, "This is only a temporary card. The board of governors has to pass on you. But you may play with this card until you get your official card."

I felt more important then than I had ever felt in my life. The LA Tennis Club! Wow! I can play at the LA Tennis Club!

Which I did for the next eight years.

At first, it wasn't easy getting a game. The older folks wouldn't play with me, but, little by little, the other juniors invited me to play or accepted my invitation to play with them.

I played whenever I could, every weekend for sure. Everyone at the club thought I was cute—always cute. But, little by little, this cute kid started winning his share of games—and from some pretty good players at that: Bob and Tom Falkenburg, Jack Tidball, Ted Schroeder, Gene Mako, Frank Parker, Les Steffon, and a redhead named Donald Budge. And I shouldn't forget to mention another little guy who could look you in the eye and beat you before the net judge put his finger on it, Bobby Riggs. Riggs, a short guy like me, was always hustling, always trying to drum up a bet, always looking for an edge.

In the month of September every year, the club hosted the Pacific Southwest Tournament. I waited to be chosen one of the ball boys for some of the biggest matches on the center court. I didn't get tapped, but I did get to watch the best players in the world: Baron Gottfried Von Cramm from Germany, Fred Perry from England, and Bill Tilden from the United States.

When I wasn't playing tennis, I was playing table tennis. I

played thousands of games of table tennis against the world's greatest players: Amanda Korea, Billy Weisbuck, Don Terry, Don Siegel, Bobby Riggs. Sometimes, I'd play table tennis from six-thirty A.M. to midnight, and, eventually, I won the Junior Table Tennis Championship of Southern California. More to the point, it was because of my table tennis that I got noticed by a guy at MGM who would become my champion and insist that MGM put me under contract. His name was David O. Selznick.

☆ 8 ☆
The MGM Family

One *Sunday* afternoon I was playing in a Ping-Pong tournament at the Ambassador Hotel in LA. It was a benefit for unemployed actors, and David O. Selznick, who was then producing independently under the MGM banner, was the referee. I didn't know who Selznick was. As far as I was concerned, he was just someone who came out of the audience to call the score. As it happened, he was not only a producer, he had married L. B. Mayer's daughter. He was the son-in-law of the studio chief at MGM.

I always had fun playing table tennis, and on this particular afternoon, I was having more fun than usual, not only because I was winning all my matches but because I had a great audience. I entertained them, with a line of picturesque speech and patter and some pantomime that had them in hysterics. One of the guys enjoying himself the most was the referee, Mr. Selznick.

As the story goes, that night Selznick could hardly sleep. He told his wife, Irene, "Metro's got to sign that kid before someone else grabs him." The next morning he went straight to Mr. Mayer's office and said, "L.B., I've found a gold mine. The most

sensational kid I've ever seen. He had the audience at the Ambassador in stitches yesterday. You have to sign him."

"What's his name?" Mr. Mayer asked.

"Mickey Rooney. He used to play in the Mickey McGuire
comedies. He was Mickey McGuire."

"Oh, him." Mr. Mayer started looking at his phone messages.
Then he looked back up at Selznick. "David, Mickey McGuire's
a has-been." Gosh, a has-been at fourteen. I wonder: what kind
of person can ever say about anybody, "He's a has-been?" Or
"She's a has-been." How can anybody ever give up on anybody?
We human beings, we're a great species, with a remarkable
ability to come back, to change, to re-form ourselves—if we
want to. Or, as O. Henry said once, in another context, "Nobody's too good to fall—or too bad to climb."

Fortunately, Selznick didn't go along with Mr. Mayer's nega-
tive thinking. He spent the rest of his day composing an eleven-
page memo, single-spaced, putting forth sixty reasons why
MGM should sign Mickey Rooney to a long-term contract. The
memo didn't make much of an impression on Mr. Mayer, nor
on any one of his minions. Eddie Mannix, Mr. Mayer's hatchet
man, came back to Selznick. "Look, David, if that McGuire kid
is so terrific, why don't you put him in one of your own pictures?"

"I will. I'll put him in my new Gable picture."

Mannix laughed. *"Manhattan Melodrama?* I don't think there's
a kid part in it."

"There is now," said Selznick, who called in the writers,
Joseph L. Mankiewicz and Oliver H. P. Garrett, and told them
to create a part for young Mickey—Clark Gable as a young boy.

They did. Two slum boys grow up together. One becomes a
gangster, the other a district attorney in the big town. Eventually, the D.A., William Powell, has to prosecute his old chum,
Gable, who walks cheerfully to the chair. "Of course, you can't
pardon me," Gable says in his patented growl. "I'll walk down
that hallway and it'll be fine, just fine."

My bit was so brief, however, that no reviewer seemed inclined to notice me. Why should anyone look at me when Gable and Powell, two of Hollywood's hottest stars, were up there on the screen?

The picture, with W. S. Van Dyke as director and James Wong Howe as cinematographer, was darn good. Arthur Caesar won an Oscar for original story (and Mankiewicz and Garrett should have gotten one for figuring out a way to get me into the picture). In addition to all that, the movie got an extra break at the box office. Two months after its New York premiere, on a hot, sweltering night in Chicago, John Dillinger, the FBI's public enemy number one, was shot dead coming out of the Biograph Theatre. Every newspaper in the country made sure to tell its readers what picture Dillinger was watching just before he died: *Manhattan Melodrama.* By 1938 the picture had grossed almost $1,500,000, earning about one tenth of MGM's entire profit for the year.

All this attention didn't hurt me one bit. Fans who, like Mr. Mayer, might have thought I was a has-been now realized that Mickey McGuire had grown up and become—Mickey Rooney. What's more, Louis B. Mayer had changed his mind about me. He decided to put me under contract.

My mother got the news on the phone one afternoon when I was there. I watched her face glow with pride, and, when she hung up the phone, I knew something good had happened. She did a little silent dance around the apartment and announced: "We've arrived." She was right. MGM, Hollywood's biggest studio, had twenty-two soundstages on a 180-acre lot; it had its own police and fire departments, its own hospital. It even had its own pumping oil well. Furthermore, it had four thousand employees representing 150 crafts and professions. They were all there to help young actors like me. And, finally, there was this: MGM paid the biggest salaries. And why not? MGM had some of Hollywood's most glittering stars: John and Lionel Barrymore, Wallace Beery, Robert Montgomery, Clark Gable, William Powell, Frederic March, Jackie Cooper, Joan Crawford, Jean Harlow, Greta Garbo, Norma Shearer, Rosalind Russell, Marlene Dietrich, Jeanette MacDonald and Nelson Eddy, Claudette Colbert.

What's more, MGM took care of its stars, giving them the best commissary in town and any and every kind of lesson you could think of. The studio paid top dollar for the kind of literary properties that would bring out the best in each of its stars. Mother said L. B. Mayer was the best studio chief any actor could want. "He could be like a father to you, Sonny. I hear he worries about his studio kids like they was his own kids."

Harry Weber negotiated the contract for us. I'd start at $150 a week and stay there until the end of 1934. After that, MGM had the option to keep me on, at which point my salary would go up to $200 a week. After that, options would be on a yearly basis, beginning with $300 a week, all the way to $1,000 a week by 1941. I'd be guaranteed forty weeks a year.

To a fourteen-year-old who had been selling newspapers on the corner of Melrose and Vermont only a few months before, that seemed like silver dollars from heaven. It didn't matter to me then that MGM would have total artistic control over everything I did, not only in pictures but over all my public appearances. MGM had the right to loan me out to other studios without my consent. MGM would decide when, and whether, I made any stage appearances, performed on radio, or did what we then called phonographic recordings.

Unlike Shirley Temple's mother, who got a small salary as a kind of rider on Shirley's contract with Twentieth Century-Fox, my mother got nothing for herself. Unlike Shirley, I did not get a bonus written into my contract.

But that didn't matter. The important thing was that I was under contract. It was the biggest possible boost to my career. It meant that I didn't have to go looking for parts anymore or go on casting calls or worry where our next dollar was coming from. It meant that I was now part of the MGM family, MGM, with more stars than there are in heaven. And, as one of those stars, I'd find fame and fortune. I'd be rich.

MGM had me working as hard as anyone under contract had ever worked, and I loved it. After doing my bit in *Manhattan Melodrama,* I did nine more pictures in 1934. First there were small parts in three more for MGM: *Hide-Out, Death on the Diamond,* and *Chained.*

Chained allowed me to work again with one of Hollywood's legendary directors, Clarence Brown. Brown had won his reputation for his superb handling of actresses—Greta Garbo, Norma Shearer, Joan Crawford, and Jean Harlow. He was a director of taste, energy, credibility, and imagination. He was also a consummate gentleman; he never raised his voice, never criticized anyone in front of another, dressed in impeccable, tailor-made English tweeds and white turtlenecks, and his shoes always shone, like moonlight on a lake.

Four pictures for MGM was only the beginning. MGM loaned me out to Universal for another four pictures, to Warner Brothers for another, and to Columbia for yet another. (See the Appendix for a complete list of all my films.) In *Blind Date,* Columbia cast me as the kid brother to Ann Sothern, and *The New York Times* judged me "an excellent child actor."

When I say I was "loaned out," I'm not being quite accurate. MGM didn't lend me, it rented me out at two or three times my MGM salary. (Of course, I had no way of knowing this at the time.) Since the people at MGM had me on loan-out three times more than they used me in 1934, they not only got my services free, they made money on me to boot. Figure it out: MGM paid me $150 a week for forty weeks. That means I cost them $6,000 for the year. But, since they had me on loan-out for thirty weeks, charging the other studios at least $300 a week for my services, they grossed no less than $9,000. They ended up, then, "earning" a bonus of $3,000 or more for themselves. It was something like slavery, except that slaves, at least, can feel the whip. All I got was honey-tongues telling me how great I was. (And seventy weeks of work—in one year!)

My mother was too naive to realize what was going on. All she knew was this: $150 a week was a heckuva lot of money. It gave her the kind of freedom she needed—to shed Wynn Brown. I thought we had a good thing going in the family, but then, all of a sudden, Wynn was leaving. He came to me one day and said that he and Mother were getting a divorce. "You mean," I said, "that we're not going to go fishing together anymore?" He smiled bravely and said he guessed not. "No more baseball and football games? No more fights or wrestling matches?"

He turned away so I couldn't see him cry.

But I cried. I cried like a baby.

I had lost—another dad.

☆ 9 ☆
I Play Puck

As busy as I was in the summer of 1934, I wasn't too busy to audition for the part of Puck in a superextravagant stage version of *A Midsummer Night's Dream,* to be directed by Max Reinhardt. As founder and director of the Salzburg Festival in Austria, and director of the Deutsches Theatre in Berlin, Reinhardt had done such imaginative and daring things on the stages of Europe and New York that he was widely considered one of the leading theatrical figures of the age. He was also smart enough to put his wet finger to the breeze and figure out which way the wind was blowing—Austria was no place for a Jew in 1934. Hitler's troops didn't march into Austria until 1938, but in 1934 the handwriting was already on the wall. The walls of cities like Vienna and Salzburg and St. Anton were defaced with crude slogans about Die Juden.

Reinhardt headed for New York, where there was already a sizable contingent of German and Austrian Jews in the American theater. But Reinhardt wanted to direct movies, so he tried, and failed, to get a directing assignment, largely because he spoke hardly a word of English. To get closer to Hollywood, he finally jumped at an offer from the Southern California Chamber of Commerce to put on a production of Shakespeare in the Hollywood Bowl. The *Los Angeles Times,* you see, had shamed Hollywood's moguls into ponying up $125,000 to promote some real culture in Southern California; how could they go wrong with Shakespeare? Reinhardt figured that if he pulled this, he'd sweep into film production on the heels of all the acclaim.

He sent his son, Gottfried, ahead to instigate his first daring move—to sign up the biggest names in Hollywood for this play. He wanted Charlie Chaplin for Bottom, Greta Garbo for Titania, Clark Gable for Demetrius, Gary Cooper for Lysander, John Barrymore for Oberon, W. C. Fields for Thisbe, Wallace Beery for the Lion, Walter Huston for Theseus, Joan Crawford for Hermia, Myrna Loy for Helena, and Fred Astaire for Puck. He didn't understand Hollywood, of course. These stars weren't available or, at least, not available for this production— which was scheduled for a long run in the Hollywood Bowl, every night for a full month under the stars.

But a lot of other stars and would-be stars wanted to work with Reinhardt and they started a stampede to the auditions at the Hollywood Roosevelt Hotel. Olivia de Havilland yearned to play Puck. She was a petite eighteen-year-old, and she could have passed for a boy. Mary Pickford, then forty-one, but still slight, also made a pitch for the part. I got it.

I'm still not quite sure how I got it. I sat in the back of the ballroom at the Roosevelt with my mother and luxuriated in the language of Shakespeare as, one after another, those trying out for the different roles put themselves—heart, soul, body, blood and guts—into the poetry. I didn't understand it. I'd never read Shakespeare before (or since). And I certainly didn't understand Puck's opening lines.

> *How now, spirit, whither wander you? . . .*
> *The King doth keep his revels here tonight;*
> *Take heed the Queen come not within his sight.*

For Oberon is passing fell and wrath
Because that she as her attendant hath
A lovely boy stolen from an Indian king,
She never had so sweet a changeling,
And jealous Oberon would have the child
Knight of his train, to trace the forests wild.
But she perforce withholds the loved boy
Crowns him with flowers, and makes him all her joy.

Those were the lines given me to read by Reinhardt's assistant, Felix Weissberger, who was handling this cattle call. By now, toward the end of the day, the whole place was heavy with sweat and perfume. Most of those who were going to read had already read. A few actors remained, either to do some politicking or to watch me perform. I made my way down to a darkened "tryout pit" and read. I swear I had no idea what I was reading.

But Weissberger was delighted with my enthusiasm. I was small for my age, I had an impish way about me, and, when I read, even though I didn't know what I was saying, my voice sounded—well, Puckish. "Not bad, not bad," he said, peering at me through lenses as thick as a Coke bottle. "Now I vant you should go home and memorize all this and come beck tomorrow for anozzer audition. *Verstehen sie?*" He handed me a script, with my lines marked in red.

When I got home, I fussed and fumed and told my mother I could never learn to say those words and make them sound right. She was patient with me. "You can do it, Mickey. You can do it."

I plunked myself down in a big armchair and memorized all of Puck's lines. When I was finished, my mother sat with me and fed me all the cue lines while I did Puck out loud, over and over again. Gradually, I began to get the feel of Shakespeare's iambic pentameter, if not a full understanding of all the poet's words. Many of them were words I'd never heard before, at least not like this. I knew what "passing" meant. I knew what "fell" meant. I knew what "wrath" meant. But what the heck did "passing fell and wrath" mean?

At the second audition, in a private suite, something came over me. I think it was the spirit of Puck. Shakespeare had infused a certain vitality into a character four centuries earlier. Now, magically, I had that same vitality. I was Puck. More important, Weissberger thought I was Puck. When I laughed Puck's laugh—part bray, part boy—he knew it. "*Ya, ya. Gut, gut,*" he said, clapping his hands together.

Shortly, a square, imposing little man strode into the room, looked at me and my mother with piercing blue eyes, and dropped into a chair. It was Reinhardt. In German (the man spoke almost no English), he told Weissberger to have me begin.

I wasn't scared. Gosh, I'd been onstage since I was eighteen months. No little guy with a pointy nose who couldn't speak English was going to intimidate me. I rattled off my lines. I mugged. I moved. Now and then I'd do a piece of stage business. Gradually, I could see I was winning him over. A faint smile came to his lips. Then I laughed Puck's laugh, as interpreted by me. I was almost an ass. That did it. "*Das Lachen*"—"That laugh"—Reinhardt said to his assistant. "*Ich mag ihn gern.*"—"I like it." I was hired on the spot at double my MGM salary—three hundred dollars a week.

I joined a gifted cast: Walter Connolly as Bottom, Sterling Hayden as Flute, Philip Arnold as Oberon (a role he had played many times in England), Evelyn Venable as Helena, Olivia de Havilland as Hermia. (She was just as glad, she told me, she got that part instead of Puck.) Erich Wolfgang Korngold adapted Mendelssohn's score. And Bronislava Nijinska and Nini Theilade staged the ballet.

Rehearsals began in early September, but we couldn't rehearse in the Bowl until just a few days before our opening, on September 17. Reinhardt had a whole team of set designers building a big hill right on the stage of the Hollywood Bowl. They planted grass on the hill and transplanted oak trees in it and shrubbery.

During rehearsal I learned what it was to be directed by a master like Reinhardt, who taught me how to make the most of Puck. At one point in the play, Puck would declaim:

> *Up and down, up and down,*
> *I will lead them up and down.*
> *I am fear'd in field and town.*
> *Goblin, lead them up and down.*

"*Ya, ya,*" said Reinhardt when he heard my reading. But then he called Weissberger over and told him how I could do these lines even better. Weissberger came over and explained that I should try to use my whole body as I said these lines. He wanted me to bounce up and down, up and down, as I said "up and down, up and down." I tried it, and it worked. It was a little detail. But, as I learned, of such details are great performances made.

At the dress rehearsal, I was amazed at the stage. They'd removed the shell completely and created a whole forest in its place. And they'd built a ramp from the stage area that ran about 250 yards to the west, all the way up to the hill that borders the bowl. The ramp was designed for the solemnity of the pageant that would begin the play's second act. Three hundred extras assembled there for a torchlight procession down to the glade. We had a full symphony orchestra, seventy musicians, to play music that Felix Mendelssohn had written in 1842, especially for this play. There were three dozen ballerinas. No wonder the dress rehearsal took thirteen hours.

I managed to add my bit to the delay. I had a minimal costume, just a loincloth over a green leotard over a jockstrap (plus a pair of Puck's horns glued on to two shaven areas of my head).

But I'd have done better with just a loincloth. At one point in the second act, Oberon calls up to one of the oaks and bids me come. "My gentle Puck, come hither." I was supposed to drop out of the branches and land lightly on the stage in front of him.

"My gentle Puck, come hither," he said again. When nothing happened, he said the line a third time. Now everyone was looking up in the oak tree, wondering why I wasn't coming hither.

"I can't come hither," I said. "My jock's caught on one of these darned branches."

Everyone laughed, including Reinhardt (once his assistant translated what I'd said).

We had a standing-room-only audience on opening night. More than twenty-four thousand people filled the amphitheater and the knolls above the stage. Searchlights scanned the skies above Hollywood, and cameras flashed in the aisles. Somebody came back to the portable trailers that served as our dressing rooms to tell us the names of some of the stars who had already arrived: Clark Gable with Carole Lombard, William Powell with Jean Harlow, Mary Pickford with Buddy Rogers, Joan Crawford and Franchot Tone, Charles Chaplin and Paulette Goddard. Somebody else had seen Gary Cooper and understood Jimmy Cagney was in one of the boxes, among the black ties and diamonds. The night itself, clear and warm as Hollywood often is in September, was one big sparkle.

The play went off without a hitch, not even a hitch in my jockstrap. In fact, it seemed over almost before we knew it had begun. All of a sudden, I was into my closing lines:

> *Gentles, do not reprimand.*
> *If you pardon, we will mend,*
> *Else the Puck a liar call.*
> *And so good night unto you all.*
> *Give me your hands if we be friends,*
> *And Robin shall restore amends.*

I raced up the long, flowered ramp to what I remember as thundering applause, a roar that I thought everyone in Los Angeles could hear. "My gosh," I said to myself, "they're cheering me." The applause went on and on. I said, "Thank life's plum for falling. It sure tastes great." I hoped I wouldn't get indigestion.

The press applauded, too. Next day's *Los Angeles Times* gave the play a great review and said my Puck was "one of the brightest moments of the performance." And Murray Schumach of *The New York Times*, writing from Los Angeles, said I moved with "an elfin, quicksilver grace" and "revealed a greater comprehension of his role than almost anyone in the cast."

We did the Bowl for the next twenty-seven nights. Night after night, people kept streaming in. Almost every morning, it seemed, the papers did more stories on individuals in the cast and on others connected with the production. And the society section had pictures of folks and their pre-Bowl and post-Bowl parties.

Reinhardt took the whole show on the road. We did two weeks on the campus at Berkeley, then took our *Dream* across the Bay to San Francisco's Opera House for four more weeks. The critics in the Bay Area were marvelous to us, and we were sold out for eight performances a week in San Francisco. Then we did the same kind of SRO at the Blackstone Theater in Chicago, a four-week stand. The last time I saw my father, he was in Chicago. I wondered, for a moment or two, if he might have been out there in the audience at the Blackstone, watching me, but I didn't dwell on the thought. Anyway, I was busy.

Then the whole cast flew back from New York on TWA. I'd never been on an airplane before, and I was thrilled. We didn't do it nonstop, of course. In those days, we had to make five stops for fueling. Our second or third stop was in Kansas City, my old hometown. As we took off for our next stop—in Amarillo, Texas—I couldn't help thinking of that first trip my mother and I took from Kansas City in the Model T Ford. That journey, from Kansas City to LA, took us four weeks. This last hop didn't take us more than a few hours.

In January, Reinhardt's dream of becoming a Hollywood director came true, or almost true. Warner Brothers decided to put his play on the silver screen, with William Dieterle, a German director who had been in this country for a long time, assisting Reinhardt. Dieterle was a giant, six-five if he was an inch, who always wore white gloves. It was a meaningless affectation. Dieterle was very much in charge, very creative, very competent. And Reinhardt agreed to some cast changes, at the request of the brothers Warner, who wanted to see more of their contract players in the picture: Jimmy Cagney, Dick Powell, Joe E. Brown, Hugh Herbert, Arthur Treacher, Victor Jory, Anita Louise, Frank McHugh, and Ian Hunter. Olivia de Havilland and I repeated our stage performances. I only had one thing to do differently: let my hair grow longer. Perc Westmore glued me on another pair of horns and a lot of extra hair all over my body. I was the first baby werewolf, a werewolf who smelled of glue.

My reputation for being accident-prone had preceded me, so Jack Warner called me in and tried to get tough. He told me that this was going to be one hell of an expensive picture, and he ordered me not to play football (I could hurt a knee), play baseball (I could get beaned), or do any high diving (I might hit my head on the bottom of the pool). If I breached these provisions in my contract, I'd be out of a job.

My contract didn't say anything about playing in the snow, so I arranged to do just that. I pointed out to my mother that Big Bear had just had a big snowfall, and I insisted she drive me up there.

When we arrived, my mother curled up on a couch in front of a roaring fire in the lobby of the lodge. Me, I went out to tumble in the snow.

I found some kids, much bigger than I. I spotted a sign that said, TOBOGGANS FOR HIRE: $2 AN HOUR. $10 SECURITY DEPOSIT. My newfound friends and I headed for a nearby hill. I took the front seat, and my friends piled on behind. We didn't know much about toboggans. We soon learned the darn things don't steer very well. You have to get everybody to lean one way or another, and that only veers them slightly off course. As it happened, we selected a hill that was generously scattered with Jeffrey pines, big old trees that flashed by as we began picking up speed. The others started to scream, so I stuck out my left leg to try and slow us down, but it was no use. Moments later, we hit a big tree and were scattered like a bunch of tenpins.

When I came to, flat on my back in the snow, I found that someone's leg was twisted up around my chin. It was mine. I grabbed it, angry and in terrific pain, and yanked it back down where it belonged. Then I passed out again.

The bad news: my left femur was broken. The good news: in yanking it back into position, I had reset the break. The medics at Big Bear didn't have to do much except put my leg in a big, temporary splint. One of those attending me said, "Congratulations, young man. You'd make an excellent doctor."

They laid me in the backseat of my mother's car, and on the ride home I swore in pain every time the car lurched, and Nell said, "Go ahead and swear, goddamn it, if it makes you feel better." But she was wondering if I'd be kicked off the picture.

Jack Warner didn't get angry. He went insane. The first thing he wanted to do was kill me. "Then, after I kill him," he said, "I'm gonna break his other leg." We'd already shot a third of the picture. It would cost a quarter of a million to start all over with a new Puck. No. They couldn't do that. Finally, they decided to shoot around me. If they needed me at all, it would be in a long shot. And so, for those shots, they used a stand-in. In four weeks or so, I could come back and work.

I recuperated in Hollywood Presbyterian Hospital, with my right leg in a cast. Fortunately for me, my doctor was a horse player. One morning I noticed that he'd left something on my bed called the *Daily Racing Form.* This took me back to my days at Caliente in Tijuana. I studied this paper, learned all about past performances, a horse's breeding, its speed ratings, and its odds on winning the next race. I arranged for my nurse to bring me the *Form* each morning, so I could handicap all the races in the country each day and then check the results in the next day's edition. I started making (and winning) some mind bets and soon I was sharing my good, make-believe fortune with some of the other doctors and nurses.

"Hey, I'd like to make a bet or two," said one intern. "But I don't know any bookies."

I allowed as to how I could book his bets for him.

"You?" he said. "You know a bookie?"

"Noooo," I said. "I'll be the bookie." I am sure I was not the first patient to run a bookmaking operation from my hospital bed. Nor the last. But maybe the youngest.

I ended up making a few dollars in my new, part-time profession. More important, I'd acquired a lifelong addiction to a difficult intellectual game—played with real money. What fun!

When I got out of the hospital, they gave me a smaller cast. Even though I was on crutches, I went to the studio and told Dieterle that I could work. He smiled and said that, yes, by God, I could. I played the rest of the shooting schedule on one leg, the bad one in a cast, always concealed from the camera.

Reinhardt and Dieterle went $250,000 over budget, and the picture was released in New York in October 1935. *Variety* judged that Warner Brothers would be lucky to lose only a half million on it, simply because this was Shakespeare. But it was a critical success. André Sennwald, the *New York Times* reviewer, called the movie "a brave, beautiful and interesting effort to subdue the most difficult of Shakespeare's works." He praised Warner Brothers for a work of high ambitions and said the movie was "a credit to Warner Brothers and to the motion picture industry." And he singled Joe E. Brown and Mickey Rooney as "the bright particular stars of the photoplay," who "hammered it into liveliness." He wrote: "Mickey Rooney's remarkable performance as Puck is one of the major delights of the work . . . He is a mischievous and joyous sprite, a snub-nosed elf who laughs with shrill delight as the foolish mortals blunder through Oberon's fuzzy domain."

So now I was a real actor. It was official. *The New York Times* said so.

☆ *10* ☆
School Days

I*n the fall of* 1935, my mother enrolled me in a military school in Culver City, so I could live right near the MGM studios and get a touch of military discipline in the bargain. I thought I would like it there, and I did, for a time. I played football, a 98-pounder on the 125-pound team, rode a jumper named Little Nipper, and I ate regular meals.

I lasted four weeks because I wasn't happy there. For one thing, they gave us uniforms that made us look like Russian Cossacks or at least like my Hollywood notion of a Russian Cossack. For another thing, I soon found that most of the kids frowned a lot and got into fights and cried out in their sleep at night. Some of them even wet their beds. Fact is, I learned, little by little, that a lot of these kids were there because their parents didn't want them around.

Maybe that's why my mother sent me away. She was starting to date again, and, at fourteen, I had decided that sex was dirty. I never said this in so many words to my mother, but I made it clear to her that I certainly didn't approve of the guys who were escorting her home these days. One night, I found some guy kissing her good night on the porch and I almost had a fit. Later,

I would tell myself that my mother had every right to a life of her own. But, at fourteen, a young man has funny feelings about a lot of things.

But if not the Pacific Military Academy, where would I go then? The one-room schoolhouse on the MGM lot? No. There was nothing normal about that, and I wanted to be *normal*. I hadn't had a normal childhood, but I was determined to be a normal teenager. And so, a month into the fall semester, I enrolled as a freshman at Fairfax High. For a while it looked as if I'd found the right place. The kids there accepted me, and I went out for B football. (B football was for kids who weren't big enough to play for the varsity.)

I think Hollywood High was playing us on our home field when I won my first battle scars. I was a quarterback in our single wing, or Notre Dame box formation, because I could handle the ball on our spinner plays and could call the plays and I was a good blocker. I enjoyed staying low, speeding out in front of my ballcarrier and taking out the end or the corner-back—whoever was out there waiting to tackle my man. In the third quarter, I made a beautiful cross-body block on one of their guys and took him down. I thought nothing of it when he whipped back at me with his cleats because, shoot, my tailback was already downfield for a fifteen-yard gain. Back in the huddle, however, somebody said, "Shit, Mickey! Look at your leg."

Apparently, the guy who gave me the crackback with his feet had a broken cleat. The screw underneath that hard rubber cleat had neatly sliced my calf and the cut was pouring down blood like the open Coke spigot at Schwab's. My guard Machado waved and called out to the coach, who sent in a sub. But as soon as our water boy cleansed the wound and taped it up, I was back in the game. Our water boy used iodine on my wound, just like the doctor at Hollywood Emergency Hospital, the sadistic guy who sent me through the roof, but now I didn't even wince. This was different. I was tougher. And all the guys were watching me to see what I was made of.

I don't remember whether we won the game. But I know I won. I can still see the faces of the guys who were waiting for me outside the locker-room door, clapping me on the back and laughing as we got on our bikes together for the short ride home. Sure, my calf hurt. But, hey, I belonged!

I loved it at Fairfax High, but the trouble was, I couldn't stay there. I was missing too much school, spending a lot more time on the MGM lot, and I was scheduled to do four more pictures in 1935. So my mother went to MGM's schoolmarm, Mary Mc-Donald, and told her I'd be joining her in MGM's Little Red Schoolhouse on a regular basis.

Jackie Cooper was there and so was Freddie Bartholomew, an English kid who had just made a big splash in *David Copperfield*. So were Deanna Durbin, a winsome little stuck-up songbird; Bonita Granville; Virginia Weidler; and Gloria DeHaven, whom I would end up dating for a time.

The Little Red Schoolhouse was just that, a little rural school-house right there in the middle of these sheds that housed the great soundstages. The one-story schoolhouse was white, not red, but it was made of wood and had a gabled roof and a chimney and a little front porch with a rocking chair on it. Three wooden steps led up to it from a neatly cobblestoned pavement.

We were supposed to attend classes for five hours a day, but the studio fudged on that a bit. We'd usually go to the red schoolhouse for three hours every morning, from nine to noon, then spend the other two with our tutors on our respective sets. Some of the tutorial sessions were a joke: fifteen minutes of English, then back in front of the camera for an hour, then fifteen minutes of arithmetic, then back in front of the camera again. I guess it goes without saying that we didn't develop good study habits.

No one raised any eyebrows over that or protested to the board of education. Who was going to do this? Certainly not the directors or producers, who won Brownie points if they completed their films ahead of schedule. Certainly not Miss McDonald, the schoolmarm in charge. Protests from her would almost certainly have led to her dismissal by the studio. Miss McDonald got the job because she knew how to play ball.

Miss McDonald looked like something out of Central Casting herself: a slender, dark-eyed woman with dark hair done up in a severe bun, with a gold watch pinned to her shirtwaist. She did the best she could, under the circumstances. She stuck to the basics: reading, writing, spelling, arithmetic. Occasionally, usually on those hot Indian summer days in LA that extend through the fall into December, she'd relieve our boredom—and hers as well, I think—by cranking up the Victrola for something called "Music Appreciation."

During those periods, I'd either do some first-class daydreaming or some tourist-class gawking: the young ladies in these classes were, after all, budding movie stars. They weren't too hard on the eyes, and they all wore perfume and lacy bras that evoked natural fantasies in me. Lana Turner hadn't yet arrived at Metro, but, as soon as she did, I assumed full gazing rights. I can remember many a day when Miss McDonald would catch me in fervent contemplation of Lana's bosom (and other parts) and warn me.

"Mr. Rooney!" she'd cry.

In perfect feigned innocence, I'd reply, "Yes, Miss McDonald?"

Her answering smirk needed no words. I got the message: she was on to me.

For a guy who had told L. B. Mayer I could make millions for MGM, David O. Selznick was sure taking his time about giving me good parts. He grabbed me to appear in his next picture, *Reckless,* a good vehicle for Jean Harlow and William Powell (who were real-life lovers), Franchot Tone, May Robson, and Rosalind Russell. But it was a sneezer for me. Victor Fleming (who would go on to direct me and Spencer Tracy in *Captains Courageous*) supervised this backstage melodrama about a theatrical agent who loves the glamorous star he represents. She spurns him and marries a drunken millionaire. My lines were pretty much: "Don't worry about the bags. I'll get 'em."

MGM cast me in another bit part in a movie called *Riffraff* with Tracy and Harlow. (I played Harlow's little brother, a mean little kid.) The first of many pictures I would do with Tracy, it was my last with Harlow, who died soon thereafter, at age twenty-six. Tracy was a labor leader in *Riffraff*. Harlow was his wife. They both ended up on the wrong side of the law. It was a serious part for Harlow, whose forte was comedy, and a serious bit of miscasting by the studio. They made her into a brunette and gave her a husband with an acute social consciousness. She ended up going to prison for him. Harlow had won people over by making them laugh. Now MGM had her trying to make people cry. It didn't work.

Variety's reviewer said, "It isn't art, but it's box office." Barely. *Riffraff* lost money. I guess that not every MGM picture had to make a profit, especially if the guy producing it was Irving Thalberg—and Thalberg was the producer of *Riffraff*. Thalberg, you see, had the reputation of being the one man at MGM who could put the studio's motto on his own coat of arms: *Ars gratia artis*, "art for the sake of art." As if money didn't matter.

Sure. Maybe Thalberg got that rep because he produced as many flops as he did hits, and it seemed to me that he went out of his way to put his wife in films she didn't need and wasn't right for. For instance, she was a very mature thirty-five when she tried to play the teenaged Juliet. The fact is that Thalberg did better when he didn't have his wife on the payroll—*China Seas* with Gable and Harlow, *A Night at the Opera*, the best film ever made by the Marx Brothers, and *Mutiny on the Bounty*, with Gable and Charles Laughton. They were—and are—classics. And they all made money.

Right after I did *Riffraff*, I was loaned out to do *The Healer* with Ralph Bellamy, a man with one of the most distinctive voices in the history of the movies. He was a doctor and I was a boy with polio, which gave me a chance to irrigate my tear ducts. Directors never had to pull any tricks to get me to cry; nobody had to tell me my dog had just died. I'd been crying on cue all my life.

On my next picture, *The County Chairman*, Will Rogers complimented me on my professionalism. "You handle yourself very well, son," he said after our first day's shooting. I'm sure he'd never heard of me before and was wondering where on earth I'd gotten all my self-assurance.

"Sir?" I said quizzically.

He explained. "You know your lines. You don't interfere with mine. You know how to have fun with the script. Your performance makes mine better."

On August 15, 1935, not long after we did our movie together, Rogers died in a plane crash at Walaka Lagoon in Alaska, hard by Point Barrow. When I got the news, I wondered why God took a good man like Will Rogers while He let a little guy named Adolf Hitler, who also liked to fly small planes, live to make trouble over in Europe. I also wondered what God had in mind for me. Like Rogers, I had started in vaudeville. Furthermore, I had a drunken philandering clown for a father and a chorus girl for a mother. Now, here I was, playing a good part in the movie version of a play written by the great Eugene O'Neill. Yes, *Ah, Wilderness!* was my next picture, and this, at last, was the kind of picture that David Selznick must have been dreaming about when he brought me to MGM.

Ah, Wilderness! is a story about growing up in small-town New England, a place that might have existed at one time for millions of Americans. Lionel Barrymore was a kindly dad trying to help his teenage son (played by Eric Linden) grow up as best he could; he even tried a heart-to-heart talk about sex, heartbreaking, funny, and memorable. (I was Linden's little brother in this one, but in 1948 I'd play the older brother in a musical remake of *Ah, Wilderness!* called *Summer Holiday.*) Creating this New England utopia was all part of L. B. Mayer's master plan to reinvent America.

Like most movie moguls, Mr. Mayer had spent his whole life reinventing himself. Along the way he became a super-American, more patriotic than George Washington himself, even concocting a birthday for himself on the Fourth of July. Even Mr. Mayer's wife participated in the charade by burning all of his correspondence after his death because she didn't want anyone to know that her husband couldn't spell very well. (She also concealed the fact that he'd divorced her, but that was for other reasons, connected with her own identity and social standing.)

But Mr. Mayer was not satisfied to reinvent himself. He wanted to reinvent America, too. In most of the movies that came under his control, Mr. Mayer knew that he was "confecting, not reflecting" America. Danny Selznick, Mr. Mayer's grandson, will back me up here. Selznick says that his grandfather looked upon his films as "shaping the taste of the country . . . He wanted values to be instilled in the country and knew how influential films could be."

Ah, Wilderness! was one of those films. Clarence Brown directed it from a script that was adapted from O'Neill's play by two of MGM's best writers, Albert Hackett and Frances Goodrich, and he signed up some of the MGM stock company's best people to bring it off: Wallace Beery, Lionel Barrymore, Spring Byington, Cecilia Parker, Bonita Granville, and me.

And we did it. The picture helped Mr. Mayer cast a spell on America, on its values and attitudes and images, and it made some money along the way. It wasn't a huge box-office success, but it grossed MGM $1,014,000 on an investment of $588,000.

For me the high point of making the film was getting to know Wallace Beery, a lovable, shambling kind of guy who never seemed to know that his shirttail belonged inside his pants but always knew when a little kid actor needed a smile and a wink or a word of encouragement. Beery was married to Gloria

Swanson when she was big. (I can imagine Miss Swanson rolling her eyes over that remark and saying, as she did in *Sunset
Boulevard*, "I was *always* big. It was only the pictures that got
small.")

Not everyone loved Wallace Beery as much as I did. Howard
Strickling, the head of publicity at MGM, never liked Beery—
because Beery's roistering ways tended to make more work for
Strickling. Once, Strickling went to Mayer and complained that
Beery was stealing props off the set. And that wasn't all. He
went on for some minutes about the trouble that Beery was
always causing him. Then Mayer sighed and said, "Yes, Howard, Beery's a son of a bitch. But he's *our* son of a bitch."

Strickling got the point. A family has to be tolerant of its black
sheep, particularly if they brought a lot of money into the family
fold, which Beery certainly did. Yes, MGM was a family, but it
was a family that cared a lot about money. The head of the
family, L. B. Mayer, would soon become the most well-paid
executive in America, thanks to his 43 percent of the profits in
the so-called Mayer's Group. Much of those profits would be
generated by a B picture that would set off a series that was
MGM's biggest money earner of all time. The picture was *A
Family Affair*, featuring a refreshingly simple young man named
Andy Hardy, played by me.

But, I'm getting ahead of my story.

On My Way to the Top

Because of my size, it didn't take a director of genius to cast me as a jockey. In *Down the Stretch*, I was Snapper Sinclair, the only jockey able to ride Faithful, an ultraspeedy but temperamental colt. In the picture, I fall in with bad elements and I'm ruled off every track in America. But I get another chance and prove my mettle in the English Derby.

As Sinclair, I got $300 a week for four weeks, even though Warner Brothers' records show they paid MGM $600 a week for my services. But consider the work in this picture of Willie Best. Willie Best usually played the same role over and over in a succession of pictures that helped establish a shameful Hollywood stereotype, the moronic colored boy. Doing it once more in *Down the Stretch*, Best earned $65 a week. However, RKO, which had Best under contract, got $130 for Best's work. At the same time Warners paid $50 a day to rent a mechanical horse to stand in for my ultraspeedy colt. I guess black kids were in greater supply than mechanical robots.

I got to know one actor quite well during two of the pictures I made in 1936. His name was Freddie Bartholomew. David Selznick had signed him for MGM in 1935 to make *David Copper-*

field, with W. C. Fields as Micawber. It was a big hit, and all of a sudden this nice young man was making one thousand dollars a week, about five times what I was making. I wasn't jealous, but I was intimidated before I got to know Freddie, then pleased to find out that he wasn't stuck-up at all. Quite the contrary, he was the kind of kid who was more interested in other people than he was in himself.

Freddie had already had some experience with the downside of fame. When he struck it rich, his dad, a one-legged ne'er-do-well named Cecil who had abandoned the family some years before, came out of nowhere demanding part of Freddie's loot. Freddie's Aunt Myllicent (he called her Aunt Cissy), who had become the young man's legal guardian, fought Cecil's move in the courts, so Cecil didn't get a nickel. But a bunch of lawyers and agents and revenuers squeezed a lot more than that from Freddie. After the dust settled, Freddie was slapped with $83,000 in legal fees.

For a couple of years, Freddie Bartholomew was the biggest kid star in Hollywood. MGM soon had us working together in *Little Lord Fauntleroy,* one of David O. Selznick's literary classics brought to the screen. It was a blend of sentiment, snobbery, and Victorian melodrama, but director John Cromwell made it all come together: handsome period settings (Brooklyn in the 1880s) and a cast that worked well together. Besides me and Freddie, it included C. Aubrey Smith and Dolores Costello Barrymore.

MGM quickly cast me and Freddie in another picture, set in New York but this time shot on a Culver City soundstage. It was called *The Devil Is a Sissy.* During that shoot I turned sixteen, time to get my very own car. I had already picked it out, a bright-blue 1937 two-door Ford convertible with real leather seats, and they delivered it to the studio just about the time I was getting out of the soundstage. I whooped when I saw it and I couldn't wait to get behind the wheel. "C'mon, Sig," I said to my stand-in, Sig Frolich. "Let's go."

And go we did, jamming out the studio's East Gate, out Washington Boulevard, through Culver City into Venice and on up north on the Pacific Coast Highway at sixty miles an hour. For a kid from Southern California, there is no finer sensation: driving your first car up the warm September coast, top down, sea air filling your lungs, knowing, now, that the car you're driving is your very own, and that you're free.

Free for what? Well, what does a red-blooded young man think most about in his own convertible? Right. Girls. It wasn't long before I began to meet my obligations to a good many of the gals in town who were dying to meet me. Who wouldn't want to go out with me? I had my own car. I had some nickels in my pocket. And I was somebody.

"Hey," I said to two cute little gals who were walking through the MGM parking lot. They giggled and pretended not to be interested in me as I started up my car. Their pretense lasted about two seconds. Soon, they were pressing up against my car door and wondering whether I could come to their school dance on Friday night. I said, in my most polite manner, that I'd be very pleased to come—as long as I could bring my friend, Andy McIntyre. Andy wasn't in pictures. He worked at Silverwood's on Hollywood Boulevard, where I bought my clothes, and he was my best friend for a long time.

The two gals turned out to be Gloria and Peggy Lloyd, daughters of the silent-comedy star Harold Lloyd. Andy and I double-dated them for some time, during which time Mr. Lloyd gave me some nice pats on the back; he made me feel we were both comedians together. And I did feel a certain kinship with him, especially after he told me that he'd lost three fingers on his right hand while shooting a movie. Reminded me of my dangerous days shooting slapstick comedy for Larry Darmour. Like many dads, Lloyd waved us off into the night with instructions: the usual "Be-home-by-midnight" routine, and "Don't-drive-too-fast," and "Be-careful-on-the-Palisades." "Mr. Lloyd," I said, "I won't go *near* the Palisades." And I didn't. Necking was more fun in the hills, high above Hollywood Boulevard.

But even with my new wheels I wasn't going out every night—far from it. I worked hard all week, generally from seven in the morning until five or six at night. Friday and Saturday nights were really my only nights to boogie, literally. Dancing was our only passion, and we hit all the high spots: down to the Ocean Beach pier one night, then the Pasadena Civic Auditorium the next, to the Palomar Ballroom on Western Avenue near the Bimini Baths, or the Coconut Grove at the Ambassador Hotel on Wilshire. We danced to the big band sounds of the day: Benny Goodman, Glen Gray, Woody Herman, Kay Kyser, Jimmy and Tommy Dorsey, and Glenn Miller.

And, after we danced to the last strains of "Good Night, Sweetheart," remembering my promise to Mr. Lloyd, we never cruised up the coast. We'd drive up above the Sunset Strip, park on overlooks above LA, and gaze down at the carpet of lights below and neck until we were aching with desire. Then, somewhat crippled by our stone-ache, we'd head back down the hill.

I'd drive the gals home to their place in Benedict Canyon, get Andy home, and then try to slip into the house before dawn, without waking Mom.

In those days I had no trouble falling asleep. My insomnia would come later.

☆ *12* ☆

Andy Hardy and Other Hits

T*he Andy* Hardy series didn't begin as a series. It began as a B movie, or what was then called "a programmer"—the second film on a double bill. Each of the studios churned out B pictures but they could never churn quite fast enough to suit the stockholders because these movies were real money-makers. A Clark Gable movie might cost $1 million, a B picture $200,000; but the B movie could end up producing more profit than the Gable blockbuster. At a rate of almost one a week, MGM's movie factory (it was something like the Campbell's Soup Company of the movie business) kept exhibitors' shelves stocked with enough product to keep alive an entertainment that has gone the way of the dinosaur: the double feature.

B movies presented opportunities, then, for young producers on their way up. If a young man could find a likely property that didn't cost too much, the studio was inclined to give him a small budget and tell him to go ahead. That's the way it happened with Sam Marx. Shortly after Marx became a story editor at MGM, he persuaded the studio to buy *Skidding*, a play he'd seen years before in New York. I think MGM paid $5,000 for the rights and handed it over to Marx to produce, on a budget of $185,000. The studio didn't expect much from it.

Marx changed the title of *Skidding* to *A Family Affair* and prevailed upon the studio to tap Lionel Barrymore as the lead. Barrymore didn't really want to play wise old Judge Hardy in a B movie, but he, like everyone else, was under contract, one of the many actors that MGM had on call. Since MGM had nothing else for Barrymore at the moment, he took the part.

Spring Byington, one of those marvelous actresses the studio could cast in almost anything, got the second lead—Mrs. Hardy. And for a while, it looked like a young man named Frankie Thomas would get the part of their son, Andy. As it turned out, Thomas was growing too fast. By the time production began in the late fall of 1936, he was too tall to play Andy. Fate found Rooney, then sixteen years old, with his height seemingly on hold.

We did the picture in fifteen days (seven thousand dollars under budget), and Mr. Mayer never noticed us. No doubt he was preoccupied by the death (at age thirty-seven!) of his production chief, Irving Thalberg, and by the pressure that the press was putting on him to name a replacement. (Mr. Mayer eventually proved that he didn't need another Thalberg. Without Thalberg, MGM had a succession of blockbusters from September 1936, when Thalberg died, until the beginning of World War II.)

I knew *A Family Affair* was a B picture, but that didn't stop me from putting my all into it. I'd not forgotten what Will Rogers told me about myself: that I was a pro. And I'm pretty sure that's the way all the others felt, too, even the great Lionel Barrymore. A funny thing happened to this little programmer: released in April 1937, it ended up grossing more than half a million dollars nationwide.

The critics weren't impressed. *New York Times* reviewer Frank S. Nugent, who had liked my work in *The Devil Is a Sissy*, thought *A Family Affair* just barely worth a mention. To Nugent I was "the epitome of all fourteen-year-olds who hate girls until they see one in a pretty dress." But he did allow that "we rather enjoyed our eavesdropping at Judge Hardy's home." *Daily Variety* didn't even give us a review. And a critic for the Chicago *Tribune* called the picture "a boob trap" that didn't work. But the exhibitors loved it. One guy from Rochester, New York, wired MGM: FOR GOD'S SAKES LET'S HAVE MORE OF THAT ROONEY KID STOP HE REALLY WOWED THEM STOP THE WAY HE TRIPPED OVER THAT DOORMAT AND LOOKED INTO THE EYES OF THAT POLLY BENEDICT GIRL THAT WAS REALLY SOMETHING STOP THE KID'S A GOLD MINE STOP AND SO IS THE REST OF THE CAST STOP PLEASE MAKE ANOTHER HARDY PICTURE RIGHT AWAY.

The reason why he and his colleagues, the theater owners across the country, loved the picture was clear: the public was crazy about it. Never mind the critics, they said, mind the people. But L. B. Mayer wasn't so sure he wanted to make "another Hardy picture right away." During the spring of 1937, I am told, many a conference was held in Mr. Mayer's white-carpeted office to figure out what to do about "the Hardy problem." If the fans were turned on by little Andy Hardy and his little-boy romance with Polly Benedict, then maybe they were tired of the romantic leads. Maybe this was a trend that would depreciate MGM's investment in its Gables and its Tracys and its Taylors. That could be a disaster.

Today it's hard to believe that a studio could think like that, but back then sequels were a rarity, particularly sequels to a B picture. But I think I know why doing a Judge Hardy sequel gave MGM some pause: the star of this one, Lionel Barrymore, made it known that he was, after all, a Barrymore, a member of a family that was the nearest thing to royalty in the American theater. Doing one B picture proved he was a team player, but getting stuck in a B series—well, that was asking too much.

Lionel was a class act. Not only was he a great actor, he wrote music and poetry. He painted. He sketched in charcoal. And he suffered from terrible arthritis, arthritis that literally crippled him. But there was no truth to the rumor that he wanted to pull out of the Hardy sequel because he thought I would "upstage" him.

This "upstaging" business is one of the clichés of the business, perpetrated by dumb writers who don't know what else to say. A good actor doesn't try to show up another actor, or "steal a scene," because he knows it's not in his own interest to do so. A good actor tries to help the other actors around him. If they do a better job, they can only help him do a better job and help the whole show in the bargain.

I am more inclined to believe another tale: that Barrymore might have carried on as Judge Hardy—*if* MGM had torn up his contract and, say, doubled his salary. Mr. Mayer wasn't exactly cheap. He didn't flinch if he had to reshoot huge chunks of a picture that was already in the can—if that was the only way to save his initial investment. But here Mr. Mayer decided he didn't want to double Barrymore's salary because he didn't actually need Barrymore in the part. He could just get a new Judge Hardy and, while he was at it, a new Mrs. Hardy and a new Polly Benedict, too. (Rooney would stay.) He'd put Lewis Stone in the part of the judge, make Fay Holden Mrs. Hardy, and cast Ann Rutherford, a dimpled, promising classmate of mine at the MGM schoolhouse, as Polly Benedict.

As Ann tells the story now (she is still a friend), she accepted the role with some trepidation because I'd been teasing her unmercifully in our MGM schoolhouse. My teasing was bad, but that only lasted a couple of hours a day. Now, cast in the same picture, she'd be subjected to my devilment all day long. Did she want that? Ultimately, she said yes. She said she'd be a fool to turn down this chance. She just knew the Hardy series would sail.

It did. MGM's sequel, *You're Only Young Once*, was better than the original. Screenwriter Kay Van Riper came up with a good story, producer Lou Ostrow kept a firm hand on the schedule, and director George B. Seitz was just what I needed. He gave me my head and (as the series went on) let me improvise when I was so inspired. And in this series, I *was* often inspired.

Gradually, MGM realized that I was the star of the series. The fourth Hardy picture, *Love Finds Andy Hardy,* grossed $2,247,000 and made a profit of $1,345,000, one fourth of MGM's total profit for the 1937 season. No way they could not put "Andy Hardy" in the title of each of the pictures that followed. (There were seventeen in all and MGM ended up with a profit of $111 million—in 1937–1946 dollars. That doesn't include the money chalked up to overhead. In today's dollars, that would be at least half a billion bucks.)

Still, I do not think that historians will remember Andy Hardy for the money he earned for MGM. Rather, it was because he made a mark on a whole generation of Americans. Through the years, I keep meeting people who tell me, "Andy Hardy? Hey, he taught me how to be a teenager." From remarks like this, I conclude that many American teenagers and would-be teenagers went along with the celluloid ideal fashioned by Metro's writers.

I can add this: if they followed the Andy Hardy model, they became the kind of teenagers Mr. Mayer could be proud of. To him, Andy Hardy epitomized all that he thought good about America. Andy Hardy was wholesome, engaging, youthful, full of energy and ideas. And if his ideas were sometimes misdirected, he soon got back on track, usually after a man-to-man talk with his father, whom he respected very much. He respected his mother, too, which pleased Mr. Mayer no end.

That was kind of a quirk with Mr. Mayer. Among God, motherhood, and apple pie, he preferred motherhood. Once John Gilbert told Mr. Mayer that he hated his mother because, he said, she was probably a whore. Mr. Mayer almost went nuts. "Out of my office," he screamed at Gilbert. "I'll cut your balls off."

"Go ahead," shouted Gilbert. "I'll still be more of a man than you."

Mr. Mayer never gave Gilbert another part.

Erich von Stroheim made the same kind of mistake one day, besmirching womankind in front of Mr. Mayer. He told Mr. Mayer, "All women are whores." Mr. Mayer hauled off and punched von Stroheim right in the nose. I don't know for sure if Mr. Mayer had him blacklisted, but I do know that von Stroheim didn't get another directing job, anywhere. He didn't get another big part in Hollywood until he landed the role of Gloria Swanson's chauffeur in *Sunset Boulevard*.

Mr. Mayer had programmed himself to like what sold, and motherhood sold big. Parents became Andy Hardy fans, just as much as their kids did. They liked to think that they could have kids like Andy Hardy and that they might, some day, be the kind of parents Andy Hardy had.

This shouldn't be so surprising. If we can believe the sociologists, 90 percent of American families are what they call "dysfunctional." That means modern American families don't look much like they used to. You know what I mean: a father who goes off to work every morning at eight o'clock and returns at five-thirty, a mother who cooks you your breakfast and kisses you as you go off to school and is there when you come home at three or four or five, fussing over a pot of beef stew and beaming as you spy the apple pie cooling on the windowsill. In this ideal American family, there is never a thought of divorce, nobody has a drinking problem (except maybe your Uncle Harry, who only shows up once a year, at the family's Fourth of July picnic), and your sister doesn't get pregnant at fifteen. You have rollicking good times at dinner every night, you play charades later in the living room, Dad tucks you in at night with a leisurely bedtime story, takes you fishing on Saturday mornings and off to the ball game on Sundays, buys you stereo equipment and posters and model airplanes for your room and indulges your dream of having an English sheepdog for your very own.

For most American families, this is only a dream. In our heart of hearts, we know it's unrealistic to expect something like that for ourselves. But we like to dream on anyway. And we give high marks to any show—radio, movie, or TV—that keeps the dream alive.

At a time when folks were flocking to see the Hardy family, they were also giggling along with a radio program called "Henry Aldrich." Later on, in TV's infancy, Americans fell in love with other unreal families: the Ricky Ricardos—Lucille Ball and Desi Arnaz—and Ozzie and Harriet. Ditto a few years later with the Cleaver family in *Leave It to Beaver*. And who has been topping the recent ratings? Another cute little family that is even more of an idealized stereotype than the Hardy family, because this one is black. Or are the majority of African-American families living in 1990 presided over by a wise, funny, well-spoken, educated, affluent, and loving male like Bill Cosby?

The Andy Hardy movies didn't tell it "like it is." They told it the way we'd like it to be, describing an ideal that needs constant reinvention. This is why we will always need Hollywood, the Hollywood that keeps manufacturing dreams.

I think that's why the Andy Hardy pictures broke all box-office records for MGM. And why I would soon be catapulted to the top of Hollywood's heap.

Through the next five years, from the end of 1936 through 1941, I more or less took L. B. Mayer and MGM for granted, blissfully believing that my good parts and my good luck and my good life would go on forever. As a result, I became as cocky a kid as ever cruised the Sunset Strip in his own convertible, exploding with sheer, selfish energy—and pissing off almost everyone around me. Kids from my neighborhood in Hollywood started laying for me, so they could beat me up good. I was always too fast for them, so I didn't get hurt. I also didn't get the message: that, if I kept up my cheeky behavior, I'd get my comeuppance someday.

For the time being, however, things were on track. The studio told me what to do, and I did it. So what else was new? Over at Twentieth Century-Fox, they were doing the same thing for Shirley Temple. This was the so-called studio system, whose bosses had long since learned what sold a picture: stars. Consequently they became experts in how to create them, nurture them, package them, keep them on the narrow path of virtue, and cover up their sins when they strayed.

MGM was the biggest, most prodigal studio of them all. To support its stars, MGM spared no costs. It hired the best directors, songwriters, orchestras, conductors, choreographers, cinematographers, costumers, cosmeticians, hairstylists, orthodontists, and plastic surgeons that money could buy. But its major assets were its stars—its Gables and its Garbos, its Barrymores and Beerys and Bartholomews and Tracys, its Harlows and its Hepburns. (Soon it would add some new stars to that constellation: Mickey Rooney, Judy Garland, Elizabeth Taylor.) The studio made those stars shine brighter by keeping the wattage turned up, i.e., by putting them in picture after picture after picture. I did four in 1936, seven in 1937, eight in 1938.

Anyone who wants to know what that did for me should take a look (by contrast) at the career of Tom Hulce. This superb actor (so much like me in so many ways) won an Academy Award nomination for his work in *Amadeus* in 1985. We have hardly seen him since on the silver screen, except in small films *(Dominick and Eugene)* or small parts *(Parenthood)*. Why hasn't he landed more big movie roles? Not because he can't act. Obviously, he can. I don't know all the reasons for his being in the doldrums since *Amadeus,* but I do know that if Hulce had come to Hollywood during the days of the great studio system, he'd have been working regularly. The studio would have seen to that. That's what the studio was for: to make money stars and to make money.

Speaking of money, would you like to know what I was making in 1936, just entering my prime? First, let me remind you I had helped MGM triple its investment (at least!) with *The Devil Is a Sissy* (it grossed $1.18 million on a budget of $396,000). And I helped make a bundle for Selznick in *Little Lord Fauntleroy*, which cost Selznick International a half million to make and cleared $2 million. In the next nine months, I would rake in more big bucks for Metro with two Hardy films that grossed more than $1.2 million and five others that grossed a total of more than $7 million, including *Captains Courageous,* one of the best films MGM ever made.

You'd think MGM might have thought it fair to pay me a million. No? How about a half million? No. Well, then, maybe I was worth eighty thousand dollars, less than 1 percent of Metro's gross on my pictures? Well, no, apparently I wasn't worth that, either. MGM was paying me sixteen thousand dollars a year—four hundred dollars a week times forty weeks.

My mother and I went to see my agent, Harry Weber. Couldn't he renegotiate the contract MGM wrote for me in 1934? As it turned out, Weber was gravely ill. He put us in the hands of his assistant, David Todd, who went to MGM and pointed out that young Rooney, now a big star and getting bigger, was still slaving away under a contract that was written three years before, when he was a virtual nobody.

So Mayer, admitting I was underpaid, dug deep into his capacious, tailored, pin-striped pockets and came up with the munificent sum of $250. That's right. He said he'd add that to the salary steps contained in my 1934 contract. Not bad. From $400 a week to $650 a week, almost a 40 percent raise.

But it was peanuts compared to the earnings of Norma Shearer and Greta Garbo, who'd been making one money-loser after another. Then there was Shirley Temple's salary. In December 1935, after the *Motion Picture Herald* reported that Temple was the biggest money-maker of the year, Fox announced it was doubling Temple's salary from $1,250 to $2,500 a week.

I'm furious about it now, but at the time I couldn't have cared less. I had enough to support my mom. I had a new car. Gas was ten cents a gallon. I could afford a new tux if I needed one and the price of a gardenia corsage on Saturday night. What more did I need? More important: I was working, and my name was up in lights. I'd been programmed for this, practically from birth. What else could I possibly want? In effect, I was saying, "Hey, Mr. Mayer, I know you're making more than a million a year and now I'm making twenty-six thousand. No matter. What's my next part?"

I was not so much of a student of the language to know, then, the meaning of the word "irony." But my next part was a picture called *Slave Ship*. Wallace Beery and I and a nice character actress named Jane Darwell (who would later win an Academy Award for her role of Ma Joad in *The Grapes of Wrath*) were on loan out to Twentieth Century-Fox for this one. God only knows what producer Nunnally Johnson and Fox paid Mayer for my services. I can bet you it wasn't $650 a week, which is what I got. Still, I plunged right in, with energy and enthusiasm, playing the role of Swifty, a bad-tempered cabin boy on the barque *Albatross*. Tay Garnett directed the story, adapted from a George S. King novel by William Faulkner.

That's right. I'm talking about *the* great William Faulkner, who would win the Nobel Prize for Literature in 1949, a crotchety guy from Mississippi who didn't even finish high school. Apparently, Faulkner would come to Hollywood every so often looking for some freshly killed money, grab it for a few weeks' work, then get drunk for a week in order to obliterate the memory of his sin. ("Bless me, Father, for I have sinned. I committed fornication three times and cheated on my taxes, and, uh, uh—" Yes, son? "I, uh, committed two Hollywood scripts.") Faulkner did seventeen scripts in the 1930s and 1940s, many of which were unproduced. He did two notable films with the great Howard Hawks for Warner Brothers, *To Have and Have Not* (with Jules Furthman) and *The Big Sleep* (with Leigh Brackett), but he earned peanuts for his efforts. At Hollywood parties, Jack Warner used to boast, "I've got the best writer in America working for me for three hundred dollars a week."

In *Slave Ship*, the captain of the *Albatross* (played by Warner Baxter) runs slaves from Africa to the U.S. He does, that is, until he falls in love with a Miss Nancy Marlowe (Elizabeth Allan), who persuades him to give up the black ivory trade. Not so fast, say the other members of the crew, led by a villainous first mate (Wallace Beery) and an even more villainous second mate (George Sanders). There's a full-on mutiny and I end up siding with the good guys.

The best thing about *Slave Ship* for me is that the geniuses at MGM who saw me in it decided with their usual perspicacity that if I played a cabin boy in that one, then playing a cabin boy in *Captains Courageous* mightn't be a bad idea.

They decided to put me alongside Freddie Bartholomew in the film version of the Kipling novel, about a spoiled little rich boy on a luxury liner who falls overboard and gets picked up at sea by a fishing schooner out of Nantucket and learns, under the tutelage of Spencer Tracy's Manuel, to become a man—a young man strong enough to feel. I was the son of the trawler's captain, played by Lionel Barrymore.

This was my best picture so far. It had the best actors—not just the great Barrymore, but Spencer Tracy, Melvyn Douglas, John Carradine and my new-old friend Freddie Bartholomew. It had three fine writers who took liberties with Kipling's story and made this movie better than the novel. And it had a great director, Victor Fleming. He was a fabulous character, tall, very handsome, and so competent that you just knew he could have stepped in and filled any job on the production crew because Fleming was, above all else, a real technician who understood

film and filmmaking. He had already made an indelible mark on
the history of filmmaking.

I had been hearing stories about him for years, how he had
quit school in the seventh grade and become first a bicycle
mechanic and then the mechanic for a famous racing driver
named Barney Oldfield. He got into the movie business by accident. Seems that he just happened to be passing by the old
American Film Company's lot in Santa Barbara when director
Allan Dwan was having the devil of a time with a balky camera.
Fleming fixed it on the spot, and soon he was working as a
cameraman for Dwan. And a creative cameraman at that. In
1929, while shooting *The Virginian,* an early talkie, he decided
that it made sense to rig the microphone right on the camera to
give audiences a feeling that they were really *there.* Later, he
helped invent the dolly, a kind of railroad track for the camera
crew, so they could move their heavy equipment forward or
backward as they followed the action.

As director of a movie called *Mantrap* with Clara Bow, Fleming invented the film montage. To tell his story, he had to get
a character from Canada to New York. In those early film days,
directors weren't quite sure how to do that quickly, how to show
the movement with a minimum of footage. Fleming decided to
try a series of quick shots, almost snapshots, that would com-
press the movement into a matter of seconds. Clara Bow, not as
dumb as her Brooklyn accent might have led some to believe,
was curious. "Will the audiences get it?" she wanted to know.
They got it.

Fleming had no trouble convincing MGM to give him all the
resources of the studio to do right by *Captains Courageous.* He
shot some of the picture at one of Metro's soundstages in Culver
City. By and large, in those days, the studios hardly ever went
on location; they tried to shoot everything indoors or on the lot.
But here, in an attempt to simulate the sights and the sounds
(and even the smells) of life aboard a fishing schooner in the

North Banks, Fleming also did a lot of shooting off the coast of Catalina in the dead of winter.

He brought a real fishing vessel, under sail, all the way from Gloucester, a four-masted schooner called the *Ortha F. Spinney.* He had the studio buy another ship, the *Mariner,* once owned by John Barrymore, which he rechristened the *Jenny Cushman.* He also leased thirteen sailing schooners from Alaska's halibut fleet and had them sail down the Pacific coast with hundreds of pounds of halibut kept alive in special tanks. He had thousands of pounds of codfish shipped in, frozen, from Boston. (When we were living out there in the Catalina Channel, I had a hard time resisting the temptation to steal an occasional fish or two and hide them in Bartholomew's bunk. Come to think of it, I *wasn't* able to resist.)

Studio carpenters converted the fo'c'sle of the fishing vessel to a classroom, where Freddie and I spent three hours a day studying with Freddie's tutor, Harold Minnear. We had a full schedule, a long shoot every morning, then art, history, social studies, arithmetic, composition, grammar, spelling, botany, physiology, and hygiene in the afternoon. No wonder Freddie was so smart.

I learned a lot about playing to the cameras by watching all these great actors around me. I also learned that Spencer Tracy wasn't the God-like figure I'd imagined him to be. He grumbled about having his hair permed every day and put in a hairnet so that he would look more like a Portuguese fisherman. "It's a wonder they don't use perfume on me," he grumped. He also complained about having to sing to the accompaniment of a hurdy-gurdy thrust in his hands. And, off camera, he drank quite a bit.

Fleming believed in action; he thought that's what movies were for. I overheard him telling someone, "Hey, Hamlet's 'To be or not to be' is great literature, but I couldn't film it to save my life." So Fleming gave us a lot of action. He even invented a new rig for his seagoing cameras: a kind of pod strapped to the mast, stabilized by a gyroscope.

On November 24 and 25, our last days of shooting, we hit a scary, emotional climax with a race between the two ships. Under the pressure of the race, our mast tumbled and fell on Tracy. (It was supposed to; the accident would send Manuel to his watery grave.) The technicians made it happen by sawing it halfway through. But it was exciting out there on abnormally high seas. As I recall, the cameramen working under cinema-photographer Harold Rosson had to climb high up in the main-mast to shoot some of the scenes, and one of them fell in the water and almost drowned.

So did Tracy. Fleming had him in the water almost four hours, which Tracy enjoyed even less than getting his hair permed. But Fleming insisted that it was for the film's sake, and I think that's why the picture hit such a degree of high realism. Critics remarked on its almost documentary flavor, the cine-matic poetry of the schooners spanking along at full sail, of the dories being lowered into a running sea, salt spray showering us all. Members of the Academy of Motion Picture Arts and Sciences agreed: they nominated Tracy, the scriptwriters, and the film editor for Oscars.

Spencer Tracy won the Oscar for his Manuel. I think Victor Fleming and Freddie Bartholomew and Harold Rosson should have gotten Oscars, too. They were terrific.

☆ 13 ☆
Lana and Judy

My mother remarried in 1937. Her groom was an accountant named Fred Pankey, and, frankly, I wasn't impressed. Fred was a big, handsome man who liked to tell dirty jokes and paw my mother in front of me. I never really liked him, but I ended up getting him an accounting job at MGM. Gosh, I thought, wasn't it wonderful for MGM to do me this favor? Later, I realized this was just a way for Mr. Mayer to be one-up on me. If I asked him for a raise, he could get on his high horse and say, "Didn't I just do you a favor by hiring your stepfather?"

Of course, I didn't ask him for a raise. That's what agents are for, and my agents weren't in the asking mood. Funny thing about many agents. Often enough, they're more beholden to the studio than they are to you. They've already got you your deal; if you make a fuss, then they have to make a fuss with the studio. And if they do that, they won't be so welcome there when they come along with a new client, like a Judy Turner or a Frances Gumm.

I introduce these people in my story now because it was just about this time that both young ladies made their appearance on the lot at MGM. You know them better as Lana Turner and Judy Garland.

Funny about the ways of Hollywood. The name "Judy" didn't fit the smoldering beauty that Miss Turner was and would become, but it was a perfect new name for the young fifteen-year-old singer named Frances Gumm. "Judy" was just right: cute, peppy, and full of bounce. When I knew her at Ma Lawlor's Professional School, she had more bounce to the ounce than everyone else in the school put together. And I will never forget her performance back then on the stage of the Pantages Theatre in Hollywood. She planted both feet wide apart, almost as if she were challenging the audience, then sang "Zing Went the Strings of My Heart" with the kind of verve that made our heartstrings, all ninety of us from the Lawlor School, go bing, ding, ping, ring, ting, and zing.

As for Garland, George Jessel, the vaudeville impresario dreamed that up for Judy, just as a press agent dreamed up "Rooney" for me, when she and her sisters were doing a gig at the Oriental Theatre in Chicago back in 1934. "Garland" was a good choice. "Gumm" was the wrong image: sticky, soft, chewy, tutti-frutti. "Garland," on the other hand, was full of joy. It smelled of pine needles and sounded like sleigh bells and tasted like Christmas morning.

When Judy arrived at Metro and saw me in the commissary, she pointed at me, grinned, and shouted, "Ma Lawlor's!" I went right over to her and hugged her. It seemed like the most natural thing I could do. Even then, I really *liked* Frances Gumm. It seemed as if we'd known each other forever, that we were destined to be best friends. But the sexual chemistry wasn't there.

Judy—soon to become Lana—Turner was a different story. I first met her before she came under contract, at Curry's Ice Cream Parlor near Hollywood High. She was a sophisticated fifteen, with the kind of reserve that you might expect of a girl who had attended a Catholic academy in San Francisco. She wasn't the kind of girl who had much to say or *had* to say much. Her body said it all, and I got the message, loud and clear. Her auburn locks, her deep green eyes, her long lashes, the tip of her nose, her pouty lips, her graceful throat, the curve of her shoulders, her tiny waist, and, yes, the nicest knockers I had ever seen. When I first saw her at the malt shop on Highland Avenue, she was *not* wearing a tight pink sweater; this was before her Hollywood handlers put her in sweaters—and I thought, Here is a woman.

My fantasies about her soon came true. When I asked her to go out with me, she said yes. And I soon found out that she was as oversexed as I was, warm, passionate, soft, and moist in interesting places. You may wonder what she saw in me. I don't know. You'd have to ask her. I do know that on a dance floor I could make her breathless. And that in the front seat of my convertible, parked high up on Mulholland Drive, I could make her laugh. (I could also make her laugh on the dance floor and make her breathless on Mulholland Drive.) For a time, that was enough for her.

By the time she arrived at MGM, in 1937, she had been discovered by my old friend Mervyn LeRoy, a pretty big guy in the industry by then. He had just been signed to take Thalberg's place, and clearly he could help Lana's career much more than I could. I had no more dates with Lana. At the time I thought Lana had just outgrown me, but later I learned from Lana that the real reason we stopped dating was this: Lana had become pregnant. The only people who knew at the time were her mom and the doctor who performed the abortion. I don't know why Lana hadn't told me, and I'm not sure about how I would have reacted, knowing I had fathered a child. It wasn't until sometime later that I found out about it, almost in passing. Lana and I met at a fund-raiser. I smiled and said, "I can't really believe we went out together." She said, "Did you know I was in a family way with you?" I was stunned, and grateful at that moment that I hadn't known back then. I might have wanted her to have the baby. And maybe that's why she didn't tell me. She and her mother probably knew, deep down, that a child made no sense at all for either of us, then. We were both children ourselves.

But, after Lana and I stopped seeing each other, I wasn't exactly dateless on a Saturday night. In fact, sometimes, on a given night, I had *two* dates. It happened this way: after several evenings out with a very proper girl whom I shall call Katherine O'Kelly, her mother met me at the door and told me that Kitty was still getting ready. She sat me down on the couch, then leaned over me and whispered, "How come you don't ask me out sometime?"

"Huh?" said I, a little thick. She explained it to me nonverbally, by giving me a warm, wet kiss. "Oh," I said, a little bug-eyed now that I understood. That night, after I brought her proper daughter home at a proper hour, I went out to my car, drove down the street, and waited. When Mrs. O'Kelly came trotting up about a half hour later and climbed in the front seat, there was no mistaking her intentions. She showed me how to do it in the front seat. She showed me how to do it in the backseat.

Then there was the budding young starlet who shall be known here as Laura Smith. My affair with Laura ended as soon as it began—at a drive-in movie in the Valley. Drive-ins were very new then, but not so new that they didn't already have a certain notoriety about them. They were, supposedly, passion pits, and the very thought of going to one might have made any girl nervous. Laura must have been nervous.

About ten minutes into the movie, I moved my right arm up on the seat behind her head and then in a gentle but carefully calculated way, I put my hand on her right shoulder to urge her closer. I guess I scared her. She let out a big, fat fart.

We both froze.

Silence. For an eternity.

Then I put my foot in my mouth. I looked her straight in the eye and I said, "Excuse me."

Well, I knew I hadn't done it. She knew that I knew. And I knew that she knew that I knew. That made me something of a smart-ass. And nobody likes a smart-ass. She said nothing, nothing at all.

So we watched the movie. Period. In silence. And, as the minutes ticked on, it became increasingly difficult to make any amends. I didn't even try. I drove her straight home, without stopping at a malt shop or anything.

In Judy Garland's first years at MGM, the bigwigs didn't really know what they had. In fact, after she and Deanna Durbin did a two-reel short called *Every Sunday*, MGM dropped its option on both Deanna and Judy. Deanna went off to become a big success at Universal (a loss for MGM but not for me: she never indicated that she felt anything for me but pity). Judy just moped for a while, thinking that her movie career was over almost before it began. But a producer named Arthur Freed (who was also quite a good songwriter) persuaded Mr. Mayer to bring her back and put her under a small contract. "We know she can sing," Freed said. "Now we just have to see what else she can do."

Judy was no glamour girl. In the first place, she had a bad bite and her teeth were out of alignment. This, of course, was something MGM's dentists could fix. In fact, they fitted her with shell caps that slipped on and off her teeth like thimbles. But there were some things about her that the studio couldn't fix. She was a little too short, a half inch under five feet tall. Her legs were long, but they seemed to be hitched to her shoulders, which were too broad for her body. She looked, well, different. And so, not knowing how to deal with Judy's individuality, MGM put her on ice.

While Freed finagled, trying to find a part for Judy, Metro loaned her out to Fox for a college football comedy called *Pigskin Parade*. That didn't do Judy much good. She sang bits of three songs, but she didn't have a very big role: she played the freckle-faced kid sister of Stuart Erwin, a country bumpkin quarter-back, and she took a dim sixth place behind the other stars: Betty Grable, Jack Haley, Patsy Kelly, and Tony Martin. There were two other pretty girls in the cast, Arline Judge and Dixie Dunbar. Compared to this crowd, Judy, wearing long braids and a gingham dress, was little more than comic relief.

Judy told me that when she saw herself in this flick, it was the most awful moment in her life. I took her to the screening, and, as the picture wore on, she sat lower and lower in her seat, until she was almost sitting on her neck. She didn't even want to talk about it afterward. "Frightful," she said. "I'm a fat little pig in pigtails."

It was pointless to argue with her, so I decided the best thing I could do was make her laugh. I ordered her a chocolate malt at a special place on Sunset Boulevard called Coast Ice Cream. "They take all the fat out of their malts here," I said, with such a straight face that Judy believed me—for a minute or two. She'd almost finished slurping hers down when she announced, "It sure tastes like the good old fattening malts I've been getting all my life."

Of course, Judy was never "fat" or "a little pig," though Mr. Mayer insisted on calling Judy "the fat kid" and "my little hunchback"—sometimes to her face. Trouble was, she bought the notion, manufactured in Hollywood, that good looks were of a certain ideal type—like Lana Turner's, for example. I think Judy believed that anyone who didn't conform to that type could either turn in her actress's license or get in line for character parts behind Marjorie Main.

In fact, Judy was an American beauty in more ways than one. She had marvelous, warm eyes that invited you to share her secret mirth and a cute little nose that wrinkled when she laughed. She had an expressive, generous mouth that hardly ever uttered a line that wasn't funny, or, in her later years, outrageous or filled with feeling. If I had not been tainted with the same phony Hollywood notions about who was beautiful and who was not, I would have fallen in love with her myself.

After *Pigskin Parade*, Judy returned to MGM without an assignment. All the other MGM kids—Jackie Cooper and Freddie Bartholomew and Virginia Weidler and I—were going from part to part, but there seemed to be nothing for Judy except classes in the Little Red Schoolhouse. Then she got her big break—and I'm glad to say that I played a small part in bringing it about.

It happened this way. One day, somebody came into the Little Red Schoolhouse and invited us to set aside five o'clock Friday afternoon, February 1. Mr. Mayer wanted us all on Stage 25, MGM's largest soundstage.

"What's the deal?" I hollered. Miss McDonald frowned at my outburst. But that didn't stop me. I still wanted to know what was happening at five o'clock on Friday.

The emissary from Mr. Mayer's office said, "Clark Gable's thirty-sixth birthday. We've got a cake. Everybody's gonna sing 'Happy Birthday.' " He turned to me. "And Mickey?"

"Yeah?"

"Maybe you can do some of your imitations. We'd kinda like to put on a little show for Mr. Gable."

Naturally, I thought. Gable was MGM's number-one guy. The studio would make up in cake what it didn't want to give him in cash. And more than cake. It would give him our love. But that was okay. We loved Gable. On the lot, on our way to or from lunch, he'd always give us a big smile, like he was really glad to see us.

But now, Judy was in a quandary. "Sure," she said to me, her voice full of enthusiasm, "you can do some of your imitations. You can do Lionel Barrymore. You can even do Clark Gable. I dare ya."

"You think I'm afraid to do Gable?" I said. "Nawww. I'll do it."

Judy laughed and clapped her hands. But then her mood changed. She said, "But, umm, what am I gonna do?"

"Well," I said, putting on a serious, reflective face. "I don't know. What can you do?"

She looked surprised.

"I know," I said. "You can do a little dance." (Later, Judy—whose legs may have been her best physical asset—would become a pretty fair dancer. But she was no dancer then.)

Now she was crestfallen or, at least, pretended to be. And then she realized I was teasing and socked me on the arm.

I hugged her. "Okay, Judy. Sing? Sing?"

She laughed. "Unh. Yeah. But, umm, what am I gonna sing?"

We went over some titles. "My Man." "Be Still My Heart." "Stormy Weather." "The Man I Love." Songs Judy had done before, onstage, to great effect—partly because it was a sensation to see and hear a kid singing these grown-up songs as well or better as anyone had ever sung them. But none of them seemed quite right for this occasion.

But then a light went on over my noggin. "Hey, Joots, we've got some great songwriters right here on the lot. Why don't we ask one of them?"

"Of course," said Judy. "Roger Edens." Judy not only knew Roger Edens, she was already working very closely with him. He'd been serving as musical director of a big radio program called "The Chesterfield Supper Club" and had gotten Judy some guest spots on the show. Edens would end up writing some of the best stuff that Judy and I ever did together.

"Come on," I said, "let's go see Edens."

Soon the three of us had our heads together. Judy suggested "Drums in My Heart," a song he'd done originally for Ethel Merman.

Edens shook his head. "Too sophisticated for you. I want you to sing something that is you, Judy, really you."

Judy wailed, "Yeah, Mr. Edens. But what?"

"Let me sleep on it," he said.

He must have slept well. He came up with a smashing idea. He'd have Judy play herself in a little skit, a little recitation, then a song.

And here is what Judy did:

After we'd sung "Happy Birthday" to Clark Gable, with Mr. Mayer beaming in the background, Edens, at the piano, struck up the band and nodded to Judy, who was wearing a little brown straw hat and a black and white dress with puffed sleeves. She approached Edens, sat down on a wooden box beside him, and then, gazing at a framed photograph of Gable, started talking to his picture, as if she were a star-struck little fan:

Oh, gee, Mr. Gable, I just had to tell you about the time I saw you in *It Happened One Night.* That was the first time I ever saw you, and I knew right then that you were the nicest fella in the world. I guess it was because you acted so—well, so natural-like, not like a real actor but like any fella you'd meet in school.

The orchestra was playing softly during all this.

And then one time I saw you in a picture with Joan Crawford, and I had to cry a little, because you loved her so much and you couldn't have her—well, not until the end of the picture anyway. And then, one time, I saw you in person.

Her voice rose with excitement:

You were making a personal appearance in the theater and I was standing there when you got out of your car, and you almost knocked me down. Oh, but it wasn't your fault. I was in the way. But you looked at me and, umm, you smiled. Yeah, you smiled right at me as if you meant it, and I cried all the way home just because you smiled at me for being in the way.

Now she was almost in tears.

Oh, I'll never forget it, Mr. Gable, honest Injun. You're my favorite actor.

Then Judy stood up and went into her song.

> *You made me love you.*
> *I didn't want to do it.*
> *I didn't want to do it.*
> *You made me want you.*
> *And all the time you knew it.*
> *And all the time you knew it.*
> *Gimme gimme what I long for.*
> *You know you got the kind of kisses*
> *That I cry for.*
> *You know you made me love you.*

Gable, normally impassive, was moved. He hurried right over to Judy and hugged and kissed her. Then Judy broke into tears (maybe because Gable had such terrible halitosis!) and threw her arms around Gable. They held the clinch and flash bulbs were popping all over the place. Judy wasn't so overcome as to lose her senses. Out of the corner of one eye, she spied Mr. Mayer, beaming with his arms held out to her. She left Gable's side, went over, and climbed into Mr. Mayer's lap. At that, everyone just about went nuts.

I didn't even give another thought to going up and doing my imitations. Who could have followed an act like that? I was just happy for Judy. I thought, now they've *got* to find a good part for her.

Judy repeated the same performance a few weeks later in front of MGM's national exhibitors, who were in Culver City for their annual meeting. This time Stage 25 was transformed into a giant nightclub, and, once again, she got a tremendous ovation.

Since, this time, the applause came from all these exhibitors, the guys who had to sell MGM's product week-in, week-out, there didn't seem to be any question about Judy's future at Metro.

The very next day, Judy was called into Mr. Mayer's office, where she was told by Mr. Mayer himself that they were making a place for her in *Broadway Melody of 1938*. She would sing "You Made Me Love You"—to a picture of Gable.

From that day on I could see Judy's confidence swell. It took director Roy Del Ruth and the cast some six weeks to do *Broadway Melody*, and I saw Judy grow more glowing, more attractive every day, working alongside the two glittering stars, Robert Taylor and Eleanor Powell, and her stage mother, Sophie Tucker, and George Murphy and Buddy Ebsen, two dancers who would go on to much greater fame later, and Willie Howard, a fabled comedian of the Broadway stage. I think she even got a little thinner, too.

On the Fourth of July, we went to Mr. Mayer's birthday party together along with Ann Rutherford, my costar in the Hardy series, out at the Mayers' place in Santa Monica, right on the beach. It was a command performance. None of us who were invited dared beg off. And when we got there, we knew, without having to be told, first to make a fuss over Mr. Mayer and then to *have fun*. If we didn't have fun, then Mr. Mayer would be disappointed. So we did, eating more hot dogs and toasted marshmallows than we should have and having a hilarious time in the pool and on the diving board. All the while Mr. Mayer's dark, sharp eyes appraised us behind his shell-rimmed spectacles.

Judy couldn't have wanted any more than this. At last, she was launched, really launched, and certain, too, that, in the eyes of the most important man at MGM, she was something special. *Broadway Melody* wouldn't be released until the early fall, but we all knew it would be a hit. (The first *Broadway Melody* had won MGM its first Oscar for Best Picture in 1929. And the sequel, *Broadway Melody of 1936*, had been big box office.) This *Melody* had the same stars, the same director, the same songwriters from the 1936 production—plus Judy Garland. It couldn't miss.

Nevertheless, Judy turned morose. What was she going to do next? What if she never worked again? Judy told me, "If Mr. Mayer can let me go once, he can let me go again."

I told Judy that was crazy.

"Well, maybe they won't find another good part for me?" She was wrong. They did. They featured her in her first movie with me, a racetrack picture called *Thoroughbreds Don't Cry*.

For a moment or two she was elated, but soon she started wondering and worrying again. "Sure," she said to me one night as we were headed for a party at Jackie Cooper's house, on Jackie's seventeenth birthday, "it's great to be working, if *Broadway Melody* is going to be so good for me, why are they putting me in this picture with you? *Thoroughbreds Don't Cry* is a horse-race picture. There's nothing in that for me. Not one song."

True, on its face, *Thoroughbreds Don't Cry* didn't hold much promise for her career, but as I told Judy, this was just part of the studio system. "We're under contract, Joots. That means we take whatever comes along. We oughta be glad we're working."

I knew I was right. As far as the studio was concerned, we were just a couple of kids on the lot. So we ought to be working. Separately or together, it didn't matter. As it turned out, all of a sudden Judy had almost more work than she could stand. The studio had her doing two pictures simultaneously: *The Ugly Duckling* (later titled *Everybody Sing*) and *Thoroughbreds*.

But *Thoroughbreds* turned out to be good for Judy's career after all. We had a pretty good script, by Lawrence Hazard, a race-track movie with kids as the heroes. And putting us together in a movie would help establish something else: that Judy and I were able to perform some screen magic together. (In fact, *Thoroughbreds* would lead to seven more Mickey-and-Judy pictures.)

MGM had bought the story with me and Freddie Bartholomew in mind. But Freddie Bartholomew was busy, so to take his place, the studio brought in this kid from New Zealand named Ra Hould (some press agent would change his name to Ronald Sinclair) and cast Sophie Tucker as the nice lady who ran a boardinghouse for jockeys, Judy Garland was her nice niece, Cricket West, and I was a not-so-nice jockey.

It seems that a British lord, Sir Peter Calverton (played by C. Aubrey Smith), has come over to America with his grandson, Roger (Ronald Sinclair), to win a big-stakes race with their prize thoroughbred, Pookah. In prepping for the big race, however, I pull the horse—that is, I see to it that he loses. I do this because my movie father has conned me into believing that he'll die unless he can buy an iron lung, which he can do if I help him win this big bet by throwing the race. Sir Peter dies of disappointment. And I wander off, disgraced and despondent.

But Judy (who did, after all, get to sing one song in the picture, "Got a Pair of New Shoes") comes to the rescue. She persuades me to return and help Pookah win the big race. I do better than that. I steal my dad's ill-gotten winnings (enough for the entry fee to get Pookah in the race) and have everything straightened out, it seems, until my dad turns me in to the track stewards for throwing the earlier race. They sit me down. I am not allowed to ride Pookah. Big crisis. But Judy comes to the rescue again. She persuades Roger that he can take the mount himself. He does, and he rides Pookah to victory.

We shot some of the picture at Hollywood Park and some at Santa Anita, but we made most of it on the lot at MGM, where they practically built a replica of Santa Anita. We were finished shooting on October 15, 1937, and the picture was edited and scored and ready for a preview on November 18. Judy and I went to the preview together, and as we watched ourselves on the screen, I sneaked a look every so often at Judy. She seemed rapt by what she saw up there: her own movie persona taking shape. And she started to accept that being, part of it created by God, part by her scriptwriters. Looking back on it now, I think it was that night that Judy's star was born.

In this picture, she was the same winsome honest, feeling, wide-eyed little believer that she was on Stage 25, singing to the picture of Gable. It was a part she would continue to play during all her glory years at MGM, until she (and I) were orphaned by the studio's decapitation.

According to a reporter from the *Motion Picture Herald,* Mr. Mayer attended the same screening. And he strode out of the theater, the reporter said, "with the air of a man hurrying to a parimutuel window to place a bet on a 'sure thing.' " The reporter's hunch was right. The picture didn't make a huge profit, but it was a critical success.

And it launched me and Judy Garland as a team.

☆ 14 ☆
Good Behavior

In the spring of 1937, I really started to hit my stride as an actor in a picture called *Hoosier Schoolboy*. It was not an expensive production. But the direction by William Nigh was good and the script by Robert Lee Johnson even better. I had a good role, and I knew it, and I played it for exactly what it was worth; in fact, I underplayed it and won some critical acclaim for my acting.

I was learning something about acting: good acting, for me, was learning to accept my own individuality, learning how to be myself. I don't think I could have learned that by going to an acting school. Am I against acting schools? Yes—with one qualification. If an acting school can teach you how to accept your own individuality, then it might work. Think about it: you were all great at make-believe when you were children. That greatness stopped when you became aware that someone was watching you. You became self-conscious, frightened that someone would catch you in the act, even though you were playing make-believe, of being yourselves.

Can a good director help? He can if he will encourage you to be yourself. Naturally, when you are playing a part, you are, also, someone else. But you become that someone in your own way. How do you cry on camera? You get into the story, you react to the story, you learn to listen.

That's what I was doing in my Andy Hardy pictures. Creating Andy Hardy. Becoming Andy Hardy. Being Andy Hardy. And I could do this in my own way because I had a director on the Hardy pictures who encouraged my individuality—partly because he was such an individual himself. His name was George B. Seitz. In 1918, he got his first movie job as a writer by presenting himself one hot summer day at the old Pathé studios in Jersey City wearing a tweed, raglan overcoat, a blue suit, yellow tie, yellow gloves, and a Panama hat with the brim turned up.

"I'm looking for a writing job," he said with a smile.

I guess he looked crazy enough to be a writer. He got the job. And soon he was writing, producing, and directing his own scripts. In an era when writers took a week to do a script, he did his in one day. And then, in addition to writing, producing, and directing, he would sometimes take on an acting job. He even played a lead in one series called *Bound and Gagged*, starring Pearl White, part of a series better known now as *The Perils of Pauline*. It was he who did most of those fabulous screen silents with Pearl White.

In 1919, he produced a Broadway musical called *La, La Lucille*, which was written by an unknown from Tin Pan Alley. "What the hell," said Seitz, "I think we oughta give the kid a chance." The kid was George Gershwin.

In seven years, Seitz did thirty-four features for Universal, PDC, Tiffany, RKO, Mayfair, Columbia, always ahead of schedule. With a record like that, it was inevitable that the MGM factory would want him.

Mr. Mayer hired him in 1933, and in seven years there he did forty-two films. I think he was able to work fast because he had the kind of overview of his films that allowed him to cut scenes in his head. (Otto Preminger had the same kind of film genius.) That's one of the things I admired about him. I have another reason for thinking of him as a great director, one of the best I ever had: he didn't take himself too seriously. He didn't try to play the tyrant. He let things happen.

One of his friends, Frank Leon Smith, who had worked with him for years, once called George Seitz "a journeyman." By that, he didn't intend anything but the highest praise—like calling an officer a soldier.

And so, bang, bang, bang, under Seitz's direction, we did three Hardys in a row, each bigger at the box office than the one before, each featuring this cocky (but always ready to be humble) kid who didn't mind listening to his dad, the judge. Those father-and-son chats became fixtures in every Hardy film. People liked them. There was something refreshing about a kid like me being so candid with his dad.

In *Judge Hardy's Children*, I asked my dad whether it was normal, my wanting to kiss every pretty girl I saw. The answer was, and would be, in each and every Andy Hardy picture I was in: yes, it was normal—but not always wise. (And in real life, well, yes, kissing every pretty girl I saw was pretty normal, too. Only later did it prove to be unwise.)

Andy Hardy flicks always had a flock of pretty girls in them. In fact, the studio realized that the Hardy pictures were a great showcase for young actresses. Lana Turner ended up in *Love Finds Andy Hardy* as the knockout newcomer I just had to invite to the Christmas Eve dance. Trouble is, I've already invited another girl, too (Polly Benedict, played by Ann Rutherford) and I end up with neither of them. I have a bitterly introspective moment in the movie when I reckon that I'll have to give up all this polygamy. But I manage to go to the party, anyway, with none other than Betsy Booth, a girl who was a real good sport and, boy, could she sing and dance, too, and just be, well, like a girl you knew and liked and could just talk to and be *real* with.

I am writing here (I guess you've already figured this) about Judy Garland, who took this part while she was waiting for Arthur Freed to put together the team that would make *The*

Wizard of Oz. MGM's writers seemed to know the movie Judy; wisely, they wrote the emerging movie Judy right into their scripts, the little girl lost, the wide-eyed true believer, the team player who'll do anything for the show, the vulnerable creature who has nothing to see her through except her talents and her feelings.

Off the set, I never gave Judy even a romantic nudge, though I think there were times when she wanted me to. The first day we reported to work on *Love Finds Andy Hardy,* I noted that Judy was watching to see what my reaction might be to having Lana Turner on the set. I think she was relieved to see that Lana and I only nodded and smiled at each other, period, and pleased to discover that we had outgrown our adolescent love affair. I thought I detected in Judy a slight sigh of relief.

Not that Judy didn't envy Lana's glamorous good looks. I had occasion, once or twice, to note a wistful smile on Judy's face when Lana passed her on the set. I imagined her saying, "If only I could look like Lana!" But of course she couldn't, not in her own eyes, at least. Or mine, either.

God! If only I could have told Judy, then, that looks are the last thing a young man ought to care about in a young woman, that they ought to be way down on anyone's list of priorities, far below intelligence, a sense of humor, and a sense of self-esteem and generosity and selflessness and warmth and caring for others. But I couldn't.

I couldn't because I was caught up myself in all the wrong values. Judy and I were both Hollywood kids, caring more about what other people thought than what we should have known in our hearts. We'd made Tinseltown's phony ways our own ways. It would take me years to see through them and years more to reject them completely.

I doubt that Judy ever did.

As I've said, the Hardy pictures were great box office—and getting greater. We grossed $3.7 million for Hardy numbers two, three, and four, on an outlay of a half million. Was Mr. Mayer happy? He was delirious. The only trouble was, Mr. Mayer wanted me to be Andy Hardy off the screen, too, which was pretty unreasonable of him, considering that this was the same Mr. Mayer who once tried to put the make on Shirley Temple's Mom, and on the couch in his white-carpeted office, if you please.

I remember his calling me to his office in early 1938. It was just after the release of *Love Is a Headache*, just after he'd seen a review in *The New York Times* that said I was threatening to run away with every picture I appeared in. I had been in Mr. Mayer's office only once before, and then only briefly. (We'd exchanged greetings from time to time, of course, in the studio commissary at lunchtime.) Now I had a chance to memorize every detail in his big white room—big white grand piano in one corner and a white carpet so deep it seemed to come to my knees. I noted that the room was filled with the rich aroma of his Havana cigars. It was not an unpleasant sensation. Neither was it unpleasant to be the focus of his warm, crinkly eyed smile. He looked down at me from his large, white, circular desk and told me how pleased he was with my work. "The critics," he said. "They love you. And I must agree with them. I love you, too."

"Well," I said, "thank you very much, Mr. Mayer."

"But—"

I said to myself, "Uh-oh."

"I've been hearing stories around town."

I nodded very seriously, just as I nodded at my father on the screen, Judge Hardy. I'd been taught to respect my elders. And I did. This was no act. "Stories, Mr. Mayer?"

He was taken aback by my tone, so polite, so deferential. "Well," he said. "Yes. I hear—" He laughed with embarrassment over the silliness of what he was about to say, but he said it anyway. "I hear you've never met a pretty girl that you didn't kiss."

"Kinda like the song, huh? 'When I'm not near the girl I love, I love every girl I'm near?' " I grinned.

He frowned. Obviously, we were getting too buddy-buddy. This wasn't what he had in mind. He wanted to be stern with me. "Look," he said. "I'm not talking about kissing. I'm talking about fucking."

My mouth dropped open. I couldn't believe that a man wearing such expensive suits would use a word like "fucking." I said nothing.

"That's about the size of it, isn't it?"

"Well, size has nothing to do with it," I retorted, deliberately misunderstanding his meaning. I quoted something I once heard in a pep talk, maybe from Victor McLaglen: "It's not the size of the boy in the fight. It's the size of the fight in the boy."

He waved his hand. "No. No. You don't understand. I'm talking about your public image."

"Image?" I asked. "Image?"

He told me MGM's publicity department had given him a whole file of newspaper clippings and things from fan magazines, too. He had the file right on his desk. "You're everywhere. The Palomar Ballroom, the Ocean Park Ballroom, Ciro's, the Coconut Grove, the Trocadero. Blondes. Brunettes. Redheads." He pointed at one picture of me holding a glass. "Is this champagne? Champagne?"

Very respectfully (for I was afraid of him), I said, "It's a champagne glass, Mr. Mayer. But it isn't champagne."

"No?"

"No. It's ginger ale." (It really was.)

He grunted.

"You ought to know I'm too young to order—or get—champagne at Ciro's. The sheriffs would call in the ABC. I'm only seventeen." I *was* only seventeen. But I was old enough to know that it wasn't the police who patrolled the Sunset Strip, it was the sheriff's office. And that it was the Alcohol Beverage Control

Commission (otherwise known as the ABC) who could take away Ciro's liquor license for serving a minor.

Obviously, this wasn't getting him very far. He decided to change his tack. He climbed down out of the high desk chair he was sitting in, waddled over, and put his face about three inches from mine. "Look, you like being Andy Hardy?"

Now I was more than a little frightened. This was one tough guy. I'd heard that he'd actually had some fistfights with more than one of his stars, and I didn't want to start slugging it out with him, even though I'd boxed a little myself. I knew I could beat him, even though he was taller than I was and a lot heavier. But beating the boss in a fistfight? A boss who was now paying me $750 a week? No way. I had to get out of there.

He wouldn't let me. I turned to go, but he spun me back by the shoulder. "I asked you a question. You like being Andy Hardy?"

"Yes, Mr. Mayer."

"Then," he said, "be—Andy—Hardy."

"Off camera?" I shouted. "You want me to be Andy Hardy off camera?"

"That," he said, "would be nice."

"Well," I said, "it would be nice for you. But not for me. I work like a dog when I work. And I work a lot. How many pictures did I make for you last year? Six? Seven? Eight? And I work real hard. I give a hundred and ten percent."

"That," he whispered, "is what I pay you for."

"I'm not the one who's getting rich off my movies," I said. I was *mad.*

"Why you ungrateful runt," he growled. "I'll show you."

"No, you won't," I screamed. "I'll show you." I stalked out of his office.

But he came running after me and caught up with me on the catwalk that ran between the new Thalberg Building and the old administration building. "Mickey," he said. "Mickey."

I could sense something else in his tone now, something softer, something that was almost pleading. It was the first time in this conversation that he'd called me by my name. I stopped.

"Yeah?" I said.

He grabbed me by my lapels, not roughly, just tight enough so I wouldn't get away before he had his say. "Look," he puffed. He was a little out of breath and emotionally upset. "I don't care what you do off camera. Just don't do it in public. In public, behave. Your fans expect it. You're Andy Hardy. You're the United States. You're the Stars and Stripes. Behave yourself. You're a symbol."

I nodded soberly. I was glad that he'd softened. A moment ago, he was going to show me. I didn't know how he was going to show me, but it wasn't going to be pleasant. Now, he wasn't threatening me. He was begging me, and in the name of the flag, no less. How could I argue with him anymore? I hugged him and I grinned and I said, "Okay, Mr. Mayer. I'll be good. I promise."

He liked that. He let go of my lapels. He smiled and straightened his tie and said, "All right, then."

We stood close for a moment more, he looking into my eyes, I into his. We had an understanding. He'd be Uncle Sam. And I'd be the Stars and Stripes.

But Louis B. Mayer's mama didn't raise no morons. He knew, despite my good intentions, that I was a young man filled with more than my share of piss and vinegar. What I needed was a keeper. So he went back to his office and called in Howard Strickling, the head of publicity. He wanted to know if Howard had a good man on his staff he'd like to reward with a promotion.

That man turned out to be Les Peterson, a tall, handsome guy who looked like he might have been a banker. Les was given one job, to follow Mickey Rooney around and keep him out of trouble—in public, at least. Les did a good job, never made himself obnoxious, never made a fuss. When I was shooting on a soundstage, he'd be standing by. When I emerged from my dressing room, he'd be on guard. Whenever I did any press interviews, there he was. He tried not to be an obvious presence; he lurked in the background, nodded when I was saying the right thing, frowned when I was getting myself into trouble. And if the reporter was Louella Parsons, I was in double trouble. She never seemed to show up unless and until she had a juicy bit of gossip.

This was about the time when everyone was trading Mickey Rooney stories, none of them true. If I had a bottle of beer somewhere, somebody would make it a case of beer. And the story would grow in the telling. "Hey, Cholly, you hear about Rooney the other night? He drank up a whole brewery." So when Louella came around, Les would tell me, "Mick, you don't have to try and explain how you think the rumor might have gotten started. Don't tell her you had only one bottle of beer. Turn her around. Tell her about the songs you're writing between takes. Tell her you're taking Peggy Lloyd to her junior prom. As long as you give her something. You give her a story, any story, she's going to go with that." With Louella, I soon learned to do just that. Les said, "The main thing is you want her to be on your side." But heck, what was so new about that? I wanted everyone to be on my side.

Les Peterson could have become a nuisance, but he had a nice, easy way about him. He seemed to be there when I wanted him and invisible when I didn't want him. I soon learned that if I invited him to go to dinner with me at Chasen's or Romanoff's, he'd pick up the tab. If I had a chance to break early and make the track at Santa Anita or Hollywood Park, Les would drive— and place my bets for me because I was still too young to bet. He'd also collect on my winning mutuel tickets. I thought this was too good to be true. MGM would pay for my losing tickets

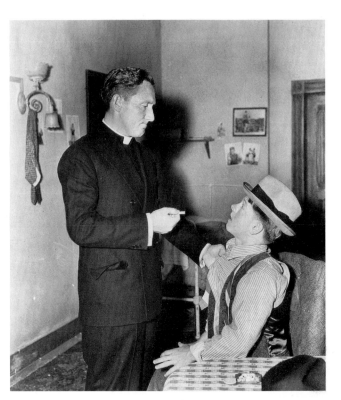

Spencer Tracy played the famed Father Flanagan in *Boys Town* (1938) and won an Oscar for his trouble. But, as Whitey Marsh, the tough kid who gets religion, I stole the show.
(MGM)

With my big-screen family, the Hardys, in *You're Only Young Once* (1938).
(BETTMANN ARCHIVE)

As a midget in 1927, with Colleen Moore in *Orchids and Ermine*. I was already being programmed to put the make on a pretty girl.

From 1927 to 1934 I was Mickey "Himself" McGuire. We did sixty-three Mickey McGuires until cartoonist Fontaine Fox sued us, and I had to give my name back.

In the late twenties and early thirties I played the vaudeville circuit, generally wearing a tux, and sometimes
oversized boots, for some reason, and singing "Pal o' My
Cradle Days."

With my dad, Joe Yule, in *Andy Hardy Gets Spring Fever* (1939). It was a reunion for us—I hadn't seen him in fourteen years. (MGM)

My mother and me in 1940. (AP/WIDE WORLD)

Judy got an Oscar this year
(1941) and a bid at concrete
immortality here at Grauman's
Chinese Theatre.
(MICKEY ROONEY COLLECTION)

Ava and me in 1941, before we were married. I am copping a feel
here instead of eating my dinner, but that didn't stop Ava from
eating hers.
DES MOINES REGISTER

Ray McDonald (left) and I and Richard Quine danced our fool heads off in *Babes on Broadway* (1941).
(MGM)

Judy and me in *Babes on Broadway*.
(MGM)

Here I am with Ann Rutherford and Judy at the premiere for *Life Begins for Andy Hardy* (1941).
(MGM)

Judy and me on location during the filming of *Girl Crazy* in 1943, the last big movie we did together.
(MICKEY ROONEY COLLECTION)

and I'd pocket my winnings. As it turned out, it *was* too good to be true: at the end of that month, I found that the studio had deducted the losing tickets from my salary. Oh, well.

Peterson even got Howard Strickling's permission to chauffeur me to the Coconut Grove if I needed to kick up my heels a bit. Ciro's was off limits because that's where Mr. Mayer liked to rhumba himself with a variety of young ladies, now that he'd sent his wife to a sanitarium in the East.

Les and Howard Strickling took it upon themselves to go a bit beyond protecting my image and move on to creating a new one. They wrote a studio biography for me that had little or nothing to do with reality. Instead of collecting blondes, brunettes, and redheads, they had me collecting stamps, coins, and matchboxes. My favorite author, according to this studio fantasy, was Eugene O'Neill. That would have implied that I read books. But I didn't read books; I barely read the plays I starred in. To burnish the studio biography a little bit more, Strickling decided I needed to have some solid aspirations, too. He had me wanting to be a chemist (if I were not in pictures) because "Rooney likes to mix things." But the only chemistry I was interested in was body chemistry, and the only things I liked to mix were ice-cream sodas.

That studio biography said nothing about my playing sandlot football—too rowdy for the MGM image, I guess. In fact, I had organized something called the MGM Lions (over the objections of Mr. Mayer), a group of guys my age and about my size to play pickup games with other sandlot teams around Southern California. But football hadn't yet gained the glamour it has today, and the MGM publicity department didn't see how Mickey Rooney's exploits as a quarterback would help sell its movies to the people of Middle America.

The carefully concocted image of Mickey Rooney seemed to work. My fan mail continued to pour in—three or four mail bags full every day. I hardly even saw the letters, much less answered them. Strickling's department handled that. I certainly couldn't have handled them myself, even if I'd wanted to. (I was too busy collecting stamps!) Occasionally, however, Les Peterson would hand a note on to me, if he thought I'd be amused by it, like this one.

Dear Mickey,

    I know that you are busy all the time and never have a chance to take a breath. But we have a cabin up here in Coeur d'Alene. You could have your own room. And nobody would talk to you. You could even make your own breakfast. You could just be yourself and get some badly needed rest, if you felt like it.

    But I know you wouldn't, you rotten son-of-a-bitch, because you're too stuck up and your head's probably so blown up you probably wouldn't come up and be a regular guy, would you? No, you phony Hollywood bastards are always the same way. Well, I've said what I had to say.

    With love and respect,
    Mrs. Ellie Jones

I couldn't worry too much about the Ellie Joneses of this world because I was busy making movies, the quicker the better. *Hold That Kiss,* with Maureen O'Sullivan and Dennis O'Keefe, took twenty-one days to shoot. I played Maureen's kid brother. She works in a dress shop, O'Keefe in a tourist bureau. They meet at a fashionable wedding and, attracted to each other, try to beef up their résumés. Comic complications ensue, of course, but, as in all Hollywood movies of the time, the characters unravel the knots and live happily ever after. I sometimes wonder whether, seeing and playing in these idealized versions of life, I didn't start thinking this *was* life.

Don't ask me why. I guess we were giving the public what it

wanted. And, on the eve of another terrible war, what it apparently wanted was more of Mickey Rooney, a name that was becoming synonymous with energy, optimism, and schmaltzy good feelings. I was about to float into my golden years. I was almost eighteen.

☆ 15 ☆
Boys Town

O*ut in Nebraska,* Father Edward J. Flanagan's model community for wayward boys had done some marvelous work, helping to rehabilitate no fewer than five thousand apprentice criminals from America's inner cities. After twenty years of struggle, however, most of America didn't even know where Omaha was, much less Boys Town. Then, early in 1938, Eleanore Griffin and Dore Schary discovered the place and the people that made it go and wrote their story, one that would go on to win them an Oscar for Best Original Story. Schary and John Meehan, who did the screenplay, might have won an Oscar for that, too, but they were beaten at the wire by another pretty good writer named George Bernard Shaw for his adaptation to the screen of *Pygmalion.*

MGM knew they had a winner—and a perfect vehicle for two of its brightest stars: Spencer Tracy and Mickey Rooney. Tracy would play the estimable Father Flanagan, endowed with patience and love—and a great left hook. Rooney would be Whitey Marsh, a combination of Jimmy Cagney, Humphrey Bogart, and King Kong, with a pack of butts in one pocket and a deck of cards in the other and his mind made up to blow this joint as soon as the padre's back was turned.

Mayer assigned director Norman Taurog to bring _Boys Town_ to life, giving him three weeks on location at Boys Town and six weeks on an MGM soundstage. Taurog had the help of MGM's answer to the Dead End Kids, a group that included Gene Reynolds (later to become the producer of TV's "M*A*S*H") and my old chum from the Lawlor School, Sidney Miller.

Miller was starting to write songs then and, in fact, would go on to write some very fine stuff, including "Come to Baby, Do," "I Waited a Little Too Long," "What Do I Have to Do to Make You Love Me?" and "There They Are." (At seventy-five, he is still going strong.) In fact, between takes, Sid and I collaborated on a song called "Love's Got Nothing on Me."

Even today Sid likes to talk about how I acted on the set of _Boys Town_, especially my ability to turn myself on and off "like a faucet." In one scene, I had to plead with Father Flanagan not to be sent away because, although the good father had been able to handle a lot of bad boys, he couldn't handle me. "Please, Father," I cried, "let me stay. The guys are beginning to like me. Let me stay. I'll be good. I promise." I started to bawl at this point, and my tears were so convincing that they triggered tears in everyone who was watching—the cameramen, the grips, even the director.

After the take (as Sid remembers the story), I spied Miller standing behind the cameras and pulled him aside. "Hey, Sid, I got the bridge to the song we've been working on. Listen to this." We went over to a nearby piano and I tried to show him what I'd worked out:

> _I'm not afraid of the moon._
> _Love's got nothing on me._
> _My heart's humming a tune._
> _And I'm still free as can be._

"You see?" I said, banging these bridge notes on the piano. "You see? Like this: da da dum de da?"

Just then Taurog came over and told me I'd have to do the scene again. "Why?" I said. "I thought it was pretty good."

"Mike shadow," he said.

I sighed and went back to the set and did the whole thing again, just the way I did it before, maybe better, with the tears rolling at just about the same place. Then, without missing a beat, I returned to the piano and resumed my song with Sid:

> *I'm not afraid of the moon.*
> *Love's got nothing on me.*

This nonchalance was all calculation on my part. During breaks in the shooting, I made it a point to clown around with whoever was on the set, telling jokes to the camera crew, playing the piano with Sid. Then, when the director called, I'd throw a gag over my shoulder and time my approach to the set just as the camera was ready to grind away. I did this to throw myself into a state of shock. It was like running a car in high gear, then suddenly shifting to reverse. It was an awful wrench and it busted me up a bit inside, but it got results.

In *Boys Town* Sid played Mo Kahn, the Boys Town barber. What was a Jewish kid doing in a place run by a Father Flanagan? Well, that was part of the charm of Boys Town and part of the charm of this picture: Catholics and Jews, friends together. Schary even gave Father Flanagan a Jewish friend, a pawnbroker (played by Henry Hull) who believed that Boys Town was worth backing. So a Jewish money man was helping a Catholic priest; they were working together on goodness and justice. Ecumenically speaking, we were about thirty years ahead of our time.

Boys Town was big box office, my biggest. It grossed $4,133,000. And now, in videocassette, it will keep on generating profits forever (for Ted Turner, who bought the MGM film library in

1986 or for the guys who buy the film library from him). The movie also put the real Boys Town on everyone's map and helped Father Flanagan raise millions in contributions. *Boys Town* not only made friends for Father Flanagan and money for Mr. Mayer. It won an Oscar for Spencer Tracy, his second Oscar in as many years; the first was for *Captains Courageous.*

That year I won an Oscar, too, along with another kid star, Deanna Durbin. Actually it was a miniature Oscar, about five inches high, which the Academy gave us for our "significant contribution in bringing to the screen the spirit and personification of youth." Whatever that meant.

One day not long after we finished *Boys Town,* my keeper, Les Peterson, showed up at the Little Red Schoolhouse and called me out of class. This was no ordinary event—Miss McDonald had us there so seldom that she wouldn't allow interruptions except in grave emergencies. Les had a pretty serious look on his face. I knew something was up.

He had a tear sheet in his hand from the *Los Angeles Examiner,* an ad for the Follies Burlesque. On it was a big picture of a cutie wearing tassels and fringe, along with a picture of a burlesque clown. A big headline read, EVELYN WEST'S TREASURE CHEST! A little headline promised 20 BEAUTIFUL GIRLS 20. An even smaller line said, DIRECT FROM CHICAGO, COMIC JOE YULE!

For a full minute I didn't say a thing. I got a lump in my throat, as big as a tennis ball. I hadn't seen my father in fourteen years, or thought of him very much, either, for that matter. But I didn't share my feelings with Les. I just asked him whether my dad's presence in town represented any kind of threat to MGM.

"Noooo," he said, taken aback, I think, by the coolness of my reaction. "Not exactly. I mean, Mr. Mayer would rather he showed up as an assistant secretary of the treasury, or a v.p. for Merrill Lynch, but the Follies is pretty small onions. I doubt anyone really cares who your father is or what he does. I was just worried about *you,* Mick. I mean, having him in town after all these years."

I nodded, trying to fight back my own tears. That darn lump in my throat was getting bigger. I turned away from Les, blew my nose, tried to compose myself. Les put his hand on my shoulder. "But, Les, I can't understand why he hasn't called. I mean, he's right here in town, and he hasn't even called."

"Well," said Les, "maybe it's hard for him. Maybe he's afraid you'd just hang up on him. You could, you know, and nobody would blame you."

I nodded.

"So," said Les. "What do you want to do?"

"I don't know."

"You want to see him?"

I almost exploded. "Well, yeah! Whaddya think? He's my dad, isn't he?"

Once he understood what I wanted, Les tried to make the whole thing easier for me. He volunteered to phone Joe Yule and see if he could arrange for us to meet him somewhere.

The somewhere turned out to be a dressing room at the Follies on Main Street in downtown Los Angeles, maybe a half hour before a one o'clock Saturday matinee. We went around back, through an entrance marked "Stage Door." An old geezer in a dirty gray shirt let us in, hardly looking at us. "Joe Yule?" he said. "Oh, yeah, he's down that hall. Watch your step. Third door on the left."

We almost tripped down some wooden steps. The hall was dark, lit by one lone light bulb, and the floor squeaked. But Dad's dressing room was well lit, lights all over the place. We found him sitting surrounded by a whole circle of lights around a big mirror in front of a table covered with makeup and false noses.

"Just putting on a little red here," he said apologetically, wiping his fingers on a Kleenex and rising to his feet. He looked something like I look now, a couple inches taller, thicker in the middle and thinner on top. His red hair had become gray.

I almost tripped getting to him and hugged him fiercely. He hugged me back and started to sway me back and forth, wordlessly. For at least a minute, we held each other tight. My eyes welled up, and my throat swelled. Finally, I said the one word I'd been wanting to say—and couldn't—for more than a decade: "Dad!"

And this time I wasn't acting.

☆ 16 ☆

In the Saddle

I*n* Stablemates, Wally Beery and I were playing ourselves or, at least, playing the selves that we had become in our movies. Of course, those selves were the invention of our scriptwriters, who had combined what they knew of us and what the fans expected of us to produce ever more exaggerated versions of ourselves. Beery was the sloppy, shambling, scratching, and slightly disreputable cowboy. I was the brash, energetic, enterprising, and mostly generous kid.

Beery also had his ornery moments, and he chose the first day of shooting on this picture to play double ornery. He was monosyllabic at first, indicating to the director, Sam Wood, and to everyone on the set, that he wasn't happy with anything about this setup. We all kept our distance from him and things were very tense, until finally Beery said to Wood, "Sam, can I talk to you?"

He took Wood aside, wiped his nose with his sleeve, and said, "I just want you to know. I quit at five o'clock."

Wood, an elegant guy who liked to sip a half bottle of champagne after a day's work, said, "Well, I just want you to know.

If you quit at five o'clock, you're gonna be a little lonely. I quit at four-thirty."

Beery did a double take. Then he threw back his head and roared. That broke the tension and everything was all right after that.

We shot the picture Sundays and Mondays at Hollywood Park because they were racing there on the other days and our production would have disrupted everything. One Saturday, we did disrupt things a bit: we shot some scenes before, during, and after the running of the $50,000 Hollywood Gold Cup. That gave our picture the kind of authenticity director Sam Wood wanted.

Early one Monday morning, C. S. Howard, the owner of Seabiscuit, one of the leading stakes horses of the day, saw me standing around with the film crew. He introduced himself and told me that he was going to give Seabiscuit a short workout. Would I like to work him?

Would I? I was so confident in my own abilities (I'd done very well on a mechanical horse at Warner Brothers, hadn't I?) that I never quavered over the thought of climbing up on one of the greatest horses in the world. In my suede jacket and Levi's and sneakers and a cap turned backward, I breezed Seabiscuit for five eighths of a mile in 1:01 and 2/5, with jockey Basil James breezing along beside me on another horse. You could look it up.

When we weren't at Hollywood Park, we shot indoors, on Soundstage 25, under the direction of Wood. The studio carpenters built a replica of the track right there.

Beery and I became pretty good friends during *Stablemates*, not just actor and kid actor but friends. One Friday afternoon at the studio, he asked me if I'd like to join him for dinner that night at Errol Flynn's home on Mulholland Drive. "I'll pick you up," he said. Now Beery was a guy I had never seen wearing anything but Levi's and cowboy boots. So imagine my surprise when he turned up at our home in Santa Monica wearing a dark-blue suit and a white shirt that was tucked into his pants.

And a tie, too! His hair was all slicked back, and he walked a little crippled, like he'd never worn shoes before or had sore feet.

He did have sore feet, as it turned out. Maybe that was a residual effect of his days on Broadway. As we drove up to Flynn's, Beery told me he'd been a chorus boy on Broadway, which also came as something of a surprise to me. He was full of surprises: he'd also been a wiper in a railroad roundhouse in my old hometown, Kansas City, and an elephant trainer in a circus, and a director at the old Essanay Studios before he moved in front of the cameras. Like me, he played in silent comedies first. Then he found his niche in some good character roles.

I had my biggest surprise of the evening when we got to Errol Flynn's house. When we knocked on Flynn's door, it was opened by a pair of exquisitely beautiful twins. "Heh, heh," said Flynn to us as we stumbled into his living room, a little bit bug-eyed. "You like my official greeters?"

How could we *not* like them? They were absolutely nude. I couldn't help glancing back for a second look. "It's all right, dear boy," said Flynn, showing off for us and his other dinner guests, Clark Gable, Robert Taylor, and Spencer Tracy, "you can take another look. Take two."

We took six weeks to shoot *Stablemates,* and I never had so much fun making a movie. I guess it showed because the box office was sensational (the picture grossed more than three times its cost) and so were the reviews. B. R. Crisler of *The New York Times* understood about me and my horse Breezy and gave me one of my more interesting notices:

We hate to be contradictory, but the two leading characters depicted in "Stablemates," at the Capitol, are not—as the Metro-Goldwyn-Mayer forward cautiously proclaims—"fictitious," and their resemblance to a couple of movie actors, by name Wallace Beery and Mickey Rooney, we think, is by no means just a coincidence. To put it bluntly, we doubt if any other two stablemates in Hollywood would have translated the horsy hokum of such a plot into the fine professional sentimentality that causes handkerchiefs to break out over the Capitol audience like signals presaging the storm of embarrassed nose-blowing that is to follow.

The tears must be the reason why, on looking back now, the plot comes back to us so mistily, resolves itself, in fact, less into a story than into a series of blurred cinematic tableaux: good old Wally scratching himself and yawning. Mickey (the boy Bernhardt) turning on the tears, the laughs, the hysterics, at will, like the perfect little screen virtuoso he is. "Stablemates" is Mickey's baptism of fire; anybody who can just break even before a camera with the invincible Beery is good, and Mickey, full of the fire of youth, even gets a shade the best of the encounter. You will just have to see this, of course, to believe it . . . They both pretend beautifully but they can't fool us: it's just Wallace Beery and Mickey Rooney, pretending.

I had hardly finished *Stablemates* before they had me putting on my saddle shoes again. This time it was *Out West with the Hardys*, the fifth Hardy epic. *Out West* grossed almost $2.2 million, seven times what it cost to make.

The story takes place on a ranch in Montana, where my sis has some romantic adventures with an eligible ranch foreman, who turns out not to be so eligible, and I have some mischievous adventures with his daughter, played by my classmate in the Little Red Schoolhouse, Virginia Weidler. Soon she'd play Katharine Hepburn's young sister in *The Philadelphia Story*. Weidler was a charmingly homely little actress who distinguished herself in what might have been her screen debut by refusing to remove her dress in the 1930 version of *Moby Dick* with John Barrymore. She was only three at the time. (Her death, at age forty, in July 1968, was unnoted in the Hollywood press. So much for fame as a kid star.)

Soon after Andy Hardy went west, I got ready for a red-letter day: my eighteenth birthday, on September 23, 1938. I was already driving, of course, and the drinking age in California was twenty-one; those weren't my reasons to celebrate. I whooped and hollered because I didn't have to take classes anymore, not from Miss McDonald or from any tutors when I was on location. I was so glad I didn't have to go to school any longer that I promptly enrolled at the University of Southern California. What's more, I enrolled in a premed course. I don't know what possessed me to do that. Maybe I thought that going through four years of premed and three years of med school and an internship and maybe a residency after that—ten years at least— was just about as easy as making a movie. After about two weeks at USC, I decided college was going to be a lot tougher than the Little Red Schoolhouse.

I think I made up my mind not to stick it out at USC when Mr. Mayer handed me my first bonus. I remember it this way: I was called to Mr. Mayer's office in the new Thalberg Building, where I swam through about a hundred yards of his white carpeting to find him beaming at me from high behind his white circular desk. "A little token of our esteem, Mickey," he said. He motioned for me to come up and take a slim piece of paper he was holding. It was a check, a check for fifteen thousand dollars.

"Gosh, Mr. Mayer, I don't know what to say," I said.

"You don't have to say anything," he said. "Except 'thank you.' You do know how to say thank you, don't you?"

I did a quick double take. Heck, I was gonna say thank you. I didn't need him telling me. "Er, uh—thank you. Thank you very much, Mr. Mayer."

His piercing dark eyes softened. "Mickey," he said. "You keep doing the kind of work you've been doing, and you're going to be in here often—to pick up more bonuses."

This time, I needed no prompting. "Thank you, Mr. Mayer. I try. You know I'm always trying."

He didn't say a thing about my offscreen exploits. With the help of Les Peterson, I'd learned to be discreet.

In those days, $15,000 was a lot of money to me, a cheeky eighteen-year-old, all in one lump. To give you an idea, I could have bought six or seven Ford convertibles with it. So, multiply $15,000 by seven or eight. In today's dollars, $100,000? $120,000. Gee, I thought, why be a doctor? If I can make money like this doing what I do, doing what I'd been prepping for all my life, shoot, I'll just be what I am. I'll be an actor.

I'm not sure why Mr. Mayer gave me the bonus. It could have been a reward. Or maybe he felt guilty. MGM had grossed $15 million on my last ten pictures and I had made exactly $39,000 on the bunch. When the Motion Picture Exhibitors of America came out with their year-end poll on the biggest box-office stars of 1938, guess who was number one. Not Tracy or Taylor or Cagney or even Beery (who had led the polls for a couple of years before this). No. It was Mickey Rooney.

I wasn't bitter at the time. After all, I reasoned then, I didn't make those pictures all by myself. A hundred other guys and gals collaborated to make them. And then an army of people marketed and promoted and exhibited the things. I was just glad I was able to work—and make $24,000—and take home a bonus check to my mom for $15,000.

She hugged me hard when I brought it home. "Hey, Fred," she said, "look at this." Fred Pankey pretended he'd known all about it; after all, he was in MGM's accounting department, wasn't he? But he did allow that he and Nell ought to celebrate by pouring themselves a double Scotch and soda. And then another. And another, as they talked about buying a house, a nice big house in the Valley.

I said. "No, Mom, not a house. A *home*. We've been renting for twelve years. It's time we had a home."

Before too long Nell and Fred found a place on Densmore Drive in Encino, and I'll never forget the day Dick Quine and

I drove out to see it. It was a twelve-room Spanish hacienda with a red tile roof sitting on five acres. "Hey," I said, getting out of my Ford and running down the hill. "It's got a pool!" I stripped to my shorts and dived in.

"Uh, Mick," Quine said when I surfaced. "Don't you think we'd better ask the folks who live here if it's okay to take a swim?"

"Naw," I said. "They won't mind."

"How do you know?" he said.

"I'll show you. Watch."

The house was quite a ways up the hill from the pool, but I ran up the flagstone walk, found the back patio, tapped on the glass door, and told the lady of the house who I was. She said, "Mickey Rooney! Why you darlin' little boy, you just go right ahead." She motioned down to Quine. "Tell your friend he can go in, too. Go right ahead."

"Pretty swell, huh?" I said to Quine as we floated on our backs in the pool, looking up at the English walnut trees that surrounded the place. There were lemons and oranges and a forest of gardenias, too.

I felt good about the place. The house cost seventy-five thousand dollars, but we only had to pay five thousand dollars down and make a payment every six months. (That home today might sell for $2 million. Add the five acres of land and you have to figure the value of the original property in today's inflated dollars would be close to $20 million.)

Our home was a place where I could entertain my friends. We had a nice game room, and my mom had a great sound console put in so we could play records and a piano so I could pick out my own tunes. I didn't know how to read music, but I could play the piano, and soon I was taking music lessons, learning how to play the guitar, the sax, the trumpet, and the drums.

Dick Quine, Sid Miller, Dick Crockett, and Andy McIntyre started coming over all the time to hang out. No, we didn't drink, and we didn't do drugs. These were simpler times. The only coke we knew was Coca-Cola. Sometimes, we'd just stay home, playing records in the game room. Eventually we realized we weren't content just to listen to music; we wanted to play our own. We started up our own jazz band.

A friend I didn't see anymore was Sig Frolich, my stand-in. He had wanted to break free from his stand-in status and have his own acting career. I wished him the best. He looked sad. I reassured him: "Hey, Sig, don't worry about me. I can always find another stand-in. Being my stand-in isn't a career. It's just a stop on the way up."

I found another stand-in right away. One night, I was roller-skating at an arena in Encino and I saw a guy with wavy blond hair who looked about my size and weight and coloring. I went up and started talking to him and learned he'd just moved to LA from Fresno. His name was Dick Paxton, he didn't have a job yet, but he was looking for "something in the movies."

I liked Dick Paxton. "Hey," I said to him, "you want to be my stand-in?"

"Sure," he said. "Uh. What's a stand-in?"

I told him. "You learn my part. Then, you help the camera-men get ready for each scene by walking through my moves." He didn't seem to understand. "They just want to be ready, so when I come along to do the scene for real—"

He still didn't get it, so I gave up. "Look," I said. "Just show up at the east gate of Metro on Monday morning at eight o'clock. I'll take you to the set and introduce you to Les Peterson and he'll take care of everything. And Dick?"

"Yeah, Mick?"

"Don't worry. You'll get the hang of it real quick."

I guess Paxton was wondering why, if I was getting paid as much as he suspected I was, I didn't do it myself. The truth of the matter is, I didn't understand either. I had nothing to do while they were getting ready. I wasn't taking classes any-more. I could have done it. But the studio insisted. Real stars not only rode from set to set in long, black, chauffeur-driven studio limousines. Real stars had stand-ins, too. And I was a star.

☆ 17 ☆

Babes in Arms

I *found Paxton* a real likable guy, and it wasn't long before I was asking my mom if he could move in with us. There was an extra bedroom for him, near mine. He'd be like the brother I'd wanted, but never had, eat breakfast with me, then drive with me into the studio. (I'd found out the kid didn't even have wheels and had been getting up at five A.M. so he could catch the Red Car and be at the studio when I got there. He made fifty dollars a week.)

Paxton was a quick study. He could read the script, run through a scene with the cameramen and the director, then show me, just before the cameras were ready to roll, where to move and where to stand. There was never any ambiguity. He knew. And he made sure I knew. Furthermore, he was a good athlete. He could stand in for me on some stunts, if necessary. As Mickey McGuire, of course, I had done my own stunts. As Mickey Rooney, I made it a point of honor to keep doing them, even though my directors objected. "Sure, Mickey," said Richard Thorpe, my director in *Huckleberry Finn*, "you can swim this river in February. But do you really want to? You could catch pneumonia or something, and that would play hell with our shooting schedule, wouldn't it?"

He had a point. We were shooting *Huck Finn* on the Sacramento River—in February. I stuck my foot in the stream and was shocked to learn how cold it was. But I swallowed my scream and said, "I'll do it." As it turned out, Paxton and I both did it. I'd take a turn, come out of the water sputtering and freezing. Then, on the next take, Dick would have his turn.

Other than almost freezing to death, the picture was rather uneventful for me. I met Max Baer, the boxer, on location there. He was training for a fight, and I jogged with him along a dusty road beside the riverbank a few times, just to see what it was like to train with a heavyweight contender.

Reviewers liked *Huckleberry Finn* (although one of them wondered why the screenwriter had to make Huck Finn into a premature member of the civil rights movement), and so did the public. In fact, the public still likes it; your kids and grandkids are probably watching it on videocassette, and the 35 millimeter film libraries still rent it out to schools.

I found out that I really did need Paxton as a stand-in on my next picture, *Babes in Arms,* which I was doing with Judy Garland. Arthur Freed had gone to the New York musical stage and brought an impossibly demanding director to Hollywood named William Berkeley Enos. You probably know him better as Busby Berkeley, the guy who choreographed most of the great 1930s and 1940s musicals at MGM and Warner Brothers, the ones with the kaleidoscope girls. Berkeley was a genius, but he had one small problem: he drank. In those days, of course, everybody drank. And so who was going to call him an alcoholic? He was a genius, not an alcoholic.

(John Barrymore and W. C. Fields were two other geniuses who drank. Fields seemed to hate everyone who crossed his path. Barrymore was a man of many parts: he was a comedian, tragedian, wit, caricaturist, art collector, scholar, yachtsman, and sportsman who would make fifty-seven films. But he chose to spin a downward spiral into drunkenness and disintegration. He had sixty cents in his pocket when he died. And most of the friends who came to his funeral in 1942 showed up drunk. On the way home from the graveside rites in East LA, W. C. Fields was mixing martinis in the backseat of his chauffeur-driven limousine.)

Berkeley could be charming, with his flashing eyes and huge, expressive eyebrows, and a smile that warmed everyone around him, but he had the alcoholic's perfectionism. If you couldn't toe the line, make it just so for Buzz, he'd go crazy. I can still see him, dressed in his immaculate white tennis shoes, white pants, and white sweatshirt, spending hours placing his cameras just so and rehearsing his dancers for days at a time and then doing take after take after take, of every number, from beginning to end. He shot those dancing girls from every angle and every side.

One day, after he almost fell from a girder high above the set, the grips put a rope around his waist and tossed it over a strut and held it while he moved from perch to perch. That way, if he fell, they could keep him from actually hitting the floor. They delegated Harry Walden, a gargantuan guy, to stay with Buzz and hold the rope while Buzz was in the upper reaches of the set, looking for the perfect shot. It didn't make any difference to Buzz whether he was seventy or eighty feet off the ground. He'd say, "Gee, this is going to make a wonderful shot, and the camera will move back like this—" Then he'd fall right off the beam, with Big Harry holding on for dear life (Buzz's dear life). Everyone would stop, paralyzed, and look up at Buzz swinging there at the end of the rope, his camera finder still in hand, and saying, "Gosh, I'm sorry, Harry. I didn't mean to step off."

"Hang on, Buzz," Harry would say, "I've got ya." Then he'd pull him back up, like a bunch of bananas, and Buzz would go back to work, single-minded in his search for perfection.

Buzz was tough on all of us. He was always screaming at Judy: "Eyes! Eyes! Open them wide. I want to see your eyes." To him, her eyes were his greatest asset, and he wanted them to show up on the screen, wide and sparkling.

Moreover, he wanted to do movies the same way he directed Broadway plays. No shooting a musical number in short takes as every other moviemaker did then. No. That wasn't for him. When the cameras started grinding away, he wanted us to do the number through from beginning to end, nonstop. No stand-ins could do that for us. We had to go through some very elaborate, very exhausting rehearsals before anyone even bothered to put film in the cameras. And then, sometimes, he wouldn't be ready to shoot until six P.M. Which meant that we'd have to knock off for a fast supper, then return for hours of night work, sometimes until eleven P.M. A couple of times we worked until three in the morning.

Both vaudeville kids, Judy and I were troupers enough not to complain. This, after all, is what we lived for. If we weren't working, then we'd have complained. But we *did* work.

Between *Thoroughbreds* and *Babes*, I did thirteen pictures in quick order. After *Thoroughbreds*, Judy did *Everybody Sing* with Fanny Brice and Allan Jones and a number of guest shots on some big radio shows like "The Chase and Sanborn Hour." Then her agent booked her on a twenty-five-city tour, where she often did four shows a day, ending up at Loews State Theater in New York, where she pulled in $1,750 a week. She returned to Hollywood just in time to make *Love Finds Andy Hardy* with me, and then yet another picture, *Listen, Darling,* with Freddie Bartholomew.

All that was just a warm-up for Judy's first real big hit, *The Wizard of Oz,* an elaborate production that took almost two years to put together, compared with our twenty-day shooting schedules on the Hardys. Those days began with Judy showing up at Metro at seven A.M. to get made up and squeezed into a corset. Because she was seventeen and blossoming, they bound her breasts, too, so she'd look more like little fourteen-year-old Dorothy.

In addition to all that, Judy still had to do her schoolwork *and* try to cope with all the emotional upset that goes with an unrequited love affair. Yes, Judy, at seventeen, was then deeply in love with bandleader Artie Shaw, already twice married and twice divorced at twenty-eight. Trouble was, Shaw never knew that Judy was in love with him. She was a kid and she was fun and they had gone to some parties together, but he had never looked upon Judy as she looked upon him.

How did I know? Because she told me. After all, I was her best friend.

"Golly, Mickey," she said, "he takes me places, and he comes to my parties but—he doesn't seem to understand how I feel about him."

My response should have been automatic: "Well, why don't you tell him how you feel about him?" But I didn't want her to do that. I knew that Shaw had a half-dozen women panting after him; I think he treated them like a string of polo ponies: if one went lame, he'd have another waiting in his stable. I was kinda glad Judy wasn't one of them.

The best advice I could give was this: "Judy, the right guy will come along, and when he does, you'll think it was worth the wait. In the meantime, we've got work to do."

She nodded, blew her nose, and gave me a hug. "I guess you're right, Mick," she said. "Work."

So Judy tried to lose herself in her work. In fact, she was already involved in prerecording musical numbers on the set of *Babes in Arms* before she'd finished all her scenes in *Oz.* I can still remember her with her Oz makeup and pigtails, doing a song with me, then rushing back to help the Cowardly Lion find his courage and the Scarecrow his brain and the Tin Woodman his heart.

Babes in Arms was a smash hit. It had already been a success on Broadway, so it had plenty going for it from the start. (Mr. Mayer bought the rights from Richard Rodgers and Lorenz Hart for twenty-one thousand dollars.) We had a good cast (including my old friends Sidney Miller and Dick Quine and a walk-on named Gene Kelly), great music, and a lively script that made people feel good about America.

This was 1939, remember, just about the time that Hollywood started to take the wraps off a self-imposed ban on producing films that might bring the country into war with the dreaded Adolf Hitler. In fact, even as much as a year later, in late 1940, Joseph P. Kennedy, then the U.S. ambassador to England, was telling major film executives in Hollywood to stop making anti-Nazi pictures. Some think he believed that Germany would win the war with England. So it was bad business for Hollywood films to promote or show sympathy to the cause of "the democracies" versus "the dictators." Besides, anti-Semitism was growing in Britain and the Jews were being blamed for the war. If Hollywood's Jews didn't want to be blamed for getting America into the war, Kennedy said, they'd better back off.

Kennedy could have been thinking about *Babes in Arms* when he made his pitch because *Babes* was MGM's first timid attempt to arouse some feelings in Americans about what was happening in Europe. There's no doubt this picture helped move the nation away from its prized neutrality. These were the days when the whole country was movie-mad, flocking to theaters by the millions. Those millions couldn't have helped but thrill to the patriotic sentiments expressed by E. Y. "Yip" Harburg and Harold Arlen in a song called "God's Country."

Freed ended up only $81,954 over his original estimated budget of $663,845, and *Babes* grossed more than $2 million its first year. (By 1945, it had grossed $3.3, and it's still making money.) That success would launch Freed on a glittering career at MGM, where he produced some of the finest musicals in the history of Hollywood.

Those early grosses from *Babes* moved Mr. Mayer to give me an eighteen-thousand-dollar bonus for *Babes*, but I think I earned it. I did everything in that picture except sweep the floors. I was in almost every scene in the picture. I acted my fool head off. I sang. I danced. I played seven musical instruments. I did imitations of Clark Gable and Lionel Barrymore. I even cried a little bit. It may have been the best picture I ever made.

Judy cried, too. In the movie, she is rejected by Rooney for the lead in the big show (which the kids are producing to help their down-and-out parents, refugees from vaudeville), and takes a sleeper bus to Schenectady and sings (to a picture of Rooney!) "I Cried for You."

She might have cried real tears on another count, too: she earned $8,833 on this picture (compared to my total of $23,400). I do not understand how there could have been such a discrepancy here. That is the way Hollywood was then. Trouble is, it's still that way. Ask Meryl Streep or Shirley MacLaine or Rachel Ward, or almost any actress in Hollywood. They'll tell you that Tinseltown is still a very sexist place, and that women movie stars generally earn less than half the salaries of male stars. The truth was that Judy and I deserved equal pay. We were a real team. We performed magic, the two of us, together, on film.

I don't think I knew how good Judy really was until *Babes in Arms.* Her comic timing was terrific. She could also deliver a poignant line with just the right amount of hesitation, slowly enough for the sadness to hit hard but still stay short of schmaltz. She could also turn on the intensity when she had to, memorize great chunks of script, and ad-lib, too.

With other actresses, I had to play everything straight. If I tried to clown around with a novice, fiddle with the timing, or ad-lib, I'd rattle her and ruin the scene. With Judy, it was the exact opposite. We actually tried to throw each other off track, tried to get the other one to mess up a scene. Say we had a tender bit to do together, where the script called for me to whisper something sweet. With anybody else, I really would say something sweet. With Judy, I might try, "Are you wearing a green garter belt today?" Then, when it was Judy's turn to whisper sweet nothings to me, she would say, "I hear the doctor says you have the clap."

I couldn't rattle Judy. She couldn't rattle me. In a dance number, I'd step on her foot. Then she'd step on mine. That wasn't in the script. But, often enough, Berkeley would like it, and shout out, *"Good! Great! Print it!"* He liked to see us letting our own feelings come out naturally, and that's how we happened to be doing our imitations right on screen. Berkeley couldn't help noticing how, between sequences, Judy and I were always trying to mimic the folks on the lot—not only the stars like Gable and Barrymore but the other people who worked with us: Roger Edens, Berkeley himself, even Mr. Mayer.

Berkeley came up to us one day when Judy and I were just clowning around. I was doing Lionel Barrymore, huffing and puffing and popping my eyes. "Hey, Mick," he said.

"Yeah?"

"You wanta try that in our picture?"

I gave that idea the usual time it took me to decide anything—a split second. "Sure," I said. "I can do Gable, too. You want Gable?"

To anyone watching us together, we were just two kids having fun. How natural, then, for our directors to want to get some of that natural fun up there on the silver screen. Whatever it was we were doing, it seemed to work on the screen.

Mr. Mayer knew he was on to something good. He didn't need to look at the box-office receipts (although, of course, he did). He sensed the special something between me and Judy. He would end up putting us in five more musicals together, all of them hits.

He got no argument on that from Arthur Freed because Freed knew we were part of his unit. He hugged us both after we finished *Babes in Arms* and said that he'd never seen anyone work so hard.

Freed made *Babes* in thirty-two days. And he saw that it was good.

Then he rested—while Judy and I kept working.

☆ *18* ☆
The William Morris Smile

T*hose were* the days when first-run movie houses in big American cities put on stage shows to go along with the products being turned out of the studios. If the exhibitors could get a real-live movie star on their stages (instead of a fading vaudeville star), so much the better for their box office. If the exhibitors could get *two* real stars—well, that was twice as good.

And so it was that MGM had me and Judy Garland out on the sawdust trail a few days after we finished *Babes in Arms*—to promote *The Wizard of Oz*. They sent us out with our moms and a small army of publicity guys to play Washington, New Haven, and Hartford. We'd end up on the stage of the Capitol Theater in New York.

To get our act ready for the Great White Way, we did four shows a day. I sang "Pal o' My Cradle Days" again, and Judy sang a song from *The Wizard of Oz* that would become her trademark, "Over the Rainbow." Then we sang some songs together, some Rodgers and Hart, some Harold Arlen. And we danced. I was never a great dancer, but I could fake it pretty well.

None of this performing did us any financial good. We were

on MGM records, but we got no royalties from those records, even though they sold millions. (We'd signed those recording rights away in our standard movie contracts.) We packed in the crowds in Washington, Hartford, New Haven, and New York, but we got no percentage of the box office. We received our MGM weekly salaries, period. Judy got three hundred dollars a week. I got nine hundred.

But, you see, as they explained it to us, we were promoting Judy's first big picture. That was supposed to make it okay because this was Judy's big break. It *might* have been okay if Judy had had any financial participation in the film, but she had zero percentage of the picture. And as long as she was at MGM, she never had any points.

Judy won fame, of course. That was something she'd never lose, even when that fame worked against her.

Other than that, all Judy got out of this tour was tired. We no sooner checked into the Waldorf on August 15, 1939, than we had to host one party after another for the teenage winners of MGM contests in some seventy Loews theaters around the country. Quiet lunches? Impossible. MGM had us lined up for lunch with exhibitors from all over the East. And how could I say no? These were the guys who had just voted me number-one box-office star in the nation.

If it wasn't an exhibitor, it was a member of the press. "What are your hobbies, Mr. Rooney? What are your favorite songs, Mr. Rooney? Where you do go when you and Judy go out, Mr. Rooney?"

Everyone assumed that Judy and I were an item, and Les Peterson told us to play along with it. He said, "If that's what people want to think, let 'em." Occasionally, back in LA, Les would suggest that I take Judy to a tennis match or out to the Ocean Park Pier, where we'd ride the roller coaster or wander in the fun house—trailed by an MGM photographer who'd capture us in some fresh poses. That, in turn, would provide fresh material for the movie gossip columns, which were a staple in every newspaper in the land.

I have to say the hoopla worked. Crowds turned out like we'd never seen before. They had to close the streets for several blocks around the Capitol Theater. The mounted police came out to keep some kind of order among the 15,000 people trying to get into a theater with 5,400 seats. Coming to the Capitol every day at midday, we felt like Latin American dictators inching along in our limo to the stage door. Were we bored by all this? No. We were show-business kids. This is what we'd been working for all our lives.

The management of the Capitol Theater decided that four shows a day couldn't accommodate all the crowds that were flocking in to see us, so they laid on another show. On weekends we did nine shows a day. I thrived on all this nonstop action, but Judy found it harder. One day, just before we were about to go onstage, Judy went into a slump and fainted right there on the spot. I went on without her, of course. The show must go on and all that. I did my thing. Then I did her thing. Then I did a few extra things to cover for Judy. I did a routine about a tennis match. I was the hush-voiced announcer, and I did the sound of the balls, too, and the strings. I did another routine about a Joe Louis fight: I was the radio announcer and the ring announcer and the crowd. I was Joe Louis, too, giving the postfight interview where Joe says it was a good fight and Hello, Mom and, over the body of his victim, Joe thanks everybody who helped make his night so pleasant.

When the show was over and *The Wizard of Oz* came on, I hustled backstage to see if Judy was all right. She was—a little pale and a little shaken, but all right. They'd called a doctor, who came and checked her vital signs and asked her a couple of questions about her diet. The doctor said he'd suggest Judy try eating a good breakfast of bacon and eggs and toast (instead of a piece of chocolate cake and a Coke) and getting to bed a little earlier. On the road like this, Judy liked to stay up and talk or listen to *me* talk. Anyhow, we all thought it was time Judy started taking better care of herself.

After my critical successes in *Boys Town* and *Stablemates,* I wasn't too surprised when the Rolls-Royce of Hollywood agencies pulled up to my door. Abe Lastfogel, representing the William Morris Agency, called up my mom and tried to persuade her that one of Hollywood's top stars deserved the best agency in town.

My mom sized him up. Lastfogel was short and plump with wavy gray hair, and he wore an expensive business suit, just like Mr. Mayer. He was Jewish, just like Mr. Mayer. And if he could sell Mr. Mayer on a higher paycheck for her boy, well, then, maybe she'd go along with William Morris. She said she'd like to meet Mr. Morris.

Lastfogel explained that, uh, Mr. Morris was dead.

My mother said she was sorry to hear that.

Lastfogel explained that he had passed away in 1932.

Oh.

Lastfogel said that Johnny Hyde was running the company now.

"Okay then," said my mother. "Mr. Hyde."

We went with William Morris. But we weren't to see Mr. Hyde until some months had passed. Apparently, Mr. Hyde didn't want to see us until the William Morris Agency was able to deliver on Lastfogel's promises to get us more cash. Then, toward the end of 1939, after it was clear the Hardy pictures would be churning out big profits for some time to come, after it was clear that MGM had a terrific new song and dance team in Mickey and Judy—only then did Hyde and Lastfogel make their move.

No one told us a thing. We just got word one day that our

presence was requested at the Beverly Hills offices of the William Morris Agency. When my mother and I arrived there, we soon realized that we were being ushered into one of Hollywood's establishment churches. At least, it seemed like a church to me because of all the silence and all the solemnity.

Johnny Hyde, president of William Morris, was dressed in a black suit, thin black tie, white shirt. He stood up behind his desk when we entered, smiled wordlessly, motioned for us to sit down in some low, overstuffed chairs designed to make us look up at him. Then he pushed a little button on his desk and whispered into an intercom, "Miss White, would you please have Mr. Lastfogel come in for a moment?"

I looked over at Mother. She was in awe. There was a kind of hush in this office. When Abe Lastfogel tiptoed in, he said nothing. He too was dressed in a black suit, thin black tie, white shirt.

Lastfogel remained standing and smiled Hyde's silent smile, obviously the William Morris smile.

Finally, Hyde broke the silence—not by speaking but by pushing my new contract with MGM across his desk toward my mother. My guess is that her head was swirling, but she at least pretended to study the contract.

When she looked up, Lastfogel was at her side with a fountain pen. Not a ballpoint pen, but an old-fashioned Parker pen filled with bright-blue ink. Mother took it. Lastfogel turned to the last page and pointed to the line where she would sign, again without a word. Getting into the spirit of things, Mother signed, said nothing, and pushed the sheaf of paper back across the desk toward Hyde. She nodded at Hyde and Lastfogel, then turned and smiled at me—a pretty good imitation of the William Morris smile.

Hyde rose, moved around the side of his desk, and shook my mother's hand. As an afterthought, he shook my hand, too. So did Lastfogel. I risked committing a sacrilege by speaking. I said,

"Thank you, Mr. Hyde." I compounded the crime by saying, "Thank you, Mr. Lastfogel." Mother mumbled something. And, in a few more moments, we were out on the sidewalk.

Mother surprised me, then, by ticking off all the salient details of the contract. For the first year of this new contract, I'd get $1,000 a week (for forty weeks). Second year: $1,250 a week. Third year: $1,500. MGM had an option for my services for another four years, with incremental raises, so that I'd be making $3,000 a week by the seventh year.

In addition to that, I'd get a bonus of $25,000 per picture, with a guarantee of no fewer than two bonuses a year.

Now *my* head was swirling. I hardly heard Nell tell me that we had to get the contract approved by a judge from the Los Angeles Superior Court, according to the new Coogan Law, passed by the California legislature after Jackie Coogan sued his parents for stealing all but $126,000 of the $4 million he had earned in Hollywood. And I hardly realized the implications of the new Coogan Law: two thirds of my salary as a minor would go into an irrevocable trust, not to be touched until I was sixty. And another chunk of my salary was headed into a trust for Nell.

We were to live on eight hundred dollars a month. And I was given one hundred dollars a week for my own use. Then, when I was sixty, I'd have hundreds of thousands of dollars in my trust fund. Sure I would.

☆ *19* ☆

Leading Ladies

Les *Peterson* continued to dog my every step, making sure I stayed in line, all for the greater glory of Metro, but the fact is, I wasn't leading such a riotous life. I was number one at the box office, a bigger draw than Tracy or Gable or Cagney or Flynn, and in spite of myself I had become Hollywood royalty. And I was starting to behave. As a young man, Prince Hal could drink and whore around with Falstaff and his lowbrow friends. When he became King Henry V, he had to renounce public lechery and pick up the royal scepter. Now I too was becoming more and more aware that I wasn't free to do what I damn pleased. I became a solid citizen. I made ceremonial appearances at worthy charities, and I cut some ribbons at the openings of new shopping centers. Or hot dog stands.

Did I have affairs with my leading ladies? Not during this period I didn't. Not with Ruth Hussey or Ann Rutherford or Lana Turner or Esther Williams or Kathryn Grayson or June Allyson or Donna Reed or Gloria DeHaven. It was pretty much business with these young women, who regarded playing in a Hardy picture as a stepping-stone to bigger things. According to the MGM recipe: take one young actress, pluck her eyebrows, cap her teeth, shape her hairline, pad her bosom, and throw her into a Hardy picture. Then wait and see. If the public liked her, the starlet became a star.

Ann Rutherford, a cute, dimpled brunette who was wholesomeness itself, was my steady girl, Polly Benedict, in the Hardy pictures. Naturally enough, to keep the plot moving, I would always fall for another girl, then lose her and come running back to Polly. But I didn't date Ann offscreen. Offscreen, I had other things to do, other women to squire around.

Lana Turner found a showcase in two different Hardy pictures, but by then Lana and I weren't an item any longer. Sure, I had dated Lana years before, before she started going with Mervyn LeRoy and a succession of others. Now, cast in the same picture, we went into a chaste little clinch, and that was it. Then I hurried off to my dressing room to finish handicapping the day's card at Santa Anita and Lana got right back on the telephone to talk to someone who was ten times as sophisticated as Andy Hardy and at least five times as sophisticated as Mickey Rooney.

I never dated Esther Williams, a former swimming champion, because she was married. We only did one Hardy picture together. She swam and said some lines. Her swimming was excellent. She was pleasant to work with—and unprofessional. If someone flubbed a line, she went to pieces, even if the flub wasn't hers. With work, later, she improved. She had to. It was either that or go back to swimming. Kathryn Grayson was a sweet young thing when she landed a part in a Hardy picture. Once or twice, I tried to get her to go out with me, but she gave me the impression she had something going with one of the higher-ups at MGM. Donna Reed was probably the best young actress who ever played in a Hardy movie. She had a nice range—marked at one end by her hooker in *From Here to Eternity* and at the other by the loving mom she played in *It's A Wonderful Life*. On the surface, Donna was sweet and demure. Inside, she was a tough dame. She had to be. I never met a successful Hollywood actress who wasn't.

June Allyson had unusual blond good looks and a sexy, almost croaky voice, but she was never anything more to me than a little sister. (I was surprised when I heard she was having an affair with a much older man, Dick Powell.) Gloria DeHaven was the daughter of Carter DeHaven, a good director who used to work with Charlie Chaplin. Blond, buxom, a fine broth of a girl, she gave Frank Sinatra his first screen kiss (in *Step Lively*). We were good friends—we enjoyed going to tennis matches together, dancing at the Coconut Grove, whatever—but we weren't lovers.

I had the normal young man's fantasies—and desires—but unlike many normal young men, I had money in my jeans. If I wanted to get laid, I just went out and got laid, with no romantic illusions. I did, that is, after Milton Berle showed me the ropes. It was he who took me to my first brothel, a one-flight walk-up off Santa Monica Boulevard called T&M Studios. (I don't remember what the initials stood for, but Berle and I used the code to kid around. "When we gonna be called to T&M," I'd say to Berle, "for another performance?")

I remember it vaguely as candlelit, with red and yellow satin wallpaper and a small bar. As soon as we gave the password and were invited upstairs, Berle introduced me to the madam, a stout, highly painted lady who might have been Sophie Tucker's twin sister. She poured us each a drink and called for the girls to come out. Then Berle tried to help me pick someone out of the lineup.

I was confused. Each of these young women was a dead ringer for a Hollywood star. Here was a Greta Garbo look-alike. There a Jean Harlow. A tall, elegant brunette reminded me of Norma Shearer. Another gal could have been Clara Bow. (Maybe, I thought for a moment, maybe she is Clara Bow; after the movies started to talk, Clara had come on some hard times.) When I couldn't seem to make up my mind, Berle tapped the little brunette who looked like Miss Bow and went off to one of the rooms with her. "C'mon, kid," he said to me, "I wanta show you how this is done."

I shook my head and held back at first, but eventually my curiosity got the better of me. Cautiously, I swung open the door behind which Berle had disappeared and found him with his clothes off and towel around his middle. "Clara Bow" (also wearing nothing but a towel) was kneeling in front of him holding a washbasin. In the basin was a purple solution and a bar of Camay soap. Berle grinned up at me. "Look, kid," he said. "Borscht and a boiled potato."

I ducked back out of the room and said to myself, "If the Andy Hardy fans could only see me now."

Milton Berle wasn't the only show-biz elder who was looking out for my sexual interests. One night when I was at Phil Silvers's apartment with Dick Paxton and Sidney Miller, Silvers got the bright idea of getting a call girl to come in and service all four of us. "Sure," said Silvers. "You, too, Mickey. You gotta lose your cherry sometime."

I grinned a shy grin. If Silvers wanted to think I was a virgin, that was okay with me. I said, "Well, shucks, Phil, if you say so."

Silvers negotiated a cut rate. After all, one trip and four Johns meant less expense and less traveling time. And then, while we were waiting for the young lady to arrive, my gambling instincts took over. "How about a little contest?" I said. "I don't know much about things like this," I said, "but how about the winner is the guy who stays in the longest? The three losers pay for him?"

They bought the plan, with the stipulation that no one could tell the girl about the bet. When she arrived, Miller went into the master bedroom first, then Paxton, then Silvers. None of them lasted more than five minutes. When I emerged from the bedroom after twenty minutes, the guys all laughed and sent me on my way a winner.

Later, Miller told me what had happened next. When the gal, fully dressed and ready for her next appointment, came out to pick up her honorarium, Silvers cornered her and demanded to know the truth. "Did Mickey really last for twenty minutes?" he asked.

"Are you kidding?" she said. "Four minutes of fucking and sixteen minutes of imitations."

She had the numbers right, but the order was wrong. I've always found that it's better to get a woman laughing first.

☆ *20* ☆

1939:
A Very Good Year

I*n 1939, I was* the number-one box-office attraction in the world. What was my appeal? I was a gnomish prodigy—half-human, half-goblin, man-child, child-man—as wise in the ways of comedy as Wallace Beery and twice as cute. I didn't play romantic leads. Clark Gable and Robert Taylor and Tyrone Power could make women sigh. I made people laugh.

In 1939, the studios cranked out almost four hundred movies. Some were junk, as always, but others were among the greatest films ever made. (And the audiences responded. Theater owners were selling an average of 85 million tickets a week, about four times the number of movie tickets sold each week these days, when there are almost twice as many people living in the U.S.).

The fact is, Hollywood moviemakers had been picking up momentum, year by year, for a decade, ever since the silents turned into sound, until this culmination in 1939.

Film students (and the rest of us, too, those of us who have access to good videotape libraries) are still watching some of that year's classics. David O. Selznick cast Clark Gable, Vivien Leigh, and Olivia de Havilland in *Gone With the Wind*, George

Cukor put Norma Shearer, Joan Crawford, Rosalind Russell, Paulette Goddard, and Joan Fontaine in *The Women*. John Ford saddled up John Wayne for *Stagecoach*. Bette Davis and Humphrey Bogart did *Dark Victory*. Sam Goldwyn hired William Wyler to direct Laurence Olivier and Merle Oberon in *Wuthering Heights*. Ernst Lubitsch made Greta Garbo laugh with Melvyn Douglas in *Ninotchka*. Ingrid Bergman made her Hollywood debut in *Intermezzo*. Frank Capra cast Jimmy Stewart as a stammering, honest senator in *Mr. Smith Goes to Washington*. MGM introduced Greer Garson to American audiences in *Goodbye, Mr. Chips*. Judy Garland did *The Wizard of Oz*. Tyrone Power starred in *Jesse James*. Cecil B. DeMille opened up the West in *Union Pacific* with Joel McCrea. Douglas Fairbanks, Jr., Cary Grant, Sam Jaffe, and Victor McLaglen cavorted in India with *Gunga Din*. Don Ameche invented the telephone in *The Story of Alexander Graham Bell*. Gary Cooper was a French Foreign Legionnaire in *Beau Geste*. Spencer Tracy plunged into darkest Africa to find a lost doctor in *Stanley and Livingstone*. William Holden made his debut as a violinist-turned-boxer in *Golden Boy*. Marlene Dietrich and Una Merkel had an unforgettable barroom brawl in *Destry Rides Again*. And Henry Fonda was the lead in *Young Mr. Lincoln*.

In that same year Hollywood's entries in the series sweepstakes were as good as they get: Paramount launched Bob Hope and Bing Crosby in the first of their "Road" pictures, *The Road to Singapore*. Lew Ayers did *Calling Dr. Kildare* and *The Secret of Dr. Kildare*. Sidney Toler took *Charlie Chan* to Reno. And Gene Autry sang under a *Carolina Moon*.

Critically and financially, I held up my end with two of my very best pictures, *Babes in Arms* and *Young Tom Edison* and another that came close, *Huckleberry Finn*. I also did numbers seven and eight in the Hardy series, *Andy Hardy Gets Spring Fever* and *Judge Hardy and Son*.

The accountants at MGM were also pleased to ink in huge

profits from those films of mine. In fact, my pictures in the 1938–1939 season accounted for more than 75 percent of MGM's profits in the best season that Loews Inc. ever had.

And each of my pictures that year made people feel. Those feelings were mainly feelings of joy and wonder and triumph. I know. Some modern film historians have written condescendingly about the never-never land of Carvel (where there was no mention of World War II until it was all over). But, maybe, precisely because of the darkening clouds of war, people did not want their spirits dashed, but raised. I think Mr. Mayer was shrewd enough to know that at this moment in history, people wanted to be lifted up, not cast down.

I think Charlie Chaplin, one of the greatest film comedians of all time, maybe the greatest, knew that, too. But he let his outrage get the better of him in 1939, when he did *The Great Dictator*, a satire featuring that great comedy team of Adolf Hitler and Benito Mussolini. Chaplin deserved better reviews than he got for that picture: the comedy, though bitter, was brilliant (with Chaplin playing Hitler and Jack Oakie playing Mussolini), balanced on the borderline of tragedy.

Jack Oakie called the result "dramady." He told me once that no one had a better talent than Chaplin "for putting a tear in your throat and making you cough it up with a laugh." It was a talent, however, that seemed lost on America's moviegoers of that time. In his satire on Hitler, Chaplin was "ahead of the curve." People weren't ready for his genius. And they stayed away from *The Great Dictator* in droves.

I was having dinner at Chasen's when I first met Charlie Chaplin. Gloria DeHaven was my date; her dad, Carter DeHaven, was one of Chaplin's directors, and she had known Chaplin all her life. So she took me over to his table and introduced me.

"I've always admired your work, Mr. Chaplin," I said. "And I just wanted to shake your hand."

"Well, I've always admired your work, too, Mickey," he said.

"Gosh," I thought. "The great Chaplin. *He* admires *me.*"

He not only admired me, he invited me and Gloria over to his mansion in Beverly Hills for tennis the next Sunday morning.

He lived in a great old brick mansion on a hill, on Summit Drive in Beverly Hills, a six-and-a-half-acre estate, with the Mary Pickford–Douglas Fairbanks Pickfair above and the Harold Lloyd estate below. The place had a high wall on three sides and was planted with fir, hemlock, cedar, spruce, and pine. On the fourth side was a lawn, sloping away down steep giant steps to a tennis court and swimming pool.

Chaplin met us in his tennis whites. He served tea in a huge, magnificent silver teapot, while Big Bill Tilden was giving someone tennis lessons out in back.

When Tilden was finished, Chaplin and I played some singles. He was very good, which shouldn't have surprised me: he knew how to move onscreen, so why shouldn't he know how to move on a tennis court? After we finished, he wanted to play with Gloria (I think he had eyes for her).

While they played, I inspected the house. The living room that opened out on to the terraced lawn behind the house was dominated by a fireplace and a huge coal bucket alongside it. A holdover from his English days, perhaps: Chaplin burned coal in that fireplace, not wood. There were bookcases everywhere, with photographs stuck in between the books. An Oscar stood on top of one of them, plus some figurines, quaint little foot-high equestrians on their prancing horses. There was a Steinway grand piano, with a big Webster dictionary on its own stand nearby. One mahogany-and-glass cabinet held some mementos of a trip to Japan, including two heavy ceremonial swords. This was the home of a man who obviously read a lot and traveled, the kind of man who could, and did, think deeply and seriously about what was happening in the world about him.

By midday, others guests started arriving: Katharine Hepburn, Greta Garbo, Ronald Colman, Gary Cooper, John Garfield, Errol Flynn. Chaplin took us to a kind of vestibule on the first floor, where he had a pipe organ. We flanked him on the bench of that organ while he played some music from one of his classics, *City Lights*. And then we talked a bit about the business we loved. "Acting," he said to me, "is ninety-nine percent sweat and one percent talent. But that talent had better be good." I nodded. That was the story of my life. I understood.

When Mr. Mayer learned the Follies was billing their top banana, Joe Yule, as "Mickey Rooney's Father," he suggested I ask my dad to retire from burlesque.

I refused. "For one thing," I said, "I wouldn't consider telling my father what to do. For another, burlesque is a noble profession in my family."

Mr. Mayer sighed and bought his way out of the problem, for cheap. He offered Joe Yule a three-year contract at Metro for $100 a week. You want to know what peanuts that was to L. B. Mayer? I can recall Mr. Mayer's inviting me to join him on a trip to Chicago (I guess I had to do some kind of promotion there) on the Santa Fe Chief. He was going back to Washington Park to see some of his thoroughbreds run, and he thought I might like to come along, along with three of his henchmen, Al Lichtman, Eddie Mannix, and Howard Strickling. I stayed up all night and watched with fascination as the three of them rolled craps on the floor of their private car—with as much as $100,000 on the carpet at one time. That was how the filthy rich lived then. Impromptu trips to Chicago in a private railroad car on the Chief to see their thoroughbreds run. One-million-dollar crap games.

And Mr. Mayer was offering my dad $100 a week.

Dad accepted Mr. Mayer's offer on the spot and signed a contract with MGM. The MGM press releases, prepared by Les

Peterson, were euphemistic. Mr. Yule wasn't retiring from burlesque, but from "the legitimate stage." And it wasn't because
MGM had offered him more money, but because Mick and Joe
wanted to work on the same lot together. But Dad was more
honest with the press. He conceded that "Mick might have had
something to do with my contract."

Deanna Durbin and I had already won miniature Oscars the
previous year, one of those honorary things awarded by the
Academy, but it wasn't quite the same as the real thing. In 1939
I got my first grown-up Oscar nomination, for my role in *Young
Tom Edison.*

In the Edison story, I had a great screenplay to work with,
written with heart and wit by Bradbury Foote, Hugo Butler,
and Dore Schary, the same writer who had done such a fine job
with *Boys Town.* I had a good director, Norman Taurog, who
had directed *Boys Town.* And I had some of the leading members
of the MGM stock company in the cast with me.

As young Tom, I was intrepid. I dived in front of a train to
save a toddler. I stopped a train from crashing over a washed-out
trestle by blasting SOS warnings with the whistle of a locomo-
tive. And I almost blew up my own train with some nitroglyc-
erine, whipped up on my own chemistry set. I saved my
mother's life by breaking into the general store and borrowing
a mirror that would reflect the light from dozens of candles and,
thereby, give the doctor the illumination he needed to perform
his delicate operation. As you can probably tell, there was a lot
of melodrama here, and there's no question the writers took
some liberties with young Tom's story. But the Tom Edison
they created was high entertainment.

I *became* young Tom. I imagined what and how this young
genius would do things and did them that way. When I wanted
to show Tom deep in thought, I pulled furiously on my left
eyebrow. That piece of business seemed to work. He loved his

mom? Well, I loved my mom, too. I looked at Fay Bainter as if she were my real mom. It worked.

As I said, I got an Academy nomination, along with Clark Gable, Laurence Olivier, Robert Donat, and James Stewart. Donat won the Oscar.

But I didn't come away from the *Young Tom Edison* experience empty-handed. In *Young Tom Edison,* MGM celebrated Edison's Port Huron years. Port Huron is pretty close to Detroit, which was then the center of the automobile business and the home of Henry Ford, who idolized Edison. It was Henry Ford who put together a lot of Edison's memorabilia in a museum in Dearborn. We had the premiere of *Young Tom Edison* there in Dearborn, on February 9, 1940, with Henry and Edsel Ford and Harvey Firestone, the tire magnate, playing host afterward at a big dinner in the executive suite of Ford's River Rouge plant.

After dinner, Henry Ford came up to me and asked me if I'd like to take a little walk with him. I said, "Certainly, Mr. Ford." So we trotted off, just the two of us, through a lot of hallways, and across a snowy, blowy parking lot, with guards saluting us all the way, until we came to a kind of hangarlike building, where they were putting the finishing touches on a prototype of the classic Lincoln Continental.

"How would you like one of these?" said Mr. Ford.

My eyes bugged out at the sight of this beautiful automobile. I had loved my 1937 Ford convertible. But this car was to my old convertible as an orchard is to an apple. I said, "I'd be a liar if I said I wouldn't, Mr. Ford."

He said, "How would you like a blue one?"

I said, "Mr. Ford, I would love a blue one."

A couple months later, one of Mr. Ford's men drove my new, blue Continental, with blue leather seats, right up to my dressing room at Metro. It had a special plaque on the dash: TO MY FRIEND MICKEY ROONEY, FROM HIS FRIEND HENRY FORD. It was one of the nicest gifts I have ever received. That first Continental is still considered one of the finest cars ever designed anywhere. I loved it. I drove it proudly.

Word about Rooney's Continental got around the studio very quickly. Clark Gable came to see it and, after eyeballing it as thoroughly as he would a fine woman or a fine racehorse, he said, "Mind if I take it for a spin?" Gee, this was really something. For months now, I had affected some Gable-isms: not only could I do a fairly good imitation of Gable's growly voice, I also started wearing his kind of loose cashmere sweater-vests and loose camel's hair jackets and a gray fedora with the brim turned up in front. Now, here was Gable lusting after something that was mine.

I grinned and tossed him the keys. He drove it off the lot, sped up Washington Boulevard, and then, in about fifteen minutes he was back. "Thanks, kid," he growled. "Gotta get me one of these." The Ford Motor Company had only made about two hundred of these Continentals. But Clark got one of them. Just like mine. Blue, too, like mine. Only difference was, he had to pay cash for his.

That year, I got another great gift, this time from Mr. Mayer himself. It was one of Mr. Mayer's thoroughbreds, a bay mare called Stereopticon. She was ready to foal, sired by a stud called Port O'Prince, and I had a fantasy that, maybe, I'd have a colt like Seabiscuit. We called the colt she foaled Inintime.

The name came from an aborted practical joke. My stepfather, Fred Pankey, thought he'd sneak a zebra into Stereopticon's stall before I got there, hoping I'd think that, somehow, my mare had been bred by a refugee from Barnum & Bailey's circus. I moved too fast for him, though: when he finally arrived with the young zebra, I was already toasting the birth of a beautiful colt. I had gotten there in time, and Fred hadn't. So Fred suggested I name him Inintime, and I agreed.

Inintime was a bay, like his mom, and he made his first start as a two-year-old on May 27, 1941, in the first race at Hollywood

Park with Johnny Longden up. He went off from post position thirteen at seven-to-one odds, and I would like to tell you that he was a winner that day, the first of many winning days. In fact, though he jumped off to a seven-length lead, he finished dead last. In the rest of his career, this colt ran in the money once.

In September 1939, the war began in Europe with Hitler's march into Poland. I wanted to join the fight then and there. But we weren't officially in the war yet, and Mr. Mayer wasn't about to lose his biggest star. He squeezed the draft board in Culver City, persuading them that I could help the war effort more by going out with the MGM stock company and selling war bonds coast to coast. I put up no objections, and I did get out and sell.

In 1940, Judy Garland and I and a gaggle of other actors and actresses started crisscrossing the nation on something called "The Metro Bond Train." We'd entertain, and we'd sell bonds. Judy would sing, I would tell jokes or do imitations, and both of us would dance together. Sometimes we'd do ten shows a day, then get on the train and move on to the next city. It was absolutely exhausting. It was also pretty eye-opening, for me at least. For the first time ever, women were throwing themselves at me, hurling themselves at the windows of our limousine, crying out, "Mickey! Mickey!" I know it seems funny. I wasn't Gable or Taylor or Tyrone Power, but women seemed to want me anyhow. It was the war, I guess.

In New Orleans, I went out after a show with three of the guys—Fred Astaire, Jimmy Cagney, and Dick Powell—and got as drunk as I have ever been in my life, before or since. We started out with a couple Sazeracs, a famous New Orleans drink made out of bourbon, absinthe, bitters, and sugar. A couple of them are enough to numb anyone, and we were no exception. Then, numbed, we went on a pub crawl, mixing more Sazeracs with champagne. In one bistro, all four of us ended up dancing on the bar as a band played "There's Going to Be a Hot Time in the Old Town Tonight."

I fell off first. When I looked up from the floor, Powell was going down. Then came Cagney, laughing to beat hell. Astaire broke into a big grin. He'd won, so he decided to keep on dancing. The last thing I remember that night was Astaire, leaning out a cab window shouting at the top of his lungs, "AH, SHIT! AH, SHIT!" The rest of us were too ossified to even cry out. I woke up the next morning lying crosswise on a big bed in this hotel, naked, with the sun shining in the window. I looked around and saw three other naked bodies: Astaire, Cagney, and Powell. There was nothing lascivious about it. We were just four drunks who ended up passing out together in a hot humid hotel.

"I'm afraid," I said, when I opened one eye and found Cagney staring at me, "I'm going to die."

Cagney answered, in a croaking voice, "I'm afraid I'm *not* going to die."

☆ 21 ☆
Strike Up the Band

For his encore to *Babes in Arms,* Arthur Freed didn't take any chances. He brought Judy and me back together in *Strike Up the Band,* a property that had already been a hit on Broadway, largely because of the songs written for it by George and Ira Gershwin. He hired Busby Berkeley to direct, and he put Fred Finklehoffe and John Monks, Jr., to work on the adaptation for the screen. In their version, I was the leader of a high school band that enters a nationwide radio contest. The band doesn't make it, but I do. Then I turn the offer down to stay with the kids. We all end up playing with a big time orchestra in New York.

The movie was huge; it grossed $3.5 million for MGM. I got paid $1,000 a week for twenty weeks, plus a $7,500 bonus. (My contract said I was to get $25,000 bonuses. Hell, where was the William Morris office when I needed 'em? Judy didn't get *any* bonus.) But we didn't know enough to mind. We just loved working together. If you see *Strike Up the Band* on videotape (it's in all the stores), you'll see how much we all enjoyed what we were doing. We did a show within a show, a send-up of the old stock plot about the villain and the mortgage and the poor working girl, in which Judy and I were absolutely manic. We did one number, "La Conga" in one take, after thirteen days of rehearsal: Paul Whiteman and his orchestra, a singing group called the Six Hits and a Miss, 115 dancers, and me and Judy. I did a furious turn on the trap drums called "Drummer Boy," and Judy vocalized alongside me. Judy did a torch song called "Nobody." Judy and I sang a duet, one of the most beautiful love songs ever written, "Our Love Affair"—by Roger Edens. And the whole cast joined together for "Strike Up the Band," a big, let-out-all-the-stops production number, which later became the UCLA fight song.

The critics loved the movie—and me. *The New York Times* called me "the Pied Piper of the box offices, the eighth or ninth wonder of the world, the kid himself—in short, Mickey Rooney."

All things considered, I did my best not to let my good press change me. I didn't insist on extra perks. I was born a trouper. A trouper I would remain. One Saturday, the studio was rushing through the last takes of *Andy Hardy Meets Debutante* with Judy and Ann and a glamour girl named Diana Lewis when George Seitz told me he had orders to finish a sequence that day, even if it meant holding the cast all night. I nixed that. I had a date to go dancing that night at the Palladium. "I won't break it," I said, "for all the money in—in Mr. Mayer's bank account." Seitz called for Carey Wilson, an early father confessor of mine on the lot, who drove over and persuaded me to work until eleven o'clock—at which time the studio would chauffeur me over to the Palladium, where my date would be waiting, courtesy of another studio limo. I said okay.

But it seemed that Seitz had misunderstood his orders. He completed the whole damn picture that night. And it took until

3:30 A.M. I drove straight home, up an empty Sepulveda Boulevard, resolving to have it out with Wilson on Monday morning, which I did.

He was profusely apologetic. "Look," he said. "Seitz misunderstood. That's all. We'll make it up to you, Mick."

"It's okay, now," I said, finally. "I missed my date, but the main thing is that we finished the job. I just want you to know I'm a trouper."

He nodded, and he smiled at me and gave me a look that I can only recall as respectful.

I added, "But you wouldn't have done this to Gable."

When Wilson told Mr. Mayer about the exchange, Mr. Mayer told Wilson, gazing out the window of his office, "Hmmm. I don't suppose we would have done it to Gable."

But that didn't stop the studio from continuing to ask more of me. When Mr. Mayer said he wondered if I'd go to New York with Judy to promote *Strike Up the Band*, I didn't hesitate a minute. Deep down, I probably resented going. But I wasn't allowing myself to express my real feelings. I was programmed to please. Best way to do that: smile and ask, "When does the train leave?"

Somehow, I ran into Norma Shearer in New York, still the Queen of the Lot at MGM, although her husband, Irving Thalberg, had been dead for several years now. She was staying at the Waldorf. "New York City," I said, "can be a lonely place." So we dined together at Club 21, then went off to the theater to see *The Streets of Paris*, with Bobby Clark, Abbott and Costello, and Carmen Miranda. It was a wonderful evening. Then, getting out of the taxi on Park Avenue, Norma asked me if I wanted to come up "for a nightcap."

A nightcap? I thought. Did she want to put something on my head? I almost said, "I don't wear one."

We had a drink, sitting on the couch together. She edged closer to me, getting very kittenish, very languid. When she turned her face toward mine and closed her eyes, I finally realized what was up. "Uh-oh," I said to myself, "how can I put a move on Marie Antoinette?"

I picked up her hand, kissed it, and said, "Well, Miss Shearer, I must be going." Good God, the lady was almost twice my age. (She was thirty-eight or thirty-nine, I was nineteen.) I was scared to death.

I was learning something: everybody—even people who seem to have everything in life that anyone could want—everybody wants to get fucked. Norma, now a pretty young widow, wasn't getting the love she needed. And she didn't give up. She made it very clear to me, once we were back in Hollywood, that she wanted me. She was hotter than a half-fucked fox in a forest fire. Once I realized what it was she wanted me for, I put up no further resistance.

A couple of years before, she had had a fling with Jimmy Stewart, six years younger than she. Jimmy gave Norma what she wanted: proof that she was still young, beautiful, and desirable. But that wasn't enough for her. She also wanted Jimmy to play a more public role, as her beau. She didn't need me in that way, not as a public escort. She just wanted my body. We confined our lovemaking to her dressing room on the lot at MGM, an elaborate trailer that had been built for her during the filming of *Marie Antoinette*. Her French boudoir was entirely appropriate for our kind of liaison—lovemaking French-style, with me sitting on her couch, my pants at my ankles and her on her knees. Here was the grand lady herself copulating with Andy Hardy!

Inevitably, Mr. Mayer found us out, and Eddie Mannix (who was delegated to bring me that news) reported that Mr. Mayer had gone crazy. (He didn't know that Norma had me half-crazy.) The fan magazines had already reported that two of MGM's stars were involved in adulterous relationships (Clark Gable with Carole Lombard, Robert Taylor with Barbara Stanwyck), and Mr. Mayer didn't even want to think what Hedda Hopper and Louella Parsons would do with this piece of juicy gossip.

We were to cease and desist, Mannix told me. Immediately. "You can't tell me what to do with my private life," I told him in a most uncharacteristic whisper, for emphasis. And then I went right off to tell Norma.

"Dear, dear, Mickey," she said. "You can talk to Mannix like that and get away with it? I can't. I want to keep working, Mickey."

"Ohhh," I said, doing a quick bottom-line analysis in my head. My last two pictures, *Young Tom Edison* and *Strike Up the Band*, had made millions. She'd been making losers.

And so, after one last lovely session together, we parted. Norma went on to land her best role ever—the ultravirtuous Mary Haines in *The Women*.

And when she left Metro, she made arrangements with the studio to give me her dressing room. The French boudoir wasn't exactly to my taste, but it was the best dressing room on the lot at the time, and I had some fun with it (and in it). But I never did without thinking of Norma, and the recollected warmth of her soft, soft lips.

I was getting ten bags of fan mail a day. One of them I remember went:

Dear Mr. Rooney,
    I loved you in "Strike Up the Band" with Judy Garland. I've seen all your pictures. You're absolutely wonderful. I guess I've been in love with you since I saw your first picture. I'll always love you, I guess, and, who knows? Maybe some day, we can meet.

    Yours forever,
    Bruce

Not everyone loved me as dearly as Bruce. In 1940, the week that MGM released *Young Tom Edison*, *Time* magazine saw fit to give me a cover story, a signal that I had truly arrived. But *Time*'s story was not a kind one. James Agee had no other choice, of course, than to tell his readers about my unprecedented rise in the Hollywood hierarchy, surpassing in popularity such matinee idols as Clark Gable and Robert Taylor and James Cagney and Spencer Tracy and Tyrone Power and Jimmy Stewart and Errol Flynn. Mr. Agee also predicted that I, "a manlier kid than any other who ever achieved stardom," would have a long life in the films.

But Mr. Agee didn't *like* me. He'd never met me, but he thought he knew me as a "rope-haired, kazoo-voiced kid with a comic strip face who until this week had never appeared in a picture without mugging or over-acting it." He decided that "to a large part of the more articulate U.S. cinemaudience, his name was becoming a frequently used synonym for brat."

But I couldn't let that notice bother me. As long as millions were paying their way into my movies, it didn't really matter what one critic wrote about me. My peers—the Gables and the Tracys and the Stewarts—liked me. So did Cecil B. DeMille. One of Hollywood's fabled directors, he was also the host on CBS Radio for a long-running series called "Lux Radio Theatre." DeMille presented radio versions of the biggest movies of the day, often (though not always) with the actors and actresses who appeared in the original film. He had a fine, resonant voice—I always figured it sounded something like God's—and, for forty million Americans every Monday night, he *was* God, bringing them for free on the radio what they had to pay for at the cinema.

Judy and I went on Mr. DeMille's show six times (in *Strike Up the Band, Merton of the Movies, Young Tom Edison, Stablemates, Boys Town,* and *National Velvet*). We did the shows before live audiences at the old Music Box Theatre near the old Hollywood Brown Derby, with four or five mikes and a sound man and a script, and they went on the network live, too. I think Lever Brothers paid us a thousand dollars apiece for these guest appearances, but Judy and I would have done them for nothing. Imagine: a live audience of 40 million people!

I don't think anybody had a bigger one, except maybe President Franklin D. Roosevelt for his periodic fireside radio chats with the American people.

And, speaking of FDR, he was a Rooney fan, too. After the *Time* magazine cover story appeared, the President's press secretary phoned me to see if I'd consider coming to Washington, D.C., for another of the President's birthday balls in January.

AMERICA'S FAVORITE MOVIE ACTOR STEALS THE SHOW AT PRESIDENT'S BIRTHDAY BALL was the *Life* headline. The *Life* writer noted that I was among seventeen other Hollywood celebrities who had come to Washington to help the President raise money for his favorite charity, the March of Dimes. *Life* gave me a special citation for my contribution "to the spirit of fun and ballyhoo and warm generosity that helps put the president's birthday appeals over the top."

Well, it was, after all, a birthday party. So I did my best to enjoy myself and bring all the others along with me on the joy ride. I arrived in Washington three days early to meet with the President. I attended official and unofficial luncheons. I went down to the station to meet some of the other Hollywood stars who kept trooping into town: Tyrone Power, Edward G. Robinson, James Cagney, Pat O'Brien, Edward Everett Horton, Olivia de Havilland, Dorothy Lamour, Lana Turner, Maureen O'Hara, George Raft, Lucille Ball, and Wallace Beery.

Even the starchy *New York Times* gushed: "And the movie actors! Formerly, three or four were all the fans could hope for, but this week almost the entire movie colony has moved to Washington. This week, if the mob does not go stark, raving mad trying to see all the celebrities at once, 'twill be a wonder."

The President wasn't going to the balls on the big night, but he did attend lunch, where there was an extra, empty place at every table. FDR then proceeded to wheel himself over to join each of the tables in turn and chat for a while before moving on. When he joined my table, he talked about Judge Hardy and the Hardy family. My Hardy series was breaking box-offices records; the nation had adopted the Hardy family as its own ideal American family, and President Roosevelt had apparently done so, too. "You'd better stick with that Polly Benedict," advised the President.

Playing along, I put on my most earnest face and said, "Golly, I sure will, Mr. President."

The other stars and I had an early dinner at the Carlton Hotel, and then we made a grand tour—of five separate birthday balls at five other hotels in the District of Columbia.

The *Life* photographers caught me (in a tux) at the Mayflower (where Mrs. Roosevelt had taken herself to cut the President's red, white, and blue birthday cake, which was five feet high and three feet across). I was hooting and hollering and dancing with a cross section of socialites from Washington and its environs— having as much fun with the older dowagers from Maryland and Virginia and Delaware as I was with their daughters. More maybe. Without embarrassment to Mrs. John Hay (Liz) Whitney (or to myself) I plunked myself right down in her ample lap—to the delight of the *Life* photographer (and, later, to *Life*'s 30 million readers).

Shortly before midnight, the Hollywood contingent was supposed to join the President at the White House, where he was scheduled to give one of his famous radio chats. He went ahead as planned—telling the nation how pleased he was that people could put aside their partisan political passion to work together for a cause—"the chief quality that distinguishes the American electorate from the political masses of the Old World."

But I wasn't there. Toward the end of the dancing at the Mayflower, a sleek, sophisticated brunette in a long silver gown caught my eye. And I caught hers. We met each other about halfway, eyes locked, then met in the middle of the dance floor.

We did some jitterbugging. Then, when we closed in together for "Always," she breathed an irresistible invitation in my ear. "I want you," she said.

When I took her back to her table, she grabbed her silver evening bag, fished inside it, found her room key and pressed it into my hand. "Give me five minutes," she said. "Then come on up."

I found Les Peterson. I said, "Little tired tonight, Les. Go on to the White House, won't you? And tell the President I'll be listening to his chat on the radio."

I let myself into a rather large, mostly darkened suite on the twelfth floor. She was kneeling on a couch in the sitting room. "You came," she said.

"Yes," I said, grinning, "and so will you."

She smiled and opened her arms to me. I went to my knees and buried my face in her bosom. She sighed and eased the thin straps of her gown from her shoulders. She was braless and I admired her breasts with enthusiasm. Soon, we moved toward the bedroom, leaving a trail of our evening wear along the way.

She spoke with an upper-class whisper, the kind they teach the girls at those exclusive academies on the Eastern seaboard. "Oh, Mickey," she said at one point, "I do so love your bools."

Since she was fondling them at the time, I had no difficulty figuring out what the hell she was talking about. But her choice of words wasn't upper class; she talked rather like a Winnemucca whore: "Oh, Mickey," she sighed, "deeper, harder, faster."

But then, in the morning, after a full night of this, I was not at all surprised when she told me her name. She was an heiress to the DuPont chemical fortune. She followed me to the West Coast.

☆ *22* ☆
Babes on Broadway

Just *a few* months after *Strike Up the Band* won all those accolades, the Arthur Freed unit was finished with another musical. This one, *Babes on Broadway,* was an even bigger smash hit than *Strike.* Judy and I, of course, were the Babes, the leaders of a group of kids trying to make it on the Great White Way. According to the script, we were also an altruistic bunch: we wanted to raise money to send underprivileged kids to the country, even if we had to do our show in a barn.

We had all our old gang of MGM kids back in this one, a lot of the familiar, energetic faces who tended to turn up in the Hardy pictures and in the Mickey-and-Judy musicals, including Dick Quine, fresh off his triumph as the kid brother of *My Sister Eileen* on Broadway, and Dick Paxton (who was more now than just a stand-in), plus a newcomer in Ray McDonald, a dancer, and Sidney Miller.

Judy and I were still good friends, but she had other things going in her life. She was, at last, in love with someone who loved her. (Her first great love, Artie Shaw, had left her for Lana Turner.) And so I was not at all surprised when Judy told me one day in the spring of 1941 that she was going to get married, to David Rose.

"Rose?" I said. "The orchestra leader who does all that la-de-la?" Rose had made a name for himself with one song, "Holiday for Strings," playing pop music as if it were a symphony written by Mozart. The Boston Pops Orchestra did it later, but David Rose thought of it first.

Judy giggled. "Uh-huh. We're getting married in September." Then, a week later, she told me she and Rose were going to elope right away.

That news bothered me and I couldn't help thinking about Judy's move as I drove home that afternoon to Encino. I just couldn't see how Judy would be happy with Rose. I thought, "Is this what Judy really wants?" I grabbed a quick snack, then told my mom I was going to drive over to see Judy. She brightened at that. She loved Judy, and she, like many of our fans, always expected that Judy and I would get married one day. But her face darkened when I told her Judy was going to get married to a bandleader. Tomorrow.

Mom seemed surprised at that, and said so. "I thought she was in love with you, Sonny."

"Uh huh."

"Maybe still is."

"Gosh, Mom," I said. "I doubt that. I doubt it very much. I just never gave her any reason. What we had going, maybe still have going, is something a lot different than 'love.'"

Still, I had to see her. I had to know whether this was what Judy wanted, really wanted. (I don't know what I would have done if she'd said, "No, Mick, it isn't what I want at all. I want you.")

Early that July evening, I drove over to Judy's in a new blue Buick convertible and knocked on her front door. She answered the door herself, with one of her sisters at her side.

"Judy," I said. "I didn't want to run away from you today. But—"

She hugged me, with her head canted to one side, so she didn't jab me with the curlers she had in her hair. "We're going to have a family dinner party tonight," she said. "But come on in for a minute or two." She winked at her sister, who scurried out of the room, sat down on a living-room sofa, invited me to sit down beside her.

I didn't ask her the question I'd come to ask. Instead, I said, "Joots, I just want to wish you all the happiness in the world."

She pressed a forefinger to my lips. "Hush, Mickey." She didn't want me to say anything more. For once, I shut up. The lull gave me a chance to focus, for a few moments, on her. I saw a kind of sadness in her eyes, and I noted a kind of excitement in her breathing that told me she was upset at, well, yes, at leaving me. Then her eyes began to glisten.

"Joots," I said. I didn't finish my thought.

She caught hold of my elbows, pulled me closer and gave me a very wet, very meaningful kiss.

Gosh, I thought, what would Andy Hardy do in a situation like this? Nobody had ever written a script like this for me before. I simply didn't know what to say. Or do. So I rose, quickly, and said, "Joots, I'd better go. I just wanted to say that, no matter what, we'll always be friends, won't we? Forever?"

She nodded, eyes wide and glistening.

I eased away from her. "It's just, just— Aww, Judy, I just want to wish you all the happiness in the world, Joots, forever and always. And all the love."

I'd broken the spell. She hopped up, giggled, and I was out the front door, into my convertible, and down the drive. I hadn't spent five minutes there with Judy. It seemed like an hour.

God knows what would have happened if we had ever gotten together, romantically. We would have been an incandescent couple, no doubt about that. Maybe we would have gone off like Roman candles, lighting up the sky for a moment or two, then fallen in a fizzle of sparks. Or maybe we would have become the longest-playing real-life romance in the history of the movies.

It's a cinch that I'd have respected Judy in a way that I did not respect some of the other women I have been involved with in my time. And that that respect might have kept me on the straight and narrow when everything else around me might have tempted me to stray.

I do not think anyone needed divine gifts to predict what kind of kids we might have had together. We would have laughed a lot together, and, I hope, cried very little. We would have had riotous family dinners and taken venturesome trips. The kids would have been tennis stars, volleyball players, golfers, gymnasts, with a whole flock of friends crowded around all the time. And we would have always had enough recruits for a softball game. I don't see how the kids could have avoided "the business"—in one capacity or another. I think they would have ended up on the stage. And if they didn't become entertainers (we wouldn't have forced that on any of them), they would, at the very least, have been entertaining.

But enough of this dreaming what might have been. Fact is, Judy went off and married David Rose. And that was that. She spent the weekend in Las Vegas, then showed up bright and early Monday morning on Stage 25 to continue shooting *Babes on Broadway*. And we went on as before, friends who didn't mind stepping on each other's feet.

On that set, I had more fun than I ever had on a movie, before or since. With Buzz Berkeley in the director's chair (actually, I hardly ever saw him sit down), making a movie was always a frenetic thing, but I thrived on it. This is what I was born for. Moreover, I had my gang around me. (Later, when I didn't have my gang around, my audience, I suffered all the pangs of an addict needing a fix. Applause, too, can be an addiction. And I caught mine so early that I could never kick it.)

The critics weren't unanimous in their praise for *Babes on Broadway*. They complained that MGM had tried to overload the picture with some pandering to the onrushing war effort, really nothing but propaganda. (The *New Yorker*'s critic observed that "this is an MGM musical and the MGM people seem to consider their musical pictures as an opportunity for ethical dissertation.") For instance, Freed threw in a production number designed to cheer up the British. He intercut a marching scene urging a universal British solder named Tommy Atkins to keep his chin up with the teary faces of some little English visitors to America talking to the folks at home on a wireless radio.

But maybe MGM knew what it was doing. Seeing the movie, the London critics were agog. The *Daily Sketch:* "If Mr. Rooney ever goes beyond the stratospheric heights he achieves here, he'll be way out of sight—in heaven, maybe, giving a virtuoso performance on a harp." The *Daily Telegraph* talked about "the terrifying talent of Mickey Rooney." It particularly liked his imitations.

It was harder for me to find praise in my own hometown: Edwin Schallert of the *Los Angeles Times* thought the picture "embarrassing and at times nauseating" because it was "coated with ten different layers of sickening glucose." *Time* didn't actually review the movie so much as editorialize over the fact that I wasn't in the army—yet. On the other hand, the *Chicago Sun*'s Wolfe Kaufman wrote, "Here is pep. Here is youth. Here is courage." And *Variety*'s critic said that if all Rooney's energy in this picture could be packaged as fuel, "there would be enough to sustain a flying fortress through the stratosphere from Hollywood to New York and return, non-stop."

Judy and I did a duet, "Babes on Broadway," and a dance number, "Hoe Down," in which I played the banjo. We did "Chin Up, Cheerio, Carry On" (more war propaganda), "Franklin D. Roosevelt Jones," "Blackout over Broadway," "She Is My Daisy," and a dance number featuring Dick Quine, Ray McDonald, and me called "Anything Can Happen in New York." The most notable song was a huge production number called "Bombshell from Brazil," in which I dressed up like Carmen Miranda—wearing a long slit skirt, a bolero blouse with phony boobs, huge platform shoes, and a headdress that might have been three feet high: what looked like a whole truckload of fruit piled on my head. You have to see it to believe it.

Babes on Broadway cost MGM a total outlay of $940,068. I earned a bit more on this one. By then I was drawing $1,250 a week. With the $25,000 bonus Freed gave me, I earned $53,333, my biggest paycheck so far. In its first few weeks, *Babes on Broadway* broke box-office records. Theater owners in thirty-seven key cities held it over after reporting they were doing anywhere from 200 percent to 369 percent of their usual business. By August 31, 1946, MGM had grossed $3.85 million on it. God knows how much it has earned since. And since there are plans to colorize *Babes in Arms, Strike Up the Band,* and *Babes on Broadway,* the earnings ain't over yet.

Probably never will be.

For Ted Turner or his assigns.

That's show business.

☆ 23 ☆
Ava Gardner

Ava Gardner was wearing a wispy summer dress and high heels and apparently little else (except a perfume called "Joy") when she came to visit the set of *Babes on Broadway* in August of 1941. Coincidentally, I was wearing a dress and high heels, too—my Carmen Miranda costume. But that didn't stop me from going right over to her after a take and extending my hand to her escort, Milt Weiss.

"Hello," I said. "I'm Mickey Rooney."

"This is Miss Ava Gardner," said Weiss, a smott New Yaw-kuh who figured I wasn't clopping my way over to see *him*. "She's one of our new contract players." Contract players. The studio was full of them, sexy young women who wanted to make it in Hollywood. Most often, Hollywood ended up making them because some of the women were there, first and foremost, as potential pussy for the executives at MGM.

"Hello," said Ava. That's all. Just hello. And without a smile. But she said it in the soft drawl of her native rural North Carolina, and I was a goner. I had known many beautiful women in my lifetime, but this little lady topped them all. She was five feet one, but she invariably wore high heels, so she was about my height when I was wearing five-inch wedgies. She had narrow ankles, perfect calves, full thighs, a tiny waist, a bosom that rose like two snowy, mountain peaks, an alabaster throat, a dimpled chin, full red lips, a pert nose, wide blue eyes beneath dark, arched brows, a wide, intelligent forehead and chestnut-colored hair that looked as if it had been stroked a thousand times a night ever since she was old enough to handle a brush. She was eighteen.

I asked her if she could have dinner with me that night.

She said she was busy.

I nodded, forced a smile, and retreated. I was hurt. Mickey Rooney being turned down? Flat? This was something new. But it only hurt for a little while. When she walked into the commissary at lunchtime, I told my cronies that I was going to marry this girl.

My technique in those days was a combination of early Neanderthal and late Freud. I'd approach a pretty girl with confidence ("cheek" would be a more exact word) and confess that, yes, I was the one, the only, the original Mickey Rooney. Then, instead of waiting for her reaction, I'd launch into a comedy routine that gave the girl only one option. She'd have to laugh. Sooner or later—generally later, after a candlelight dinner and some violins—she'd say, "Gee, Mickey, you're wonderful."

When I found a lady who liked my impersonations and was willing to accept me, I was elated. But I was young, and my instant elation quickly turned to instant boredom. I'd move on to someone else as quickly as possible. I admired a pretty face, a voluptuous body. Then I left before bothering to learn if, behind the face and the body, there was also a person.

Ava Gardner turned down my first five requests for a date. That only made me want her more, not just so I could go to bed with her. I wanted to make her the mother of my children.

On the sixth day after our first meeting, I was determined to make one more try, then give it a rest on the seventh day. On the set of *Babes on Broadway,* I sent Dick Paxton out to find Ava and see if she might consider dinner that night. Paxton found her in MGM's still-picture studio, where she was posing for some cheesecake. After she won a beauty contest in North Carolina, MGM had signed her on as a contract player for seventy-five dollars a week. Now the studio was working up some publicity shots. Tough work for the still photographers, but somebody had to do it.

"Mickey sent me," said Paxton.

She looked down at him, not unfriendly, apparently amused. "I don't think so," she said.

Paxton shook his head. "I think you're crazy, Miss Gardner. Don't you realize how much good Mickey Rooney could do for your career?"

She said she didn't. But, then, after she'd finished her stint with the photographers, she consulted Milt Weiss. "Will it really help my career, Milt, if I'm seen with Mickey Rooney?"

"You'd better believe it," said Weiss.

When I called her that afternoon, she seemed warmer, friendlier. We talked a little bit. She said she'd liked me in *Boys Town,* even more in *Babes in Arms.* I said I was really pleased to know that MGM's scouts had found her and brought her out to Hollywood. "But now," I said, "how about dinner tonight?"

She was still reluctant to go out to dinner. Her sister Beatrice was with her, you see, and—

"Well," I said, "I'm inviting you *and* your sister, too. I'll call Dave Chasen right now and make a reservation for three."

Ava paused. For once, I was silent. I let her think it over. She said yes.

At Chasen's, I took charge—of the dinner, of the conversation. I ordered champagne and caviar. From the moment we arrived, I was on. I went into my well-rehearsed routine. And even to myself I began to sound decadent. I thought I saw a twinkle in her eye, but she didn't crack a smile.

I introduced Ava to crêpes suzette that night, and even if she didn't love me, she loved them. She ordered them again and again whenever we dined out. After dessert, I grabbed her hand and took her around the room to show her off to my friends and acquaintances, who couldn't have helped noticing her and wondering who she was. She went along with me on this. After all, there had to be some big-shot producers sitting there in Chasen's front room, people who might help her someday.

Afterward, we went dancing at Ciro's, then the most popular nightspot in town. On the dance floor, she was taller than I, but we weren't dancing cheek to cheek anyway. I liked, as they say, to cut a rug. This was something I did well.

This way, we didn't have to talk, which suited me just fine. When I wasn't telling jokes, or doing imitations, or recounting the latest studio gossip, I didn't really know what to talk about. And it didn't really matter: I had one of the most beautiful women in the world on my arm.

When I saw her to her door, about two A.M., I said the only honest, sincere, feeling thing I could think of. "Ava," I said, "will you marry me?"

That broke through her cool. She hooted and said I must be crazy. But she smiled (a nice, if somewhat enigmatic, smile), said good night, and ducked into her apartment.

She didn't kiss me, I said to myself as I stood there in the dark. But she did go out with me, and we did dance at Ciro's, and, well, who knew what would happen next?

After that I saw Ava every day, and every day I proposed marriage. She didn't say yes, but her no began to sound less firm after a time. She went from "You're crazy, Mick, I hardly know you" to "Marriage is a serious thing, Mick" to "What'll our life be like?" It was clear to me that I was making some progress.

I could see that Ava was enjoying the pleasures of life at the top. She was a starlet who was yet to appear in her first picture, but now she was seeing her name in the gossip columns. She enjoyed dancing at Ciro's until closing time. She found she had a tremendous capacity for liquor and started drinking anisette.

Ava was undergoing the classic Hollywood transformation from small-town simplicity to big-city sophistication.

We might have gone on like that for some time—my proposing, Ava wanting to talk about it some more—but I started getting impatient. I was not used to the celibate life, and, unless I got Ava in bed, I knew I'd burst. Something had to give. What gave was rather unexpected.

On December 7, 1941, the Japanese bombed Pearl Harbor. The next day, I heard the official reaction to that on the radio in Norma Shearer's dressing room (where I was yacking with her after lunch about the pros and cons of her next picture). We'd declared war on Japan and Germany. There was something new in the air all through that dark December: war and the specter of war, maybe even on the West Coast. There were even reports, unconfirmed, that the Japanese had dropped some bombs off the shores of Santa Barbara. And with the change in climate came a change in the way men and women thought about marriage. Kids who were only dating ended up rushing down to city hall for their marriage licenses.

I bought a big diamond ring, then waited for the right, romantic moment to pop the question. This time, Christmas eve, after a big dinner party I'd given for Ava on her nineteenth birthday at Romanoff's, I was as serious as I'd ever been in my life. "Ava," I said when we got in the car. "Will you marry me? Come on. I'm not kidding." She gave me a long look.

"All right," she said very softly. "I'll marry you, Mickey."

Cannons exploded in my brain.

When the roar of cannons stopped, I leaned over and embraced Ava. I moved my lips close to hers and then, for the first time, she opened her mouth to mine and we tasted each other. I explored her mouth and she explored mine. Our passion grew, but we didn't make love that night.

I wanted to, but Ava didn't. Ava was determined to be a virgin on her wedding night, and, I confessed, I agreed with her that this was the right decision. "But," I added, trying to get comfortable in my car seat, "let's get married tomorrow."

Ava thought we ought to wait until we had time for a nice honeymoon, after I'd finished shooting *The Courtship of Andy Hardy*.

"Ummmm," I said.

The reactions at the studio were pretty cool. I told my producer, Carey Wilson, that Ava and I were engaged. He said he didn't think Ava was right for me. What he meant was, no one was right for a kid, just twenty-one, who was still a convincing teenager in MGM's most lucrative property, the Hardy series. *His* Andy Hardy series.

I was hoping Mr. Mayer would understand.

He didn't.

He was ready to talk me out of marriage as soon as I strode into his office with Ava on my arm. He hardly looked at her, didn't greet her, even though I was holding her hand. He just launched into a tirade. "How dare you destroy the studio's best investment?" he said.

I just stood there shaking my head. I didn't think I was destroying his investment. "The Hardy series won't last forever," I said. "I'm growing up."

He didn't want to hear that. "You don't see reason?" he said. "All right. I simply forbid it. That's all. I forbid it." His voice was soft. But his eyes were hard. And he was starting to flush.

"You've got no right to do that," I said. "This is *my* life."

"It's not your life," he shouted. "Not as long as you're working for me. MGM has made your life." My God, I thought, I was talking to Dr. Frankenstein.

By then Ava was cringing in the corner. She'd never met Louis B. Mayer before this. Now she was seeing him at his worst. On the other hand, she'd never seen me any better than this, standing my ground against the most powerful man in my world. "Then maybe," I said, "I shouldn't be working for you.

If you don't want to give us your blessings, Mr. Mayer, I'll be glad to go to another studio."

Mr. Mayer blanched at that, and his voice softened. "Mickey, it would break my heart to see you unhappy."

For a moment, I was surprised. I don't think I knew until that moment that *I* had some power, too. Sure, MGM had had a lot to do with my accession to power, but now I had it. I was the number-one box-office attraction in the world, making more money for Mayer than all his other stars put together, and MGM wasn't the only studio in town.

Mr. Mayer relented, but he and his people did their best to control the damage (as they termed it) of my getting married by decreeing that Ava and I would become man and wife in Ballard, California, a former mining town way up in the mountains of Santa Barbara County, far, far away from the concentration of the world press in Hollywood. And that Les Peterson would go along on our honeymoon. Mr. Mayer was nothing but a bully. But he saw himself, I am sure, as my benefactor. To prove that to himself, at least, he even threw me a bachelor party, a luncheon at Metro, just a few days before the big day. Every one of MGM's male stars showed up except Leo the Lion. Clark Gable, Spencer Tracy, Robert Taylor, Lewis Stone, Bill Holden, Jimmy Gleason, Robert Montgomery, Lionel Barrymore, Wallace Beery, William Powell, Fredric March, Jackie Cooper. This was supposed to be a roast. I spun on the spit.

Lew Stone didn't try to give me any fatherly advice. He just sipped his cocktail and listened gravely as the others tried to make me feel that, now, I was a man among men. Taylor said I'd be using some new muscles. "Take it easy at first," he said. "A sprained back will be hard to explain to Louella." Gable had some suggestions on technique. "Nibble her ear but not too much. It ain't like it was a steak sandwich, kid." Tracy reminded me of the story about the sink and the marbles. "You'll never have a year like your first year. Every time you make love to her, then, you put a marble in the sink. After that, every time you make love to her, you take a marble out. But, Mickey, you know what? You'll never empty the sink." Everybody roared. Leo the Lion would have roared, too, if he'd been there.

Early one Saturday morning in January, our wedding party headed north toward Santa Barbara in two cars, with Les Peterson and his wife in the front seat of my Lincoln Continental and me and Ava in the back, and the rest of the wedding party following us in a studio limousine: Ava's sister, Bappie, my dad and his new wife, Theota, my mother and her husband, Fred Pankey—and a studio photographer. I was trying to make everyone feel good, singing and telling jokes, but somehow I couldn't help thinking that we were doing something wrong—in the eyes of Mr. Mayer, at least. And in that total MGM culture in which I lived, when Mr. Mayer disapproved, could God's own disapproval be any different?

Bappie was maid of honor and Les was best man, and we were married in a 150-year-old church by Pastor Glen H. Lutz, who looked like a marine. After the ceremony, we kissed our families good-bye and headed for our honeymoon in Carmel, at the Del Monte Inn, with Les Peterson still playing chauffeur.

We didn't have a normal, sexy wedding night. I was a nervous wreck. Getting there had been more than half the fun. Now I didn't quite know how to savor my victory. To quiet my nerves I drank too much champagne at dinner and barely made it back to our room before I took off my pants and sank into bed. By the time Ava emerged from the bathroom, all dressed in white satin and lace, I was snoring heavily—dreaming, no doubt, about how nice it was, being married to the most beautiful woman in the world.

That was just the beginning of our troubles. Chapter two began the next morning when I headed to the Pebble Beach Golf Course.

"Golf!?" Ava said when I went to the car and pulled my clubs out of the trunk.

"Of course," I said. "Why do you think I brought my clubs?"

"But I don't play golf," she said.

I said, "That's okay, honey, I'll play. You watch." I wasn't kidding.

She did watch, for the first day, and she saw me card a confident seventy-nine. That night, I demonstrated the same confidence, more than making up for flaking out the night before. Ava, I was pleased to tell myself, was a virgin, and I was, by turns, alternately tender and tremendous, and that helped. All night long, she had my undivided attention, and I hers, and together we ended up performing our own sexual symphonies: Bach, Brahms, Beethoven, the whole gang. Oh, yes. Even Ravel was there.

We had a four-day music festival, in between my rounds of golf. Mornings, Ava would sleep in, while I played eighteen holes, then she'd join me for lunch at the clubhouse, then play some gin rummy with Les in the afternoon while I trotted the back eighteen. After thirty-six holes of golf, I'd shower and swim and then be ready for an early-evening concerto with Ava. Then we'd do dinner. Then Ava and I would retire early to practice our Mozart. It was an ideal honeymoon: sex and golf and sex and golf. Ideal, that is, for me. It never occurred to me to ask Ava what she wanted.

☆ 24 ☆
A Divorce

I n 1942, I did two more Andy Hardys—*The Courtship of Andy Hardy,* and *Andy Hardy's Double Life,* which helped launch the Hollywood careers of Donna Reed and Esther Williams. The pictures did well at the box office—they grossed more than $5 million—but anyone could see the series was beginning to wear down. Predictability is always the death of comedy, and this comedy was becoming a little too predictable. Besides, my fans were beginning to wish out loud that I'd grow up *on* screen. They assumed, now that I was married to Ava Gardner, that I'd grown up offscreen.

They were wrong. The truth was, Ava and I were just kids. And besides, we had very little in common. I liked classics, she preferred jazz. I loved the track, she was bored by the horses. When I got tickets to a USC game, she asked me why I couldn't get a box for the pops concert at the Hollywood Bowl.

Oh, we told ourselves that we were very much in love, and our sex life helped us in that particular piece of self-deception. Once Ava got into the spirit of things, she wanted to do it all the time. And she quickly learned what it was that turned me on about her. Let me count the ways: a smoldering look, a laugh, a tear, kicking off her shoes as soon as she got in the house, getting all dolled up, *not* getting all dolled up, coming down to breakfast in a pair of shorts—and no top at all. In bed, let's just say that Ava was . . . well, she had this little rosebud down there at the center of her femininity that seemed to have a life of its own. I am not talking about muscles. One gal I knew had trained her muscles, so that she could snap carrots in her pussy, no hands. But Ava had something different. She had this little extra—it was almost like a little warm mouth—that would reach up and grab me and take me in and make my, uh, my heart swell. She also had big brown nipples, which, when she was aroused, stood out like some double-long golden California raisins. And when I sucked those warm breasts, I did taste her mother's milk.

We were both athletic in bed, and pretty verbal, too. Once Ava lost her Southern reticence, she seemed to enjoy using the f-word. And I didn't mind a bit, when, for example, she would look me straight in the eye, raise a provocative eyebrow, and say, "Let's fuck, Mickey. Now." Some years later, Hedda Hopper would say of Ava, "The girl was made to love and be loved." I had to agree with that judgment.

We had a small apartment in Westwood, where Ava played the good wife. That meant staying home to eat elaborate (and heavy) Southern-fried-chicken dinners. On occasion, we'd still go out for dinner and dancing, but Ava was becoming a homebody. I was a guy with tremendous energy. When Ava didn't feel like going out, I'd take off anyway.

I tried giving Ava more attention after her appendectomy, only five weeks into our marriage, but I didn't let anything interfere with my golf on the weekends and going to the track. Ava spent her time alone writing long letters home, listening to jazz, crying, and consoling herself with dry martinis, trying to dispel the lonesomeness that was growing in her soul.

Of course, we both wanted to see her career take off. I had tried to persuade MGM to cast Ava in *The Courtship of Andy Hardy,* as the girl Andy almost falls in love with, but Carey

Wilson felt Ava wasn't ready. In March, Ava got her first speaking part, as a waitress in a drive-in diner, with Marsha Hunt and Lee Bowman in *Kid Glove Killer*. Between takes, I coached her a little, showing her how to stand, what to do with her hands, and how to avoid looking at the camera.

They say that Mr. Mayer had no intention of keeping her on contract when her six months were up, but, perhaps to please me, he renewed her contract and even raised her salary (from $75 a week to $150) and gave her a few walk-on parts. Up to then, at parties, Ava spent most of her time sitting in a corner looking beautiful. Little by little, however, she started having more fun. At one party, juiced with a couple of martinis, she started dancing with Tom Drake, a handsome young contract player at Metro. It was all very innocent, I know now, in retrospect. But I didn't think it was so innocent then, and I said so as we were leaving the party. Ava said she'd dance with anyone she damn pleased.

I said she ought to appreciate me a little bit more. After all, I was getting her career rolling.

"Yeah," she said. "A big help you were getting me the part in your last Andy Hardy! *Zero* help."

"I did my best," I said.

The next thing I know Ava announced (it was probably the martinis talking) that she was moving back to live with Bappie in the apartment on Franklin Avenue.

"Go right ahead," I said. (I'd had a few martinis, too.) That only made her more furious. She said, "You know, Mick, I'm goddamned tired of living with a midget." And that was the last thing she said. Before I knew it, she was packed and out the door.

This taunt hurt me more than I wanted to admit. I didn't ask to be short. I didn't want to be short. I've tried to pretend that being a short guy didn't matter. Sometimes, it was an asset. It helped me get in and out of crowds, into movies for half price until I was thirty-five, out of fights with big bruisers. I compared

myself to Toulouse-Lautrec, or to Willie Shoemaker, the jockey
who became a multimillionaire. I joked: "I wouldn't be a bil-
lionaire if I was anything but short." And it gave me a unique
repertoire of jokes, jokes that taller guys like Milton Berle
couldn't tell. Like: "So I'm in this bar the other day and I walk
up to this big blonde and I go, 'Whatdaya say to a little fuck?'
And she smiles and stands up and looks down at me and goes,
'Hi, little fuck.' "

But, in truth, I didn't like it very much. I tried to make up for
being short by affecting a strut, like I was a guy who knew
where he was going, by adopting the voice of a much bigger
man, by spending more money than I made, by tipping double
or triple at bars and restaurants, by winning tennis tournaments
I should have lost, by dating tall, beautiful women you'd be
more likely to see on the arm of an all-American forward at
UCLA. But nothing I could do, now that Ava had left me, would
add an inch to my height. Or to my self-esteem.

I lost some of my zip. It showed at the studio. I moped around
on the set, and my Andy Hardy, dark rings under his eyes,
looked more like Oscar Levant. Producer Carey Wilson went to
see Eddie Mannix, who reviewed the dailies on *The Courtship of
Andy Hardy* and cracked, "He's beginning to look as old as his
father."

Mannix decided he had to do something. He talked things
over with Bappie, then asked me and Ava to come in and see
him. He said lovers always quarreled. He wanted us to get back
together again and promised Ava that if we did, he'd get her a
good part in a good movie. That was what Ava needed more
than almost anything: a good part, something that could help
cover up her insecurity and make her feel she was a star, too. She
needed to like herself more. If Ava didn't like herself, how could
she like me?

With Mannix's promises still ringing in our ears, Ava and I
left the lot, drove just a few blocks, parked the car, necked for
half an hour, right there on Washington Boulevard in broad

daylight, and told each other we were gonna make it together.

We moved to a nice little home on Stone Canyon Drive, in Bel Air, and Mannix kept his word. He got Ava a part in a picture at Monogram with the Dead End Kids, *Ghosts on the Loose*. She wasn't bad. In fact, she showed some flair for comedy. More important, we were back together—for a time—and the studio began to see that old Rooney flair again.

Things didn't stay rosy for more than a few weeks. Soon we started nightclubbing together, but nightclubbing wasn't the cure for what ailed our marriage: we had practically nothing in common. In fact, the nightclubbing hurt because we both tended to drink too much, and drinking doesn't help marriages. Neither does vicious gossip. Some of Ava's so-called friends were telling her that I was out fooling around on her. That wasn't true, but how do you build something when the termites keep boring from within?

That's what I called Hollywood's gossips. As soon as they see anyone happy, they try to break it up. And now, I was helping them do it, not by cheating on Ava—why would I cheat on the most beautiful girl in the world, who had promised to be mine forever?—but by not being what you might call "the perfect husband." I remember the evening when things really began to come apart. We had gone to the Palladium to dance to the music of my friend Tommy Dorsey, who invited me to sit in with the band and play the drums. I not only played the drums, I played Dorsey's trombone, too, while Ava fumed at being left alone.

Around midnight, she flounced out and drove herself home. About three in the morning, I slipped into bed, apologizing to Ava and stroking the back of her neck, something she always loved. She became aroused and soon we were in passionate embrace. Afterward, she slipped out of bed, then turned to me as I lay there luxuriating in the good feelings, watching her. She was nude and glowing. She was never more beautiful. But then, she surprised me with a snarl: "Listen, you son of a bitch," she said, "if you knock me up, I'll kill you." Then she ran for the bathroom, slammed the door, and locked it.

We continued, for a few more months, to live together. We made love as before, though a shade less frequently. But our kisses should have told me the marriage was almost over: there was less tongue involved. Secretly, I hoped she would get pregnant and was saddened when she didn't. Ava would have many men, including Artie Shaw, Mel Tormé, Frank Sinatra, Clark Gable, Howard Hughes, Robert Mitchum, Farley Granger, Robert Walker, Peter Lawford, Howard Duff, Walter Chiari, Sir Malcolm Sargent, George C. Scott, and a whole stadium full of toreros from Madrid, but she never had any children. I suspect she was barren.

When I had to make a publicity trip to the Midwest that summer, I went without Ava. I rather enjoyed going to the racetrack without feeling guilty for leaving her home alone, and I enjoyed the track most particularly one Saturday, when I made a big twenty-thousand-dollar score at Arlington Park. Later that afternoon, I bought a beautiful pair of diamond earrings as a peace offering for Ava. When I got home, peace did prevail, but not for long. Two weeks later, Ava and I drove down to Tijuana for a Saturday at the races, won a few bets, lost a few, and had fun. But Ava resented my intense interest in the *Daily Racing Form,* and she was on the attack all the way home. I sweet-talked her out of that mood and persuaded her that we ought to have a late supper at Chasen's. We did and enjoyed ourselves immensely—until, high on myself, I bought drinks for the entire bar. Once you buy for the bar, you have to stick around for the bar to buy drinks for you. Ava took a cab home.

By the time I got home, Ava had taken a kitchen knife to every piece of furniture in the house. There was stuffing everywhere, and the living room looked like the set of a horror movie. Ava was fast asleep, or pretending to be. It was only a few days later that Ava said she'd had enough. She asked me to leave, and I went.

Soon, I was plying Ava with gifts, phoning her, trying to win her back. One night, I tried to break her door down, which compelled Ava to call the studio and ask that something be done about me. Mr. Mayer responded by pushing up the production schedule on my next picture, *A Yank at Eton,* which was to be shot mainly in Connecticut and at Lake Sherwood in the Conejo Valley. Next thing I knew, I was on a train to the East.

I returned from Connecticut in October 1942 and tried to get back with Ava. She didn't even want to see me. I thank God the studio was there to help me then, rushing me into another picture almost immediately, one of the best I ever did, William Saroyan's *The Human Comedy.* Work has almost always been good therapy for me. As someone who was programmed to work, how could it have been otherwise? I think the studio knew that.

The studio also knew that I could be called into the army and *would* be called in—unless Eddie Mannix could make a case that my presence in pictures would be more helpful to the war effort than my presence on the battlefield. He did make a case. On September 3, 1942, he got the draft board to give me a three-month extension so that we could finish making *The Human Comedy.*

Mr. Mayer had loved William Saroyan's Pulitzer Prize–winning play, *The Time of Your Life,* so he found Saroyan in New York and asked him if he'd consider coming back to the coast to write a movie for MGM. Saroyan jumped at the chance. In his office at MGM, Saroyan set out to do a story about the war—not a battlefield story but a story about the war's effect on a small town in America. Thinking that the studio might consider casting me in the lead, he set his focus on a youngster who worked as a telegraph operator in a small town.

Of course, the story fit right in with Mr. Mayer's campaign to help America reflect on its own goodness. Mr. Mayer was reflecting all the time on "goodness." Could it be that he was trying, all along, to cover up his own badness, the badness that he was living behind the scenes? Mr. Mayer wanted to believe that he was good and that America was good, that its people were good, and that people would survive if only they had faith and love and hope. Unfortunately, Saroyan, a good novelist, wasn't a good screenwriter; he didn't make his ideas come alive in a dramatic way. Rather, he had his characters spouting these ideas as if they were sermons.

Mr. Mayer did the best he could to salvage the script. He hired Howard Estabrook to do a rewrite. Estabrook was only partly successful, and the reviewers couldn't help noting something was wrong. Bosley Crowther of *The New York Times* called the sermons and the tear-jerking score part of the movie's "cheap pretentiousness."

Still, I was happy with my performance (which won me an Oscar nomination). I was Homer Macauley, the messenger boy, and I tried to play him with simplicity and restraint. (In addition to that, I had been humbled by my failing marriage, and my humiliation may have given me something extra, some extra feeling in the role.) In one scene, I discover my telegrapher, a lovable old drunk named Willie Grogan (Frank Morgan), has died at his keys, with a half-finished telegram transcribed on his machine. It is addressed to my mom, Mrs. Kate Macauley, of 2226 Santa Clara Avenue: THE DEPARTMENT OF WAR REGRETS TO INFORM YOU THAT YOUR SON, MARCUS . . .

I am stunned. Moments later, I tell my boss, Tom Spangler (James Craig), "I can't take this home now. I can't tell Ma . . . and Bess . . . and Mary . . . yet. How am I going to go into the house and look at them? They'll know the minute they see me. I don't want to tell them, but they'll know."

My boss suggests we walk a while to give me a chance to work out my own feelings over my brother, killed in action (played by Van Johnson). "He said he might go. I can't figure it all out. All I want to know is . . . what about my own brother? When

my father died, it was different. He had lived a good life, the way
he wanted to. He had a family. We were sad, but we weren't
sore. I'm sore. What's a fellow supposed to do?"

"Your brother didn't want to go."

I was inconsolable. "But I want to see him. I can't help it. I
want to see him walking and standing around. I want to touch
him. I want to talk to him. I want to have fights with him,
even—the way we used to."

I'd had plenty of opportunities in my acting life to emote over
inconsequential things. And sometimes I had tried to make up
for the weakness of my material by overacting. Now, I didn't
need to do that. The starkness of a young man's loss—of his own
brother and in a war—that didn't need a lot of hype, just a quiet,
thoughtful sharing of my feelings. I thanked Estabrook for suggesting that Craig and I end the scene by doing a man's kind of
thing together: pitching horseshoes in the dark.

I also gave the director, my old friend Clarence Brown, a good
deal of credit for bringing out the best in me—by simply telling
me to be Homer Macauley, in my own way.

Van Johnson had been in only two films previously and Robert Mitchum was making his film debut in this picture, but I
never really got to know them. Funny about making a movie:
when the cast is together on the set, they're closer than the
members of any family. But after each day's shoot, they split and
go their own ways because they want to see other people, do
other things.

Here's a strange aside, related to the idea that we actors don't
really know our temporary "families." It's changed a bit now, as
things are much more out in the open, but there were always
rumors about leading men being gay. Were any of the stars I
played with gay? I don't know. I really don't, even though I used
to participate in all the gossip. In those days, gays stayed in the
closet. I do know that no man I acted with ever made a pass at me.
Neither did any of my other gay friends (and after many of them,

as they say, came out of the closet, I realized I had had more than I thought I had, a number of whom have made great contributions to the world of the theater and of film). No, wait, I just remembered. One of my gay friends did make a pass at me, once, at a Hollywood party. It was Rock Hudson, and he didn't even make the pitch himself. He had one of his friends approach me as I was getting a drink at the bar to tell me that Rock was having a few guys over to his house afterward. Would I care to come? The way this guy acted and the way he said, "Come"—well that was all the tipoff I needed. I told him, "Hey, tell Rock thanks, but I thought everyone sort of knew about me—that I like girls."

The Human Comedy opened in March 1943 to a great deal of ballyhoo, which was the way Mr. Mayer wanted it. It was, he said, his favorite picture of all time. On a budget of a million, it grossed $3,858,000, of which the Mayer unit got 40 percent. I suspected that this picture grossed a hell of a lot more than that—maybe $3 or $4 million *the first week*, and, over the next three years, about $35 or $40 million. I guess Loews Inc. never figured I'd wonder where the extra millions went. Who do they think they were fucking kidding? No wonder Mr. Mayer liked it so much.

I thought I'd be going into the service after I finished *The Human Comedy*, but I got a reprieve from my draft board. They classified me 4-F—on the basis of some medical tests that showed I was suffering from high blood pressure. That surprised me, but I didn't protest or ask for another exam because I still had some unfinished business at home (which may have been the cause of my high blood pressure). I really thought that if I had more time, if I didn't have to go into the army, I could put our marriage back together again. I just couldn't let go. I found myself driving past Ava's apartment from time to time just to see if she was there—or if someone else was there. I never saw her or anyone else, but in my imagination I saw plenty—Ava in the shower, Ava in bed, Ava sipping a cup of coffee, Ava laughing at something she saw in the paper, Ava with a whole parade of guys, singly and in bunches.

I didn't fight Ava's divorce suit when she filed on May 2, and I had to admit she was kind; before the case was over, she waived her claim on half my property. (MGM's Mannix had told her that things would not go well with her at MGM if she took Mick to the cleaners.) So all Ava asked for was twenty-five thousand dollars in cash, a car, and the furs and jewelry I had given her. She got everything she asked for.

By the summer of 1943, however, Ava seemed to have stopped hating me. She'd landed a role in one of the Dr. Gillespie pictures, *Three Men in White.* Lionel Barrymore played an old curmudgeon who wanted to test the seriousness of an intern played by Van Johnson. Ava was Dr. Gillespie's temptress, and the role, though not a big one, was big enough to throw her into a panic. She turned to me for help, and I jumped at the opportunity to see her again. Acting lessons turned into dinner dates (but they led us not into bed). Then, one night, she pulled me into her apartment, and when we awakened the next morning, we started talking about getting back together again.

(Ah, wasn't sex wonderful? What a miracle! I cannot describe the feeling. It's indescribably delicious. Songwriters and poets are the only ones who can do it justice, but it's only frontier justice: just a mere approximation of the reality. I think there's a reason for that. If we could describe the feeling, then we'd have it all canned up, wouldn't we, in one neat container. Then it would lose its charm and its mystery, and we'd end up saying, "Sex? Oh, I don't think I want a can of *that* tonight. We had pork and beans *last* night.")

When I phoned Ava that evening, however, she told me she didn't want to see me after all. "No, Mick," she said. "I can't have dinner with you tonight." I asked her why. She said, "Look, I don't think we should start up again. Anyway, I have other plans."

In my mind's eye, I saw fifty-five guys lined up at Ava's door.

☆ 25 ☆
Girl Crazy

I t *didn't take* a genius to realize that the studio wasn't going to let Andy Hardy grow up. I knew it for sure when I saw the script of *Andy Hardy's Blonde Trouble*, scheduled for the summer of 1943. I was almost twenty-three, but Andy was still at the "Gee whiz, she kissed me" stage. If the people at Metro had had their way, I'd have remained a teenager for forty years.

But I didn't have the time (or the energy) to bitch about the story, and, anyway, I was too pleased with another project that Mr. Mayer had put together for me and Judy to complain. We were going to do *Girl Crazy*, the movie adaptation of a Broadway hit written in 1930 by none other than George and Ira Gershwin. (RKO did it in 1932, with Ginger Rogers, but the guys at MGM decided they could do it better.) Producer Arthur Freed, writer Fred Finklehoffe, and directors Norman Taurog and Busby Berkeley were going to team up on one of the best musicals MGM would ever mount.

The plot was a piece of nonsense about the playboy son of a newspaper publisher (me) who gets sent out West to attend the Custer College of Mines and Agriculture, only to discover: (a) there's only one girl in town (Judy Garland), the daughter of the postmaster, and (b) the college is so strapped for money it has to close its doors. Judy and I save the college by putting on a big rodeo *cum* beauty contest and turning Custer into a coed institution.

The movie was a hit because of the marvelous music in it.

Tommy Dorsey and his orchestra, Judy, and I made the most of these melodies: "Treat Me Rough," "Embraceable You," "Girl Crazy," "I Dare You," "Could You Use Me?" "Rockabye Baby," "Fascinating Rhythm," "But Not For Me," "I've Got a Crush On You," "Biding My Time," and the smashing big-production finale, designed by Busby Berkeley, "I've Got Rhythm." Tell me, dear reader, how the hell could the producers go wrong with all this going for them?

It was hard work, but I thrived on it. I wish I could say the same for Judy. A month into the picture, Judy was down to 94 pounds and completely exhausted. I didn't have to ask her what the matter was. I knew: married life with David Rose was not so rosy. At the end of January, her physician told the studio Judy couldn't dance for six to eight weeks.

In fact, Judy was back at work in *two* weeks—only to collapse again. She was on the lot, and off, all through February and March and April, then managed to work for a solid month from April 19 until May 19, when we finished shooting—two months over schedule. Some people say the studio doped her up at this time, giving her downers at bedtime and uppers so she could get up and go to work in the morning. This was simply not true. MGM would never do this. Judy had taken to drinking, and, with her drinking, sleeping pills. No one forced them on her. She was old enough to know what she was doing. But, in reality, she didn't know what she was doing. She started with one, then, when one didn't work, she took two. When two didn't work, she took four. When four didn't work, she took eight. And, oh Christ, you lose count after eight. Later on, Judy would blame the studio or her mother or some nameless "theys" for getting her started on the road to self-destruction. Who ever wants to blame themselves? She was only human, but the most human woman I've ever known, and she didn't want to take the blame—the blame for killing Judy Garland, the Judy Garland that I (and the whole world) loved.

The fact is, Judy was not well, and she did not get good medical care. She just couldn't keep up with the studio's cost-effective shooting schedule. They were trying to save money by trying to get Judy to do too much, too soon, but they ended up going $322,000 over budget anyway. And along the way they put one of the biggest stars any studio ever had on an escalator to the basement. Movie-wise, Judy never quite made it back above the mezzanine.

For her work in *Girl Crazy*, Judy got paid a total of $28,666 on a picture that grossed $5,886,000 (in 1943 dollars). I earned $68,166, including a bonus of $25,000. She got no bonus at all. Neither of us got a dime's worth of royalties from all those great songs we recorded; MGM took all the profits through its records division. In reality, I believe *Crazy Girl* actually grossed more than $47 million worldwide. The thieves were still at work. You must remember that at this point in my life the peak of my earning pyramid, I had yet to earn my first million. This should lay to rest all the bullshit people write about how Rooney has pissed away hundreds of millions. Oh, I've *earned* more than a billion bucks. But I never *saw* very much of it.

That was the time I should have taken Judy by the hand and confronted Mr. Mayer—told him that we had to have $10 million each, in cash or else. An outlandish request? Maybe. But that's just about what Jimmy Cagney did to Warner Brothers.

As Jimmy told the story to me, he simply went on strike at Warners—until they gave him $10 million flat. Jack Warner was stubborn and let Cagney stew for a year to teach him a lesson. In the end, it was Warner who learned the lesson. He went back to New York to a board meeting and almost lost control of the company. The majority of the board was appalled to find out why Cagney hadn't made a picture for more than a year. "You know how much money we've lost because of your stupid damn silly move?" one of the board members told Warner. "You're costing us hundreds of millions. Pay the son of a bitch the ten million."

Unfortunately, Judy Garland and I made no such moves. We were just vaudeville kids. How could we stand up to a man like Mr. Mayer, the highest-paid executive in the land? Better for us to stick to what we knew best: singing and dancing for Arthur Freed and Busby Berkeley.

By early 1944 almost every able-bodied man in Hollywood was in uniform except me. I had just finished a quickie entertainment to help bolster the nation's morale, a movie called *Thousands Cheer,* about a soldier (Gene Kelly) and a colonel's daughter (Kathryn Grayson). Most of the folks under contract to MGM at the time made cameo appearances in this one, but I didn't show up until the film's climax, when I hosted a huge army camp show. Even as a 4-F I could do that much! Mr. Mayer rationalized my deferment by telling me, "Mickey, this show will do more for America than ten Mickey Rooneys in uniform."

I responded to that with a grunt. Then I went down to the Selective Service Center and asked for some new tests. I passed them this time, and my draft board reclassified me 1-A. I was already shooting *National Velvet,* starring one of the most beautiful twelve-year-olds I'd ever seen, Elizabeth Taylor, and it didn't look as if there was anything else on my horizon after that. And, even if there were, I wanted to serve my country for a change instead of my master, Mr. Mayer.

Eddie Mannix filed an appeal with the draft board, which turned him down, informing him that "Mickey Rooney will be inducted sometime in May 1944." Mannix knew that was it. He told Clarence Brown to shoot all the Rooney scenes first. That meant I had a month, more or less, to finish *National Velvet* and get my affairs in order. Knowing this was my last picture for MGM (or anybody else) for some time to come, I did my best to enjoy it.

I loved the script, about a butcher's daughter who wins a horse called "Pi" (for "Pirate") in a raffle, teams up with a jockey down on his luck to train the horse to run in England's Grand National Steeplechase, and rides him to victory. It was written by two real pros, Theodore Reeves and Helen Deutsch, based on a novel by Enid Bagnold. My favorite line, about the character I played, the unlucky jockey: "What's the meaning of goodness, if there isn't a little badness to overcome?" It could be my epitaph.

I loved Clarence Brown. And I loved the horses. Elizabeth Taylor loved horses even more than I did, and she was a lot braver than I. She'd been riding since she was three, and she had absolutely no fear—even when she discovered that the studio had purchased a son of Man O' War to play her horse in the film, a gelding named King Charles, who was too spirited for his previous owner to handle. Everyone else in the cast gave him a wide berth, but Elizabeth lost no time making friends with him.

"Keep away from that horse's head," I told her one day when I found her cheek to cheek with King Charles. "That horse is a killer. He'll eat you." She didn't listen to me (I was kidding, of course), and I stomped off, muttering for the benefit of those standing by, "Oh, God, you can never tell kids anything."

I couldn't tell Elizabeth about horses, but I taught her a thing or two about acting. I've never been a Method actor, and the only acting theory I really believe in is, "Be natural." I never liked talking about acting. I just liked doing it. And I think I communicated some of this to Elizabeth, who was so full of natural talent in this, her first major role.

She was as eager as I had ever been and infinitely more teachable. One day, I caught Clarence Brown watching me giving Elizabeth a lesson, not in acting, but in listening. "Sure," I was saying, "you have your *lines,* and those are the lines you deliver.

But you will deliver them better if you listen to what I'm saying when the cameras are grinding away—really listen, then react to *me.*" Clarence smiled and walked away. I think he approved of what I was telling her.

Clarence himself never told us how to do a scene. He'd just sit back, away from the camera, and say, with his great moon face breaking in a smile, "Okay, whenever you're ready." When we finished the scene, he wouldn't say, "Cut," or "Stop," or even "Okay." He'd just be sitting there chuckling softly. Then he'd get up and you'd hear an assistant in the background say to cut the cameras.

I met Sam Stiefel in Pittsburgh when I was touring with Judy for *Girl Crazy.* He came to the theater, a beefy guy with a raspy voice who introduced himself to Les Peterson and me and ended up taking us to dinner. That's where he made his pitch. He wanted to manage me, close his shop in Philadelphia (where he owned some theaters), and move to the West Coast. What he said, and the way he said it, impressed me. He seemed so confident. I told him to come ahead.

In the months that followed, Sam became the kind of friend who would lend me money without question. At Santa Anita, if I was tapped out, he'd offer me money without my having to ask. "Okay," I'd say. "Give me five hundred."

"Here," he'd say, flashing a big roll of hundred-dollar bills, "take a thousand."

I took his offerings, with thanks. My Metro salary, about $125,000 a year, wasn't enough for me and my mom. Two thirds of that went into my trust. Then Uncle Sam got his share. So did the William Morris Agency. So Sam's help was welcome. Soon I found myself telling him to put the wheels of my independence in motion. "Go ahead, Sam," I said. "Let's get that company started."

In March the incorporation papers came through for Rooney,

Inc. I was president, Sam was secretary-treasurer, and Mort Briskin, a long-time friend of Sam's, was legal counsel. On March 21, 1944, Briskin sent MGM a memo asking that no more checks be sent to the trust (after all, I was now twenty-three). Every cent of my earnings would now go to Rooney, Inc. If and when my mom needed cash, Sam assured me all she had to do was holler. I was due for induction at Fort MacArthur in two days, and I'd been worried about Mom. Now I wouldn't have to worry anymore. Sam would take care of her.

The night before I was scheduled to leave, I asked Ava if she'd have dinner with me. She said yes, and we went to the Palladium, then did some dancing at the Big Band Emporium. When I took Ava home, she surprised me by inviting me in, excusing herself for a moment, then reappearing in a red nightgown and red peignoir.

"Unnhhh," I said cleverly.

Afterward I chose one of the three things there are to say after sex: (1) I gotta get going, (2) thank you, (3) I wanna marry you. In this case, I said, "I wanna marry you—again."

Ava said, "I'll wait for you, Mickey. When you come back, I'll be waiting."

As I made my way to my car in the dawn's early light, I couldn't believe what a lucky guy I was. While I was off fighting for my country, Sam Stiefel would take care of my finances and Ava would be waiting.

☆ 26 ☆
In the Army Now

Τhe next morning I reported to the army induction center on Main Street, not far from the Follies Burlesque, with about fifty other recruits. Next stop, MacArthur, where they shaved our heads and gave us a pile of clothes, dog tags, and heavy boots. In three days, we were on a troop train to the U.S. Army's cavalry training center at Fort Riley, near the Republican River, which can only be a river in Kansas. The cavalry!

"Great!" I told myself. "I love horses." Little did I know I'd never get close to a horse.

Army training was tough, but I had no problem with the forced marches, the heavy packs, the work on the obstacle courses, or the hours on the rifle range. In fact, I got medals for my marksmanship. By the end of two weeks' training, I found myself a squad leader. I *did* have a problem with my fellow soldiers. Some of them thought the army gave me special treatment because I was a movie star.

"You lousy fuck," shouted a little guy named Martinez when I took over the squad. "You get to lead just because you been in a movie."

Martinez reminded me of the guys who used to come after me

on the pier at Ocean Park. "Do I have to take this?" I asked my lieutenant after three days of being hassled by Martinez.

"Hell, no!" he said.

Martinez and I had one of the goddamnedest bare-knuckle fistfights you ever saw. With the entire squad watching, we went at it in the compound outside the dayroom. After a half-hour battle, the lieutenant stepped in and ended it. He looked us over, noted our cuts and bruises, and called over to one of the noncoms. "Take these guys to the infirmary. Get 'em fixed up as best as you can. And get 'em some tetanus shots."

Later, Martinez told me, "I was an asshole. You didn't ask for nothing special. You stood up to me. And I liked you for that." I bought him a beer. He bought me a beer.

During basic, I'd been writing to Ava, and she'd been writing back to me. But her letters started getting shorter and more infrequent, and finally they stopped altogether. I tried to phone her, only to get her roommate on the line. "No," she said, "Ava isn't here." I kept calling and kept getting the same song and dance. Then, one night when I was lying in my bunk, after taps, after a long day's march with a full pack in one-hundred-degree heat, one of my sergeants called me to the telephone in the dayroom of the barracks. The room was dark, illuminated by a single light bulb on a post outside the window.

"Hello," I said, a little nervous. I thought it might be bad news from home.

"Hello, Mickey," said a shaky voice at the other end. Unmistakably Ava. "Mickey," she said. "I want you to stop writing—and phoning."

"But I love you," I said. "Ava. I love you."

She made no reply.

"Ava," I said, "is there someone else?"

There was no answer. Then I realized the phone was dead. She'd hung up.

At the end of basic, I got a ten-day furlough and took the train home to LA. I attended a Hollywood premiere at Grauman's

Chinese Theatre and got my picture in the paper the next morning wearing my uniform and my marksman medal. I looked pretty good, I must say, and I felt lucky. At about eight o'clock that night, I drove up to Ava's apartment just in time to see a guy getting out of a battered old Chevy. "So this is why Ava wanted me to stop writing," I thought. I squealed to a stop and caught up to the guy on Ava's doorstep. "Lissen, bud," I said, grabbing him by the shoulder.

Startled, he threw up his guard and whirled around. Then it was my turn to be startled. It was Howard Hughes, the rich boy genius, the inventor, the dashing flyer, the head of RKO Pictures. I was ready to back away, but then Ava appeared, so I had to fight him. I threw a punch. He threw a punch. He had a reach on me, so I ducked inside his next punch and we fell into a clinch.

Soon we were wrestling on Ava's front lawn, a gangling genius and a Hollywood gnome, swearing at each other in the dusk. Ava was swearing at both of us, demanding we stop. When we didn't she disappeared into the house, then returned with a heavy glass inkwell. I think she meant to throw it at me, but she hit Hughes instead.

"Jesus," cried Hughes, "you cut my head."

"Oh, my God," said Ava, as the blood started to flow.

I pulled a handkerchief out of my pocket and handed it to him. Ava was pulling both of us into the house.

Sitting in the living room, the three of us started laughing.

"Isn't this the damnedest thing?" said Hughes. "Getting upset over a bunch of crap?"

Ava arched an eyebrow at that. Since the fight was over her, she didn't think it was a bunch of crap, but she was a good sport. In the blink of an eye she was holding a bottle of Dom Perignon and three glasses. By the time we finished two bottles, none of us was feeling any pain.

Finally, I made a move to go. It was either that or pass out from the bubbly. "I gotta go fight a war," I said.

"Good luck," said Howard Hughes. "And Mickey—"

"Yeah?"

He smiled and, though his speech was slurred, his voice was warm. "Don't get your ash shot off."

In early September the army sent me to Camp Sibert near Gadsden, Alabama, for training in chemical warfare, but the government never taught me how to use poison gas. It put me back in show business. It seems that entertainers attached to the USO didn't want to have any part of the action on the front lines. So the army said, "That's okay, we've drafted some entertainers of our own. We'll entertain our own troops."

The army put out a call to a number of commanding officers across the land, asking them to identify their men with talent—actors, musicians, singers. My commanding officer tapped me, and soon word came through: I'd be headed for an army base near New York City. Then I'd be going overseas with a bunch of entertainers, assigned to the 6817th Special Services Battalion.

So I only spent a few weeks at Camp Sibert—just long enough for me to get married. Sounds pretty casual, but I was hurting, after Ava, and vulnerable and needing to patch up my battered ego.

It happened like this: the Loews exhibitor in Birmingham, who'd been supplying the brass at Camp Sibert with first-run films, called up my commanding officer and asked him if he could come to Birmingham for a late September premiere of *National Velvet*. There'd be a party afterward, of course, with the town's elite. And if the general could bring Mickey Rooney . . .

The general could. It was the first time I'd seen *National Velvet,* and I must confess that I was thoroughly charmed. The folks in the movie house almost went nuts when they found out I was in the audience. "Shucks," I said, when they asked me to take the stage and say a few words. But I loved the attention. I needed it, the way a drunk who's been on the wagon for a week needs a shot of booze. I grabbed the mike.

"Well," I said. "You saw the picture. We had a lot of fun making it." I lowered my voice to a conspiratorial whisper. "But you know, folks, those hills and that seaside? That wasn't really England. It was Carmel, California." The audience oohed and aahed over that piece of intelligence, pleased I would take them into my confidence.

Then I flattered them. I said, "You probably have some thoughts about this young actress, Elizabeth Taylor. I'd like to know what you think. You think she'll make it? Has she got star quality?"

They answered by bursting into applause. And when I thanked them for coming, they stood and clapped for at least three minutes. You'd think I'd just told them their history teachers had made a mistake, that the South had really won the Civil War.

Afterward, at the party, everybody seemed to be drinking bourbon and branch water. "Sure," I said, "I'll have bourbon and branch." In fact, I said it several times.

Through my drunken haze, a newspaper reporter, Lily Mae Caldwell from the *Birmingham News*, appeared at my elbow and said she had someone here with her, someone who wanted to meet me.

"Well, hello there," I said to a beautiful young woman with a smile as wide as a jack-o'-lantern.

"Mickey, this is Betty Jane Rase. She's attending the conservatory of music here. She's also Miss Birmingham of 1944."

"Well, hello, Miss Birmingham of 1944. I'm Private Mickey Rooney."

"Oh, Mr. Rooney," she cooed.

"Oh, Miss Birmingham," I snapped back, smartly.

Sometime after the seventh bourbon (or maybe the seventeenth), I asked Miss Birmingham if she'd like to become Mrs. Mickey Rooney, and she said yes.

We were married the next weekend, on September 30, 1944, to the delight of her mom and dad, Lena and Ed Rase, at the home of my commanding officer on the base. After the reception there, we had all of one day and one night for our honeymoon in Birmingham. I answered reveille on Monday morning. We had one more weekend together in Birmingham. I was charmed with Betty Jane, with her blond good looks, her refreshing naiveté, her Southern drawl. She was charmed with my energy, my sophistication, my picturesque speech and patter. We seemed good for each other, and I was happy to have someone to come home to. If I came home.

Then my unit was off to New York and the ETO—European Theater of Operations.

☆ 27 ☆
The Jeep Shows

We took the *Queen Mary* to England, but believe me, it was no luxury cruise. The army crammed seven thousand GIs into space meant for one thousand passengers, and our guys drew billets way down in the ship's bowels. (Bowels was the right word. Halfway across the Atlantic, the latrines broke above us.) They gave us an hour a day above decks, then it was back down to the bowels again.

We ended up at something called the Tenth Replacement Center in Lichfield, a small, smoke-filled, sulfur-ridden town near Birmingham. I remember peeling a lot of potatoes (the entertainers got twenty-one straight days of KP to prove we weren't getting special treatment) and doing a *lot* of shows.

Most of the entertainers in our outfit were pretty good, if not terribly well known. Bobby Breen, who'd made a name for himself as a kid star at Universal, was with us. So was Jimmy Cook, one of the finest guys to ever blow a saxophone in the Big Band era. Almost every night at Lichfield, we'd put on a show, getting warmed up for the European Theater.

When our outfit got to France, one of the first people I met was Major Josh Logan, the Broadway producer, and he was worried. It seems that we were going to have a hell of a time working out a series of shows for the American GIs. "Our troops are too much on the move," he said. "They're never in one place long enough to see a show." To make things more complicated, there were 153 men in our unit. Obviously, the logistics of moving 153 entertainers around western Europe during a shooting war were going to be tough. Then Major Logan informed us that they were going to split us up into three-man teams and give us Jeeps, and send us out all across the European Theater. "The only real problems you'll have," Logan told me and some of the others, "is finding (or improvising) your own stages."

I thought I had a solution.

I said, "They got any barns in this country?"

Major Logan looked interested. "Sure," he said, smiling in anticipation of what I might say next. He'd seen all the Mickey-and-Judy musicals. "They got barns everywhere. Little ones anyhow."

"Well," I said, "we'll just put on little shows—in the barns."

"By God," said Major Logan. "That oughta work."

It did work. We went ahead with the Jeep show idea during that winter of 1944–1945, moving along with the troops, armed with battery-powered megaphones and accordions, saxophones, clarinets, and trap drums.

Each team was supposed to have a musician, a singer, and an MC who told jokes. I was the MC for Bob Priester, hometown Hollywood, and Mario Pieroni of San Francisco. Priester sang, mostly Broadway show tunes. Pieroni played the accordion. And I did my old numbers from vaudeville, pieces of Mickey McGuire, bits from my best movies, imitations. God, the troops loved the imitations of their favorite actors: Gable, both Barrymores, Cagney, Bogart, Edward G. Robinson.

We put on our first show between two Sherman tanks in a Belgian snowstorm, with sixty guys in the audience, three miles from the front, with the sound of howitzers booming in the distance. The troops didn't know we were coming. We had to introduce ourselves: "Captain Jones, I'm Private Mickey Rooney and this is Private Priester and Private Pieroni. We're here to entertain you."

We had tough duty, and it was often chaotic. Our Jeep wasn't exactly winterized, and we lived mostly on C rations. We'd go days without shaving and weeks without a bath. One day, we walked into a headquarters company near Radonge, Belgium. It was about eighteen degrees below zero outside and not much warmer than that inside. We introduced ourselves to the officer in charge and said we were there to put on a show for the men, "if you can stand it, Colonel."

He said, "We sure could." But he didn't really know what was happening or about to happen. Just as we returned from our Jeep with our stuff, me with the electric megaphone and Pieroni with his accordion, a three-star general burst through the door. We all came to attention. He eyed the room with an imperious look and asked what the hell was going on.

"Sir," I said. "We're here to do a show for you."

He said, "Rooney, that'd be just great, except for one thing. We're about to blow hell out of this headquarters company in just about eight minutes. So, if you don't get your ass out of here, it ain't gonna be around anymore."

We scampered as quick as we could, down the dirty turns of a highway that was as slick as a hockey rink, away from this headquarters. But we'd obviously driven the wrong way. All of a sudden, we could hear an unfamiliar sound. We stopped the Jeep and the sound became louder. I said, "My God, that sounds like a tank."

Sure enough, about five hundred yards ahead, through some trees, we saw a tank with a swastika emblazoned on its side, armed with an 88 millimeter cannon. "Geez, Pieroni," I said, "let's get this thing outta here."

Carefully, quickly, Pieroni put our Jeep in gear and jammed his foot down on the accelerator as hard as he could. We spun crazily on the ice for a moment, then straightened out and hightailed back up the road.

Before we crossed the Rhine, we did about seven shows in one evening and finished our last show about three-fifteen in the morning. Then our guys went off to fight the battle of Remagen about four-ten. At five forty-five, I saw many of the men we'd entertained being brought back in, on stretchers, dead or dying. Who was winning? Nobody.

We played a lot of hospitals. Sometimes we wouldn't have the heart to do a show. We'd just go around the wards and tell the guys to keep their chins up 'cause Americans everywhere were praying for them. I can remember visiting MASH units where there'd be ten operating tables going at once, with bizarre white lights shining down on these wounded kids. I can remember one doctor clipping off a kid's fingers as if they were toenails. Next to him, a nurse was wrapping a young man's stomach to keep his guts from pouring out, while another nurse held an oxygen mask to his face and a third was pumping albumen into his arm. At the next table, a surgeon was digging into what was left of a guy's chest. I saw nineteen- and twenty-year-olds lying on the floor all covered with powder burns.

I'd go from bed to bed whispering, "Hi, buddy, I'm Mickey Rooney." I got a smile sometimes. Sometimes nothing. It didn't matter. I just wanted these men to know I was there. I'd gone down about six beds when I saw one young man motioning to me across the aisle.

He looked fifteen. I went over. "Hi, son. I'm Mickey Rooney." He said, "I know. I know." And then his eyes filled up with tears. He had a picture on his pillow of a girl who looked fourteen.

I touched it. "And who's this?" I asked.

"My girl back home," he said, choking with a hold-back-the-tears sound in his voice.

I tried to buck him up. "Gee," I said, "she's awful pretty, and don't you worry. She'll be waiting for you. You're her guy, and she'll be there."

He couldn't believe that. He was going to have his leg amputated in the morning. I told him about Herbert Marshall, the great English actor who had lost his leg in World War I, and suggested he could be as charming as Marshall. "The girls will love you. But," I added, with a glance at the picture on his pillow, "they won't be able to compete with this gal here."

Well, this young man was quiet for a moment, thinking hard. Then he smiled at me and said, "Hey, you may be right."

(Years later, down on my luck, I stopped by the bar at the Fairmont in San Francisco to have a slug of Scotch before I went on with a nothing little nightclub act I was doing there. About to toss back my drink, I heard a voice calling for me. "Hey, Mick! Hey, Mick!" this guy said. "Can I talk to you for a minute?"

I walked over to him, said I had about ten minutes before I went on, and sat down. But he said nothing. He just looked deeply into my eyes, without a word. I looked back at him. For more than a minute, we stared into each other's eyes. Then he said, "You don't remember me, do you?" I said I didn't. He said, "I didn't expect you would. I was a kid soldier once, in a hospital in Germany, and you told me I was going to be a Herbert Marshall kind of guy—"

I said, "You're that—"

"That's right," he said. "They took my right leg. Now I didn't turn out to be Herbert Marshall, but—"

I said, "What about the girl? Her picture was on your pillow, and I'll never forget how pretty she was."

"I married her," he said. "We have three children. And I'm an executive at Boeing."

At this time in my life, I hadn't had much to smile about. But now I broke into a big grin. "Jeez, I never thought—"

"Think it," he said. "You helped me come back, Rooney, at

a time in my life when I needed help. Here's to you. You're a helluva guy. Thank you."

I touched his glass with mine. "And so are you. *You're* a helluva guy, too." Now, he'd returned the favor. Now, all unwitting, he was keeping *me* going.)

I was especially touched by the soldier and his girl back home because I'd just received a V-Mail letter from Betty Jane, dated November 15. I don't know how the letter found me; we were free-lancing all over the western front, following various divisions of the 12th Army Group and the 83rd Airborne and Patton's Third Army Division, hardly ever checking in with the 6817th Special Services Battalion. But it did get to me, and I was flying high with the news: Betty Jane was about six weeks pregnant. In other words, Sure Shot Rooney had hit the bull's eye on his first try. "So now," she wrote, "you got another good reason to stay healthy. Ha ha."

Priester and Pieroni and I covered something like 150,000 miles that first year. By then, the war in Europe was almost over. I was one of the first Americans into Dachau, and it was there, staring at the piles of human bones, that my strong stomach suddenly became weak. I went over to a nearby fence and threw up, again and again. I did not want to look at the evidence before my eyes, of the horror that one set of human beings are capable of inflicting on another.

After the shooting war was over in Europe, we did fewer Jeep shows and began coming back together for bigger extravaganzas. I remember doing one big show near Berlin, one that President Truman was going to attend. He didn't show up, we were told, because he was busy conferring with Joe Stalin and Winston Churchill in a Berlin suburb called Potsdam. But Admirals King and Leahy were out in the audience, and so were Generals Marshall and Arnold. General Marshall sent me a note backstage. "Keep it up," it said. "George C. Marshall." No sweat, General, I said to myself. I assured myself I'd never have trouble keeping it up. I think that's what the general (and my fans) have liked about me: I was always up, always brimming with a lust for life. (That's an unreal expectation, of course. I'd soon make that discovery myself: that no one can be up all the time. And, even though that is what my fans would keep expecting, I'd make myself crazy trying.)

On September 19, 1945, in Mannheim, we did *Up in Central Park,* a musical comedy from Broadway. And we stayed in Mannheim to do an original musical review called *OK—USA* for six days at the end of September. I directed the show and played in most of the skits. Looking over the program now, I find the names of Corporal Red Buttons in some of the skits with me, along with T/5 Bobby Breen and T/5 Bob Priester. T/5 Jimmy Cook was in the orchestra.

I didn't come straight home after the war in Europe was finished. You see, the army didn't want to take any heat for giving me special treatment. And even when I had my requisite number of points, the army didn't want to let me go. I was transferred to the Armed Forces Radio Network in Frankfurt, Germany, where I served as a radio announcer and all-around entertainer until I got a few more points. Finally, I hopped the first boxcar I could find out of Paris to Le Havre. It was raining in Le Havre, but I didn't care about that. I was going *home.* But then, a colonel who had only been in Europe ten days confronted me.

He said, "Sergeant Rooney"—I'd made sergeant by then— "how would you like to become a lieutenant and stay over here and entertain the troops?"

"Sir," I said politely, "you could offer me brigadier general and I would still say no. I want to go home."

I was in the army one year, eight months, and twenty-one days. When I left, I was older, wiser, and still in one piece. I had one Bronze Star, a good conduct medal, a World War II victory medal, seven bronze campaign buttons on my ETO ribbon, and a sharpshooter badge with an automatic rifle bar. I had more than medals. I had memories. Those men I fought with—I will never forget them. I loved them and they loved me. Bicknell, Breen, Cook, Hetzer, James, Pieroni, Priester . . . I could go on and on. But I had no wounds and no aftereffects from a brief bout with trichinosis. Even the trich was a pleasant memory because none other than Marlene Dietrich found me recovering from it in a VAC hospital and walked over, held me in her beautiful arms, and comforted me.

I took the *General G.O. Squire* home to New York, laughingly called a troop ship, 365 feet from bow to stern and so dirty that we had an epidemic of typhoid fever on the trip. A quarantine was slapped on the boat, and we waited another twenty-five days in New York Harbor.

Finally on March 6, 1946, I walked down the gangplank and was surprised to find—not my mother or my dad or Betty Jane—Sam Stiefel, my managing partner. He wanted me to stay in New York, to see some shows. I said, "No, Sam. No shows. The only show I want to see is in my living room, where my wife and my son, Mickey Rooney, Jr., are waiting for me."

But when I saw them, I said to Betty Jane, "My God, honey!"

"What?"

I was stunned by her size. At seventeen, she had been only a couple inches taller than I. Now, more than a year and a half later, all dolled up and in high heels, she seemed to tower over me by almost a foot. "You're so—so—beautiful."

She leaned down to give me a big wet kiss. "Ah'm so happy, Mickey," she said. "So happy you're home. And safe."

☆ 28 ☆
Money Troubles

Having survived the Nazis, I thought I'd have an easier time when I got back to Hollywood. I was mistaken.

Sure, being back in Encino with my mom and Betty Jane and the baby was great. He was Mickey Rooney, Jr., a blond with blue eyes and an upturned nose; he looked just like some of my own baby pictures. At eight months, he was already a curious, active kid.

But I soon learned that while I was away, my professional life had taken a wrong turn. Sam Stiefel had taken charge of Rooney, Inc., and now he seemed to own me—*and* my family. When I was in the service he'd been lending money to my mom. Now, she informed me, she was in hock pretty deep to this friend of mine—$159,000 to be exact. The studio, of course, had stopped paying me when I was drafted, and Mom needed something to live on. She couldn't keep up the home, with Betty Jane and little Mickey, on Fred Pankey's salary alone.

I didn't object to that, in principle. After all, Sam was the secretary-treasurer of Rooney, Inc. If he couldn't help my mom, then what good was he? But $159,000 seemed a little much.

"She owes you $159,000?" I said to Sam. "How can that be?"

We were in a box at Hollywood Park, Sam and I and our lawyer Mort Briskin. Sam took a puff on his cigar and said, "Not to worry, Mick. We'll work it out in due course. That and the money you owe me."

"The money *I* owe you?"

He stopped puffing on his cigar, looked at me in mock surprise, and said, "Yeah, Mick. Did you forget the money I advanced you here at the track, before you left?"

"Yeah, Sam, I did forget. Uh. How much, Sam?"

He wouldn't tell me. "Mick," he said. "We're friends. We're business partners. We even got our own stable together." He was right. While I was gone, Stiefel had invested in some thoroughbreds on my behalf and, together with his own nags, we did have our own stable. Trouble is, those horses represented outgo, not income.

He reminded me that he had renegotiated my contract with MGM more than a year before. Now I had a contract for $5,000 a week for forty weeks, a bonus of $140,000 to Rooney, Inc., and the right to do thirty-nine weeks of radio each year.

I nodded. That seemed pretty good to me, double my old salary. (I had forgotten, for the moment, that postwar prices had gone up—just about double.) But the radio bit was a sweetener. In the old days, Mr. Mayer would never give me permission to do radio. Now, I thought, I could have my own radio show. Still, there was all that money my mom and I owed Stiefel. "Uh," I said, "about the money we owe—"

He said, "How about we just go fifty-fifty on your earnings until we're even?"

What the hell, I thought. There was no limit now to the money I could earn if I was on my own. And soon, I'd be on my own, an independent producer of my own movies and a star on network radio to boot. "Sure, Sam," I said.

I didn't get out of my contract with MGM until 1948. In the

meantime, I did four more pictures for the studio, in 1946, '47, and '48. A couple of them were okay. A couple weren't even that good.

Naturally, the studio wanted to see if anyone still remembered Andy Hardy, so we did *Love Laughs at Andy Hardy,* with a young costar named Bonita Granville. In the movie, I'm back from the war, ready to finish my freshman year in college, when Bonita jilts me to marry someone else. I flee to South America and fall in love almost immediately with a Latin American beauty.

The movie did quite well. I was asking moviegoers to believe that I was still a gee-whiz teenager. I think folks were so glad to see me (and Andy Hardy) back on the screen that they willingly suspended their disbelief. Maybe they wanted to be assured that after the war we could go back to normal again. *Love Laughs* grossed $2,389,000 (and only cost $1 million to make), which wasn't at all bad, and it came close to being as profitable as the prewar Andy Hardys. Still, the studio had to be real: Andy Hardy was finished.

Then Arthur Freed put me and Judy Garland in a superspectacular, hyper-Hollywood variety show called *Ziegfeld Follies,* from a script as thick as *War and Peace,* turned out by a team of thirty-six writers. The first cut of this film about the great Broadway impresario ran 273 minutes, which was about twice as long as it should have been, and that was the reason Freed gave me for cutting the Mickey-and-Judy numbers. I think they cut them to give me a message: I wasn't indispensable anymore.

Judy was pretty busy on other projects in 1946. She made *Till the Clouds Roll By.* She married again, after her divorce from the musician David Rose, this time to Vincente Minnelli (who directed us in *Ziegfeld Follies*). She was pregnant. She gave birth to Liza. She suffered from a postpartum depression. And she began a year-and-a-half downward slide into amphetamine abuse. We drifted apart at the time: we weren't making pictures together, we didn't see each other, we didn't even talk on the phone.

Of course, I could do musicals with any of a number of others, and MGM knew that. The studio put me and the Arthur Freed unit to work on another musical, this one very much in accord with Mr. Mayer's wish to reinvent America. It was called *Summer Holiday*, a musical remake of *Ah, Wilderness!*—a picture I had done with Clarence Brown in 1935. (This time, I played the older brother, Walter Huston played my dad, Agnes Moorehead my mom, and Marilyn Maxwell the vamp.) And Freed, as was his custom, went to Broadway to find another first-rate director, the man who had directed *Carousel* and *Oklahoma!* in New York, Rouben Mamoulian.

Mamoulian's wife was an artist who painted lovely landscapes in oils, and Mamoulian became something of a cinematic artist in his own right in this picture, simply by insisting on the kinds of scenes in *Summer Holiday* that you might find in the paintings of a Grant Wood or the posters of a Norman Rockwell. Movie audiences were treated to scenes of kids cavorting at the old swimming hole, the ladies at their croquet games, men drinking beer at a stag picnic, the whole town out to see the Fourth of July fireworks, a high school graduation (with the girls in their white dresses and the boys in their blue serge suits), and square dancing on the lush New England greens.

I sensed that I needed to prove myself all over again in this musical, and I tried too hard. The reviewer for *PM* said my part called for shyness and sensitivity; I gave the opposite impression, that of a frantic vaudevillian. The reviewer for the *New York World-Telegram* said I gave the picture "an air of surly tumult in sharp conflict to all the other apparent aims of the film." And he talked about a new Mickey Rooney, who was not so boyishly playful as he once was. Rather, he said, I displayed a rise of "ill nature" that I apparently mistook for "emotional force." *Summer Holiday* was my biggest financial flop at MGM. It lost $1.46 million.

If I displayed any ill nature in *Summer Holiday,* it wasn't only because I felt I was on shaky ground at the studio. Home wasn't what I'd imagined it to be, either. Betty Jane and I and little Mickey hadn't stayed in the Encino home with my mom any longer than we had to. A wife ought to have her own home, I told Betty Jane, and she couldn't agree fast enough (possibly because my mom and Fred Pankey had started drinking more than a little). So I arranged a loan from the studio to make the down payment on our own place in the Valley, not far from Mom's. I think it was about then I realized I was married to a hick.

Betty Jane was totally oblivious to anything that was happening in the world outside our home. She was a wife and mother, period. She knew nothing about my world, and apparently she didn't care to know. She didn't like my friends, not even my very oldest and best friends—Dick Quine, Dick Paxton, Andy McIntyre, Ray Pearson, Sid Miller, Jimmy Cook. So I gave her what she seemed to want, the old-fashioned, male chauvinist pig solution: I kept Betty Jane home, barefoot and pregnant, literally. Betty Jane conceived again, in May, about two months after I'd arrived home. I was surprised it took as long as two months. I thought all I had to do to get Betty Jane pregnant was hang up my pants.

For a while my money worries kept me from thinking about my troubles at home. If I couldn't pick up where I left off before the war, I wouldn't even be able to afford a home in the Valley. Sure, I was making five thousand dollars a week during the sixty-seven days we took to shoot *Summer Holiday*, but I didn't see much of that. Sam Stiefel took his 50 percent off the top. Then he paid the overhead and gave me what was left, generally close to nothing. Things weren't turning out the way I'd dreamed they would when I was bouncing around the war in Europe. The thought depressed me. I was even sadder when I realized that, up to this point in my life, I had never even had my own bank account, never written a check, never had my own financial integrity.

I plunged into my own special cure for depression: work. And

I was tickled beyond words when Les Peterson (yeah, he was still following me around Metro) told me what my next part would be: the title role in a boxing picture with Ann Blyth, Brian Donlevy, and James Dunn, *Killer McCoy*. It was precisely the kind of part I needed to reestablish myself in Hollywood as a serious actor. I knew I could never be another Gable or a Taylor, but I could do character roles, playing the kind of people Cagney had been playing at Warner Brothers. This was that kind of part. I was a bantamweight boxer with a driving ambition and a lethal punch—so lethal that I'd kill my best friend in the ring.

I thought I might be on my way to a second career as a character actor, but MGM disagreed. In retrospect, I think *Killer McCoy* gave me a major clue about MGM's plans for Mickey Rooney: the studio seemed to want me out. All it needed was an excuse, and I think that the director of *Killer McCoy*, Roy Rowland, had been told to set me up.

It started when I had a scene with Brian Donlevy, a close two-shot. The camera over my shoulder ran out of film, and Rowland said, "We'll reload. Stay where you are."

They doused the lights, and Donlevy and I relaxed and started telling stories until they were ready to shoot again. We kept right on talking, right up until the time the cameraman said, "Speed," which meant that our scene was ready to begin. And then I said, "So that's the way the story ended" and waited for Rowland to say, "*Action!*"

Instead, Rowland said, "Cut!" And then: "Goddamn it, Rooney, who the hell do you think you are? What do mean, clowning around when we're trying to shoot a scene?" And that wasn't the end of it. He went on like this for four or five minutes, stomping all over the set to the amazement of the fifty or sixty people who were standing around.

It was such an extreme reaction that I thought he had to be kidding, but when he kept on, I walked over to him and said, "You're *not* kidding, are you?"

He said, "You're goddamn right I'm not kidding, and I'm going to walk off this set."

"No, you're not," I said. "*I'm* walking." And out the door I went.

I wasn't home five minutes when the phone rang. It was Mr. Mayer's troubleshooter, Eddie Mannix. "Mick," he said, "what the hell happened?" His voice oozed concern.

"Nothing happened," I said. "Rowland insulted me. There was no reason for it. You can ask Donlevy."

"Uh-huh."

"I'm a professional, Eddie, and I always give respect to my fellow actors and to my directors."

He said, "Well, Mick, why don't you just apologize to him, and we can get the work done?"

I said, "Why the hell should *I* apologize? I didn't do anything wrong. He's the one who should apologize."

But I did apologize because I knew I needed *Killer McCoy*, and I was determined not to screw it up. I knew this picture could represent a turning point in my career. "After *Killer McCoy* is released," I told Les Peterson, "I'll never have to worry about another role."

The apology made me feel awful, and that night I took out my frustration on Betty Jane by growling at her and telling her I was going out—alone. In tears, she said she might as well go home to her mother. I said I thought that was the best damn idea she'd had in a long time. I didn't blame her for leaving. I was no good for her. Betty Jane was on her way back to Birmingham, three months pregnant, with one-year-old Mickey, Jr., in tow. In January 1947 she gave birth to Timmy.

We finished *Killer McCoy*. But it did no good for my new career. The movie got so-so notices, and so did I. I suspect the fight with Rowland went against me in whatever high-level discussions that were going on about me and my future.

☆ *29* ☆
Words and Music

I *made my last* picture under contract to MGM in 1948, an Arthur Freed production about the famous Broadway musical team of Richard Rodgers and Lorenz Hart called *Words and Music*. It should have been a smash hit—it featured twenty-two song hits and had fourteen stars in it, including Perry Como, Mel Tormé, June Allyson, Lena Horne, Ann Sothern, Gene Kelly, Vera-Ellen, Betty Garrett, Ann Miller, Cyd Charisse, Janet Leigh, and Judy Garland.

Rogers was Tom Drake (the handsome guy that I thought Ava had paid too much attention to a few years before), and Freed thought I was a natural to play Hart, a rumpled and amiable bachelor who was inclined to think his dinner parties were a failure if one guest went home sober. Even better, Hart had been five feet tall.

The songs from the movie were great: "There's a Small Hotel," "With a Song in My Heart," "Thou Swell," "Where or When?" "The Lady Is a Tramp," "Slaughter on Tenth Avenue," "Blue Moon," "Johnny One Note," and a duet sung by Judy and me, "I Wish I Were in Love Again." The critic for the *Hollywood Reporter* loved the music so much that he wrote, "One gladly forgives the story—which doesn't matter." But the story always matters, and others, myself included, were not quite so forgiving.

Fred Finklehoffe, the scriptwriter who had done so well for me and Judy in many of our grand musicals, failed us now. He and his fellow writers came up with a terrible turkey, and I knew it as I soon as I saw the shooting script. At the beginning of the picture, the writers had me playing a bouncing, lovable guy with a million friends. Then I turn sad, simply because I am jilted by a broad who thinks I'm a runt. I end up dying in the rain, on an agonizing walk from my sickbed in the hospital to the theater.

No wonder that Bosley Crowther of *The New York Times* called this ending "among the most inadequate and embarrassing things this reviewer has ever watched." Crowther also said that I was fantastically incompetent. Maybe I was. Throughout the shooting of this picture, I was lonely and drinking too much. I didn't show up for rehearsals, and I was truant almost every Monday morning.

Truth to tell, I was hanging out with the wrong crowd (for me, anyway). It was a drinking crowd, led, as I recall, by Tommy Dorsey, one of the great boozers of all time. Drink was poison to me, but I hadn't quite realized it yet. After a few drinks, I'd have a hangover that might last five days. I started not showing up for work on Mondays. Movie historians will be able to read between the lines of an assistant producer's notes in the Freed Collection at USC:

"5-3-48. Jimmy Cook informed us at 7:45 A.M. that Mickey Rooney is exhausted and ill and unable to work today."

"5-10-48. At 7:35 A.M., Jimmy Cook notified us that Mickey Rooney was suffering from severe headaches and would not be able to work today."

"5-17-48. Mickey Rooney called at 7:30. He could not appear but was persuaded to come in at 1 P.M."

The same assistant producer's notes reflect another sadness:

Judy Garland was calling in sick even more frequently than I. Our old friend Norman Taurog shot around me and Judy. It was a wonder that the picture went only $140,000 over budget.

I'd like to say that I helped Judy at this point, but I couldn't help myself. Our times together were rushed then and infrequent. And when we talked, there seemed to be a lot left unsaid—awkward pauses, grunts, hurried hugs. Then she'd be off in one direction and I in another.

To some of the people at Metro, it appeared that I didn't enjoy working as I did in the good old prewar days. Exactly wrong. I didn't enjoy *not* working. For the first time since I joined Metro, the studio had no plans for me. And so I got mad and told Sam Stiefel to go ahead and sever my legal ties to MGM. That was one of the dumbest things I ever did. I had to forgo my $5,000-a-week salary and my pension (I could start drawing $49,000 a year in four years). And I had to pay Metro $500,000 besides, which I was to work off at a rate of $100,000 a picture (and keep only $25,000 for myself). In other words, Stiefel negotiated me down to $25,000 a picture. I had collected $169,167 for my work on *Words and Music*. Now, I had to do five pictures for $25,000 apiece, minus 50 percent to Sam Stiefel and minus Uncle Sam's share. That would bring my take down to less than $10,000 a picture—not even enough to pay my upcoming alimony and child support.

And who knew if I'd even make a picture? The federal courts, after a decade of hearings on the movie industry, had ruled that film studios had been violating U.S. antitrust laws and must start divesting themselves of their theater chains. The courts said that theater owners didn't have to limit themselves to showing the product of just one studio; they could pick and choose what they wanted, taking a Metro film one week, a Paramount picture the next. (I never understood this. Why was it wrong for MGM to show pictures in its own theaters if it was right for Ford and GM to sell cars in their own agencies or Kinney Shoes to manufacture shoes and sell them in its own stores?)

But Loews Inc. was beginning to see what lay ahead, and the company made a few moves. First, they got rid of Mayer because he, personally, was making too much money—6.7 percent of MGM's profits. Then Nick Schenck brought in Dore Schary to oversee all of MGM's production.

Dore Schary had lots of plans for MGM, but unfortunately they didn't include me. I don't know why they didn't. Schary had made his first big splash in Hollywood as the screenwriter for *Boys Town,* and later we teamed in the same way on *Young Tom Edison.* I expected Schary to retain some fond memories of our successes together, but from him I got zilch. Maybe it was because of the scene we'd had when I'd returned from the army. I went up to his office as soon as I got home, still in uniform (because there was a rule that we had to wear our uniforms for ten days after our discharge).

"Hi," I said.

"Hi, kid," said Schary. "Where you been?"

I couldn't believe his snotty words. How had *he* fought the war? I stared at him. I was still five feet three, but I had grown a little bit and I'd seen men die, and I thought I'd learned the difference between reality and fantasy. I spoke the last words I would ever speak to this man.

I said, "Fuck you, Schary." Then I walked out of the room.

In December 1948, still waiting for a picture, I found some work on my own: I played the Hippodrome Theatre in Baltimore for two weeks (at ten thousand dollars a week) and the Stage Theatre in Hartford for another two weeks (at twelve thousand dollars a week). At least, I figured, I'd have some money for Christmas.

In January 1949, I was sitting alone one night at a table at Ciro's, not at all happy and half in my cups, when Nick Sevano, a friend who was also a friend of Frank Sinatra, came over to my table with a pretty young actress in tow. "Mickey, baby," he said. "You hadn't oughta be sitting off by yourself."

I looked up to give him a weak smile, but I brightened when I saw the girl. Her name was Martha Vickers, and I'd seen her last picture, *The Big Sleep*, with Humphrey Bogart and Lauren Bacall. She was the second lead, and she'd done a darn good job, playing an oversexed young gal who made her first appearance in the film trying to sit on Bogart's lap while he was standing up. And now, meeting her face to face and talking with her, I could see that she was interesting as well as beautiful. And she was only a half inch taller than I.

Her brightness brought me out of my doldrums that night. The three of us talked until they closed the place. I called her the next day and asked her if she'd consider joining me for dinner at Chasen's. She said yes. We went on to catch Kay Thompson's act at the Beverly Wilshire. The next day, when I phoned, I told her she was the nicest girl I'd ever met (My God! Those rehearsed words.) and asked her to have dinner with me again that night. And the next and the next.

From that day on, we went steady. We didn't go to bed together right away. We were both healthy young adults (she was twenty-four and I was twenty-eight), and we were both going through the throes of divorce. (She had been married, briefly, to A. C. Lyles, a Hollywood press agent.) We could have each enjoyed the validation that true love (and good sex) can bring, but we didn't, as they said in those days, go all the way. We both wanted this to be right, and that meant taking our time. We dated for more than two months—mostly trips to the track and to dinner afterward—and we talked a lot, about life and love and why our previous marriages hadn't lasted. And, during this period, I never looked at another lady.

Well, that's not exactly true. I couldn't help *looking* when a fantastically sexy blonde named Norma Jean Baker wiggled into my life. A friend wanted me to see if I could wangle her a part in *The Fireball,* a rollerdrome melodrama I was making at United Artists. I had made it a policy never to wangle parts for anybody. If I started that, there'd never be an end to it.

In this case, however, I wanted to do this particular friend a favor, so I took Norma Jean out for drinks early one night to see for myself. Wow! She wasn't wearing a bra, or stockings, or panties, either. Her skimpy little frock left nothing to the imagination. She was all there, right in plain sight. And the way she looked at me—with her moist, half-opened eyes and her moist, half-opened mouth! And the way she talked! Every word she uttered seemed to have a sexy subtext. "But Mickey," she said in her precious little voice, "I'm more than just a pretty girl. I can do—*any*thing!" She reached over and touched my knee.

So I helped Norma Jean Baker get a bit part in *The Fireball.* I remember her having one line: "Honey, I'll be here when you want me." Oh yes, she soon changed her name—to Marilyn Monroe, and became one of Hollywood's legendary sexpots, one of the best cocksuckers in Hollywood, according to my friends, Richard Quine and Blake Edwards. Why did she go that route? Because it was naughty. Some women love being naughty. Marilyn Monroe made naughtiness a personal trademark.

I remember one evening I was having dinner at Mike Romanoff's in Beverly Hills with Cary Grant when Marilyn sashayed over to our table wearing an ermine coat. Knowing she often spurned wearing any undergarments at all, we were prepared to discover that she had absolutely nothing on under the coat, then disappointed to find, as she eased off the coat and leaned over the table to talk to us, that she was wearing a beautiful organdy gown. "Oh, Mr. Grant," she cooed. "I do so love you in all your pictures. *Public Enemy Number One?* And *The African Queen?* Absolutely thrilling." Then, as she turned to leave, we were startled to see that her gown had somehow gotten caught up around her waist, and, as she retreated, we were treated to a unobstructed view of the two cheeks of her ass. They looked like two pink Crenshaw melons. Which is probably what prompted Cary Grant to say, "Mick, I don't know what you're going to order, but I'm going to order some of *that.*"

I was pretty naïve about what we used to call "perversions." One night at a party in Beverly Hills (I can't remember whose), I opened a bedroom door, looking for a bathroom, and found an actress I had been introduced to earlier in the evening, Tallulah Bankhead. She had her head between the limbs of a beautiful young blonde. "Oh, excuse me," I said. Tallulah never missed a bite, never looked up.

I introduced Johnny Hyde to Miss Monroe, and I was able to get a favor from Hyde in return. Hyde, the chief honcho at the William Morris Agency, helped extricate me from my association with Sam Stiefel. Once Hyde agreed to take me back into the fold at William Morris, my course was easy: I just walked into the office on Sunset one morning and told Stiefel it was all over. "You've taken me," I said, "for about—" I read from a scrap of paper that Fred Pankey had given me "—about six million, four hundred thousand, six hundred and thirteen dollars. And twelve cents. Now get out."

I had to pay a price: to get out from under Stiefel, Hyde told me, I had to do *Quicksand, The Big Wheel,* and a third picture to be designated later for twenty-five thousand dollars apiece. Stiefel had a solid, enforceable contract, and that was that.

The less said about *Quicksand* the better, except to note that it was aptly titled. We sank in it. The picture didn't make much money, and Stiefel commandeered whatever cash there was. *The Big Wheel* was a story about the son of a race-car driver following in his dad's exhaust, and it featured some pretty good work by Spring Byington and Thomas Mitchell. I heard the other day that somebody is colorizing it, a process that is costing them about three thousand dollars a minute. They wouldn't be doing that if they didn't think there was still an audience out there willing to watch what should still be my picture.

The third picture was something called *Francis the Talking Mule.* Briskin had optioned the property, but Stiefel didn't like it. When Briskin dropped his option, Universal picked it up and put Donald O'Connor in the role that was meant for me. *Francis the Talking Mule* became a big hit, and O'Connor went on to do five more Francis pictures, one each year from 1951 to 1955. They all made money.

I was glad for Donald. I liked him then, and I like him now. Like me, he is a survivor, and he hasn't forgotten his old friends. In 1989, we would tour the nation together, two old farts singing and dancing and telling jokes in a production called *Two for the Show*.

For every Donald O'Connor, there are a dozen Frank Sinatras. Sinatra had been a friend of mine, had come to little screening parties at my apartment with Tommy Dorsey and Mel Tormé and the gang, went out drinking with us, had even double-dated with me and Ava. After that he kind of disappeared from the Hollywood scene for a while, but then one day at Lakeside Country Club, I heard he was back in town, staying at the Garden of Allah. I felt happy for him, so I phoned to wish him well. I liked Frank. He was tough, he was sardonic, but I'd always thought he was a real guy. And he was funny. I thought we were still friends.

I was wrong.

"Yah?" said the surly voice on the other end of the line, one of Sinatra's entourage.

I said, brightly, "Mr. Sinatra, please."

"Who's this?"

I said, "Mickey Rooney."

Then another gruff voice came on. "Yeah," he said.

I said, "This is Mickey Rooney calling for Mr. Sinatra."

Finally, Sinatra was on the line. He said, "Hello, how are you?"

I said, "Well, Frank baby, you made it. I told you you were going to do it, no matter how much you hated Tommy Dorsey. Welcome back. Now when are we gonna have dinner or something?"

"Uh," he said, not even bothering to call me by name, "I'm kinda busy these days."

I said, "Oh, I thought I was talking to Frank Sinatra."

He said, "This *is* Frank Sinatra."

"Oh, no, it isn't," I said, deliberately misunderstanding. "Lemme talk to my friend, Frank Sinatra."

At the other end of the line, before I hung up, I heard him coughing with embarrassment. I forgave him. Later on, we became brothers-in-law, of sorts. We both were married to Ava Gardner, and he got treated worse than I did, if you can believe the rumors about his marriage coming to an end when he walked in on Ava one day at their home in Palm Springs and found her in the sack with another woman. For an Italian American to find his wife having sex with another dame—well, that can be a pretty big blow to the ego. If that's what happened, I don't blame Frank for splitting. But I really doubt that it did. When two people are fighting—and drinking—like Frank and Ava were at that time, they could say anything. True or not, it wouldn't matter, as long as it hurt.

In April, I gave Mart—my nickname for Martha—a diamond engagement ring, and we consummated our love at my little place in Laurel Canyon. It was one of the greatest emotional highs of my life, a whirling, spinning thing, like Gershwin's *Rhapsody in Blue*. We were both glad we waited.

We had a double-ring ceremony at five in the afternoon on June 3, 1949, just six hours after I picked up my divorce papers. The inscriptions on our rings read: "Today, tomorrow, always. I love you." The initials M.R. and M.V. were on both rings.

Afterward, at the champagne reception, Mart and I cut the three-tiered wedding cake and I told an inquiring reporter, "I've got me a wonderful girl this time. If this one doesn't last, there's something wrong with me."

It didn't last. You can draw the obvious conclusion.

Some of my friends said I believed I didn't have to be with my wife when I had something more exciting to do. Wally Cassell, a good friend who was in our wedding party, said, "With his wives, Mickey felt he could do anything he pleased: leave them alone, or go anywhere he wanted with anyone he wanted any time he wanted as long as it made him feel good." Dick Quine said, "Mickey was frenetic. It was impossible for anyone to keep up with him. He used to wear *me* out. In fact, I used to slip a phenobarbital into his drink every so often, just so I could get some rest."

When Mart became pregnant, she found it even harder to run as hard as I did. (Sure Shot Rooney had struck again. Our son Teddy was born nine months after we first made love. Needless to say, her own acting career had to go on hold.)

My career seemed to be stalled, too. In February, my old friend Les Peterson phoned and asked me to be one of the presenters at the Academy Awards. I said, "Les, I am so honored that the Academy would think of me." I thought, At least the Academy doesn't think I'm a has-been.

On the night of the awards, Mart and I were sitting at the kitchen table. We'd gotten dressed early and were having a bite to eat before we made the drive into town. Then the phone rang. It was Johnny Green, the show's musical conductor, who had drawn straws down at the Academy and lost. He had to tell me the bad news: the Academy had had second thoughts about my presence. "You've been married too many times to be a presenter," he said.

"Sure, sure, Johnny," I said. "I understand."

But I didn't understand. I hung up the phone and slumped down in a chair at the kitchen table with Mart and the baby. My tuxedo shirt looked soiled, I looked soiled, my life looked soiled.

"I think I'll quit the business," I said.

"Maybe that's a good idea," Mart said. "Why don't you go ahead and quit? You could be a milkman."

I stared at her, then at the glass of Scotch beside her. Ahhh, I said to myself, it's just the Scotch talking. Finally, I got up and roamed into another part of the house to see if I could find where I had left my tears.

I know—now—why I took this so hard then. From the beginning, I had been programmed to live by applause. If I got that applause, I was truly alive. If and when I didn't, I was dead. That put me in my own kind of hell, a hell where even the idiocy of others could make the fires hotter.

I think that was the night our marriage died. Martha never felt the same way about me again, and I didn't feel worthy of her. Soon, we were living apart.

On March 13, 1950, my father died of a heart attack. I was surprised at how much I blubbered when I got the news. I had no idea I missed or loved him so. We buried him at Forest Lawn, right next to Wallace Beery. I thought it was fitting that these two comedians should rest in peace, side by side. I had a fantasy about the two of them having a beer together at some heavenly dive, surrounded by towering show girls and glancing up from time to time at a mirror behind the bar, where they saw not their own reflections but images of me, in real time, as I made my own meandering way through this puzzle of my life.

"The kid's gonna make it," Beery was saying to my dad.

And my dad was saying, "They'll never count him out."

There was no way to get around it: I was on a helluva losing streak. I couldn't even pick a winner at the track. I tried dating, but I had lost my spark. I remember the names of a few gals I met—Diane Garrett, Kay Brown, Erin O'Brien—but I don't recall anything else about them. The best kind of sex for me then was just as impersonal as it can get, like the time in Tokyo when Don "Red" Barry and I booked sixteen Japanese gals into our hotel room for an Asian-style orgy. If there is something that

Californians can learn from the Asians among us it is their acceptance, without guilt, of the erotic. Even so, I'm not crazy about sex with hookers. When it came to having sex, I really preferred being in love with the lady.

So it didn't take me long to find a new love. It was on our way back from Tokyo. We stopped in San Francisco, and I met a San Francisco heiress who shall here be known as Margarita Brown. She was a twenty-seven-year-old widow with dark hair, blue eyes, and a gorgeous figure. There was instant chemistry between us. All the laws of physics seemed to apply, too. She was a great storyteller, full of tales about her family's early days in San Francisco, and she had a hearty appetite for good food—and good sex. I ended up taking her back to LA with me, and soon we were an item in the Hollywood colony.

Cary Grant stopped by our table one night at Chasen's and said to me, "This isn't the rich widow from San Francisco, is it?"

"It is," said I.

"Oh, you rascal," said Grant.

I grinned. "What do you mean?" I grinned some more. I knew what he meant. I just wanted to hear him say it.

"I'm just a leading man," he said. "But you, you really can pick 'em."

I laughed, and so did Margarita, flattered by the attention of this dashing, this handsome Cary Grant.

"If you marry her," he said, "you must remember me."

"And why is that?"

"Well," he said, "someday you may want to finance one of my pictures." Margarita laughed. I think she would have loved putting money in the pictures of Cary Grant. He hardly ever made a bad one. (You see: other stars were beginning to think about becoming their own producers. I had started a trend. I wasn't very successful at it. But I was one of those who started it.)

We did talk about marriage, Margarita and I. And I began to spend some time with her at her mansion in Carmel. But all that ended one afternoon, after we had spent almost an entire day in bed together. "Oh, Mickey," she said. "Think of it. When we get married, you won't have to work anymore, and we'll be able to live anywhere. Hawaii. Palm Springs. Florida. Carmel."

I sat up and looked at her. "What did you say?"

"Hawaii. Palm Springs. Florida. Carmel."

"No. What did you say first?"

"Huh?"

"Your first words. You said I won't have to work anymore. Well that won't wash. You're telling me you want to take away my manhood. Working. That's what I do."

By now she was sitting up, too, and she looked startled. "Oh, well," she said. "Just forget I said that."

"No," I said. "I can't forget."

"Well," she said, "if you can't forget, can you at least forgive me?"

"I can forgive you," I said. "But I can't forget, can't forget that you'll always be thinking about my not working anymore. I can't have that."

Over her protestations, I got out of bed, dressed, and left. I got her chauffeur to drive me to Monterey, where I hitchhiked a ride to San Jose on a private plane, then caught a commercial plane home to LA.

Margarita tried to reason with me. She phoned me a million times and sent me ten thousand telegrams. But I was adamant. And I was not sorry I walked.

I began, then, to realize how important working was to my identity as a man. Intuitively, my mom realized that, too, and she took steps to help me be me by engaging a good portrait artist, Peter Fairchild, do me in oils. So I sat for him at the home on Densmore (this was just before Mom had to sell it). Imagine me, sitting still long enough for a portrait artist to do his thing? But what the hell? I didn't have anything else to do.

Fairchild became a friend. And then, one day, as friends will, he asked me for a favor. He asked me whether I minded if a friend of his could stay at my mom's for a few days. He was visiting from Spain. He didn't speak any English at all, but he could drink with us, and he did, quite a lot. Then, when it was time for him to go, he tried to tell me how much he appreciated my kindness. "Mee-kee," he said in his very primitive English, "I can geev you only painteengs for being such a good, uh, how you say?—host."

So he left me two canvases and was gone. But what was I to do with two large oils, one of them depicting a watch melting on the branches of a tree and the other dominated by a slim pyramid and a large eyeball? So I put them in the garage to gather dust. I might have put my career in there, in storage, to gather dust, too, for all the good my striving did over the next twenty years.

But things are seldom what they seem, either in the art world or in Hollywood.

Several years later, I offered those paintings to Blake Edwards, who had started to make movies with one of my oldest friends, Dick Quine. The paintings made him laugh (which is one thing that good art can sometimes do) and he took them, even though he had never heard of the guy whose signature appeared in the lower-right-hand corner: Dalí. The late Salvador Dalí's paintings are almost priceless now, but if someone could afford to buy them, these two would go for millions. In my ignorance, I gave 'em away.

☆ *30* ☆
Mrs. Rooney #4

To my surprise, Dore Schary called me back to MGM in 1951 to make *The Strip*. It was under the favorable terms that Stiefel and Briskin had arranged for me a few years back—favorable, that is, to MGM. But it was work, and I needed work.

I played a drummer in a band who is falsely accused of murdering a racketeer. This was a low-budget musical with a low-budget story. But there was enough good music in it, along with performances by Vic Damone, Louis Armstrong, Jack Teagarden, and Earl "Fatha" Hines, to bring in audiences all over America. *The Strip* made only a little more than it cost ($885,000), and I brought in just enough to pay a few outstanding bills.

Then I was back where I started, waiting to see if MGM could use me again. When it was clear that Metro couldn't, or wouldn't, I signed a three-picture deal with Harry Cohn and Jonie Taps at Columbia at $75,000 a picture. But it wasn't the money that attracted me. It was the presence at Columbia of Dick Quine, who was being given one of his first chances to direct. And he was going to direct me, his old buddy. Cohn and Taps ordered Quine's friend, Blake Edwards, to do the script, a service movie called *Sound Off*.

I didn't feel very good in those days. I was depressed over my breakup with Mart (we were divorced on September 25, 1951), and I couldn't sleep. I had discovered barbiturates, but I was afraid to use them more than occasionally. Most of the time I'd just drag myself out of bed in the morning and cruise into the studio wearing my I've-got-everything-under-control mask. I kept telling myself I was a professional and that this is the way a pro had to do it. I knew something was wrong with me. I just didn't know what.

Worse, I didn't try to find out. Instead of seeking professional help, I called my old friend Sig Frolich and told him we were flying to Houston for a while. What I wanted to do was escape, and I thought Houston would be a good place to hide. We hid out at the Shamrock, Glen McCarthy's luxury hotel, where I slept for two weeks, aided by hundreds of phenobarbitals. I gulped them by the handful.

I thought the pills could help me escape my bad conscience. I'd screwed up again. Having asked myself the usual question ("What do I do now?") and not coming up with any answers, I said, "Fuck it. There's more to life than living. Is living really life, or do we just pass through the assembly line of repetition? Kiss, hurt, hug, hurt, hate, love, love, hate. Would I keep on going, trying to pick up the broken pieces of my life when I knew that I was too egocentric to give, enthuse, enjoy, understand, care, share? No. Gimme some more pills."

At the end of the two weeks, surprised that I hadn't killed myself and grateful for the presence of my loyal Sig, I woke up and announced, "Okay, Sig, I'm through sleeping. Let's go home."

"You got any plans?" asked Sig.

"No," I said. "Nothing. Nothing at all."

"Well," he said, "just don't get married tomorrow."

I said, "Not tomorrow. Or ever, Sig. Don't worry."

. . .

I set up bachelor quarters with another friend, Red Barry. I first met Donald Michael Barry de Acosta when he came to Southern California with an all-star football team from Texas. His team lost 21-14, but he'd played a great game, so John Wayne and I went down to the locker room afterward. We both told him to look us up if he ever wanted to be an actor. Darned if he didn't show up soon after that. I got him a job in *Boys Town,* but he choked in his one big scene with Tracy. Fleming had to find a replacement for him.

But that didn't stop Red. He found his niche in what *Variety* used to call "oaters"—cowboy pictures. He was a dashing guy with rugged good looks, and he had no trouble getting dates with the likes of Joan Crawford, Susan Hayward, and Linda Darnell. Red couldn't help sharing with me the story of his first date with Joan Crawford. He'd called for her to take her out to dinner, but she insisted they go in her chauffeur-driven Rolls. That wasn't exactly Red's style, but, what the hell, he said. On the way home, however, Miss Crawford put the make on Red in the backseat, insisting they make love right there in the car, a couple feet away from the chauffeur.

"Funny thing about Miss Crawford," Red told me (he always called her Miss Crawford), "she couldn't get hot unless there was an element of danger there. Every time we made it there was a chance someone would see us. Fact is, most of the time, she'd say, right in the middle of a good screw, 'Red, do you think anybody will catch us?' " (Well, whatever turns a woman on. I had encountered this particular bit of kinkiness myself when I dated Betty Grable briefly some years before, not long before she was to marry bandleader Harry James. Betty also insisted I make love to her in the backseat of her limo, and I was pretty sure she was paying more attention to the chauffeur's reactions up in front than she was to mine.)

Trying hard to keep up my alimony and child-support payments (by now I had three boys to support) and stave off the IRS, I gave my all to three projects in 1952: *Off Limits,* a Paramount picture with Bob Hope; *All Ashore,* a navy farce directed by Quine, the second of my three-picture Columbia deal; and *A Slight Case of Larceny* for MGM, a labored comedy that brought me and Eddie Bracken together for the first time.

Living in the reality of 1952, the reality of little work, bad scripts, and none of the marketing and public relations support that I had had at MGM, I began to realize how few friends anyone ever has. All those Hollywood friends I had in 1938, 1939, 1940, and 1941, when I was the toast of the world, weren't real friends at all. Sure, we'd have dinner together, me and Spencer Tracy and Clark Gable and Jimmy Cagney and Errol Flynn. But they were as insecure as I; they only wanted me around because I was lucky—and because they thought some of my luck would rub off on them. I was lucky to have Dick Quine, Bob Hope, and Eddie Bracken. Quine was the brother I never had. Hope never failed to invite me to his annual golf tournament. And, later on, Bracken would come to my rescue when everyone else had forgotten me.

On January 8, 1952, I cut the cord with MGM. They let me out of my deal (I think that Schary was ashamed of giving anyone with my credits a mere twenty-five thousand dollars a picture), and I was free. Free maybe to starve. But God must have been watching me, watching closely enough to see that I didn't die before I'd made my deal with Him, but not closely enough to save me from myself.

I've always been attracted to strippers, and I spent some time in 1952 with Tempest Storm. Tempest and I went nine straight rounds—or rather, nine hours—on our first night together. I fell hard for her. I bought her (what else?) a floor-length mink coat, and I probably would have married her—if, that is, I hadn't met Elaine Mahnken.

Like Mart, Elaine Mahnken was another redhead. Tall, with a drop-dead figure and a hard, athletic body, she had posed for a nude calendar when she was seventeen and had been a beauty queen at Compton College.

Elizabeth Taylor was only twelve when we made *National Velvet* together in 1944.
(MGM)

Off to fight World War II on June 14, 1944. Mr Mayer tried to keep me out of the army, but I stayed in for twenty-one months and won medals for bravery.
(ACME)

Wife number two: I married Betty Jane Rase when I was in the army. Here we are in Montgomery, Alabama, in 1946.
(ACME)

Wife number three: Martha Vickers and me at our Las Vegas wedding in 1949. We split two years later.
(MICKEY ROONEY COLLECTION)

Wife number four: Elaine Mahnken and I eloped to Las Vegas in 1953. After six years she got tired of my profligate ways and headed for Lake Arrowhead.
(MICKEY ROONEY COLLECTION)

Bill Holden and I fought the Korean War together in James Michener's *The Bridges at Toko-Ri* (1954).
(PARAMOUNT PICTURES)

Wife number five: Barbara Thomason and me with our firstborn child, looking like a happy family in 1959. What happened to her is the saddest part of my life.
(AP/WIDE WORLD)

In 1958, I did my last Andy Hardy picture, *Andy Hardy Comes Home*. My own son Teddy starred in it with me, playing my son.
(MICHAEL B. DRUXMAN COLLECTION)

Wife number six: Margie Lane was with Barbara the night she was murdered. I was so drugged out then I hardly remember her now. I'm told we were married one hundred days.
(AP/WIDE WORLD)

Me in a pensive mood (something rare) in 1964.
(LEIGH WEINER)

Wife number seven: Carolyn Hockett never wanted anything *from* me and all the best *for* me. She gave me a good home for six years and two fine kids.
(AP/WIDE WORLD)

Timmy Rooney, my second son (1966).
(MICKEY ROONEY COLLECTION)

I won an Academy Award nomination for my role as a washed-up trainer in Coppola's *Black Stallion* in 1979.
(ZOETROPE PRODUCTIONS)

On Broadway for the first time in 1980 in a burlesque musical called *Sugar Babies*, a smash hit and a critical success, too.
(MICKEY ROONEY COLLECTION)

With Dennis Quaid in *Bill* (1981). I won a Golden Globe for my portrayal of a mentally retarded man.
(ALAN LANDSBERG PRODUCTIONS)

Wife number eight: Jan Chamberlin, singer, artist, homemaker, and my last wife (honest!). We've been married almost twenty years.
(MICKEY ROONEY COLLECTION, 1983)

I flipped for her—her body, her backswing, even her little dog, a Maltese terrier named Pepy. A month after I met Elaine, I asked her to fly to Las Vegas and marry me. Elaine said, Yes, I will be Mrs. Rooney number four.

I was so delighted that this beautiful woman would want me that I chartered a plane and flew off with her to Vegas. We were married in something called the Wee Kirk of the Heather on November 15, 1952. (I think they knew me there. Maybe they recognized the rice marks on my face.)

Elaine wasn't keen on the races, or about my gambling, either. I soon found out why: gambling was an addiction of her ex-husband, Dan Ducich, who had been convicted in 1949 of armed robbery and placed on five years' probation. But he couldn't stop gambling, and now he was in hock to some very shady people in Vegas. A few months after we were married, the mob killed Dan, shot him through the head because he couldn't make his markers good, and left him on the street in downtown Vegas. Elaine took it hard.

That really chapped my hide. Now I felt responsible for this guy's death. And I'd never even met him. It put kind of a pall on our marriage, right from the get-go. But we were both too insecure to call it quits so soon.

In fact, to make Elaine feel more secure, I bought her a big home on Fryman Road, in Studio City, a California ranch house that Elaine really went wild about. It cost $85,000 (and would probably bring more than $3 million in today's inflated market). I don't know how I financed it; I must have found a banker who was a fan of Andy Hardy's. But it took all the cash I had, $12,000, and now I had a mortgage I couldn't afford. But Elaine loved it. She had never had anything before, and saw a big new home as a kind of symbol.

So we moved in without much more than two mattresses—one large one for me and Elaine, and one small one for her dad, whom I had invited to move in with us and serve as a general factotum around the household. After a while, we scrounged up

enough cash for furniture. We had to. We were going on Ed
Murrow's Person-to-Person, and we couldn't do that sitting on
orange crates.

(When we appeared on Murrow's show several weeks later, so
did our neighbors, Gordon and Sheila MacRae, leaning over our
back fence. So did our pet chicken, Miss Chicken, who had the
run of the place, and laid an egg a day for seven years.)

But now I was beginning to get better parts, and better paying
parts. And I got the agent I had been needing ever since I left
MGM: Maurice Duke, a lean, keen guy who knocked on my door
one day, then limped into the living room (he had had polio; he
had a brace on his knee and walked with a cane) and told me that
he was going to manage my career. He had played the harmonica with a vaudeville troupe, then turned to managing show-
business personalities when he realized there wasn't a big
market out there for harmonica solos. Now he wanted to help
me. I dared him to try. He not only tried. For five years, he did
a helluva job for me.

In 1954, I did the third picture in my three-picture Columbia
deal, *Drive a Crooked Road.* Blake Edwards wrote a terrific script,
about a garage mechanic (me) who falls in with some bank
robbers. The film got good reviews, and it even won a Redbook
Award for the best picture of the year.

Then I did a picture for Republic, *The Atomic Kid,* a project
put together for me by Maurice Duke, who got a producer's
credit. I was a prospector accidentally left in Nevada during an
atomic blast. I become radioactive and, with my newfound powers, help to round up some Communist spies. Benedict Freedman and John Fenton Murray turned it into a cute script, and
darned if this little picture didn't win rave reviews. They found
a part in this picture for Elaine, now my wife—she played a
beautiful nurse—and she got some nice notices, too.

Then I ran into James Michener, the author of a Korean War
novel, *The Bridges at Toko-Ri.* Michener and I took an instant
liking to each other, and he wrote me into the film version of

Bridges. It was going to be, as they say, a major motion picture, big budget, with Bill Holden, Grace Kelly, Fredric March, and Robert Strauss. I jumped at the chance of playing Mike Forney, a cocky little Irishman who always wore a derby hat and specialized in jumping out of choppers to save downed navy fliers. And I rather enjoyed the thought that Bill Holden and I would die heroes' deaths in the icy waters off Korea.

Paramount made money on *Bridges,* and I almost got nominated for another Oscar. Now this was more like it. I began to feel better about myself. And, feeling better, I was in the mood to launch my attack on television.

Television was beginning to get real big in 1954 and somebody like me was seven kinds of damn fool if he didn't try to get his own series. I had already tried twice, but failed. The first was a pilot for CBS in 1951 based on the life of Daniel Boone, and the second (also for CBS) was based on the files of the Tokyo police.

I got Quine and Edwards to put on their thinking caps. I told them, "You guys are clever. Think me up a TV series." They brainstormed for a while, then wrote a comedy pilot for me. I'd be a page at a network like NBC, waiting for my break as an actor. They wanted to call it *For the Love of Mike,* but after they learned that a radio announcer named Mike Wallace had registered that title, they retitled it *Hey, Mulligan.*

The Leo Burnett Company, then one of the nation's most powerful ad agencies, bought *Hey, Mulligan* for one of its biggest accounts, Pillsbury Flour, and its subsidiary, Jolly Green Giant Peas, and I signed a contract with NBC for $3,500 a week. I felt absolutely fantastic—until I learned that NBC slotted *Mulligan* at eight o'clock on Saturday night, opposite Jackie Gleason.

We did thirty-three episodes of *Hey, Mulligan,* under the direction of Les Martinson, and they were pretty damn good. Joey Forman was my sidekick on *Mulligan,* a page like me. He got the job by walking into the casting call on his knees, wondering if he was "tall enough" to work with Rooney. Quine and Edwards had done a fine pilot, and they brought in Freedman and Murray again. They understood one important thing about me: I was very good at pantomime and slapstick. They'd both written for radio, but they understood that television was a visual medium and that if they could just give me a visually funny situation, I'd milk it for all it was worth. In one episode, for instance, they had me on high heels, so I could play a scene with a taller girl in a little theater production. Of course, I couldn't get used to the lifts, and I kept losing my balance and falling over. It was a simple idea, but the audiences loved it—those who bothered to watch it.

Gleason beat us all to hell on the ratings. While he was pulling, maybe, a forty-nine Nielsen share, we were getting a seven. I think my mother watched the show. Period. Even on nights when the Gleason show was preempted, the ratings were low because people weren't in the habit of tuning us in. But on those nights when Gleason wasn't on, he made it a point to watch me. Then he'd phone me about three in the morning, wake me up, and tell me, "Hey, Spider, I want you to know that one loyal American watched your show tonight." Then he'd cackle and hang up before I could say a word. Gleason didn't call up to gloat. He didn't have a malicious bone in his oversized body. This was his way of being friendly.

Jackie Gleason and I became good friends, even if we didn't exactly pal around together. I'll never forget the thirty-eighth birthday present I got from him. I was staying at the Essex House, in the penthouse suite of Herbert J. Yates, head of Columbia Pictures. At about seven-thirty in the evening, I answered a rap on the door to find two of the most beautiful women I had ever seen in my life. They looked like sisters, sisters who had been cloned from the likes of Sophia Loren, Ann-Margret, and Elizabeth Taylor.

"Are you Mickey Rooney?" asked one of them, somewhat unnecessarily, I thought. But I knew that this was not the time to smart off. I knew they weren't here to assault me except in the most friendly fashion.

"Yes, ma'am, I am," I answered.

"We're your birthday presents, Mr. Rooney," she said.

Her sister added, "Mr. Jackie Gleason sent us. We're here to see you have a happy birthday."

Well, they didn't bring me happiness in any absolute sense, but they were experts in the art of lovemaking, which I would have been a fool to refuse. I didn't. They were marvelous in a hundred different ways, and, a dozen hours later, I felt as light as a feather. We showered together the next morning, and I waved them good-bye until they disappeared on the elevator. Then I walked back into my suite and pulled up the shade—and went right up with the shade.

Despite the competition from Jackie Gleason, *Hey, Mulligan* might have gone on to a second season, and then maybe more, but I blew it with my sponsors, the Pillsbury family. In the spring of 1955, they invited me and Maurice Duke to attend a big anniversary celebration of the Pillsbury Flour Company in Le Sueur, Minnesota. I was supposed to play in a golf tournament, in a foursome with Leo Burnett, General Lucius Clay, and Peter Jurow, president of the company. Jurow had already ticked me off by suggesting that it was my responsibility to pick up Pillsbury sales in those places where they were weak. I told him, "Hey, Mr. Jurow, that's not my job. I'm an actor."

Four holes into the match, I came to the realization that Mr. Jurow and Mr. Burnett and General Clay were bores. Besides, they played too slowly for me. So I feigned a stomachache and walked off the course. That ticked them off.

That night, at dinner, we ticked one another off some more. They put me next to the family's number-one son, and through seven courses, he kept calling me Charlie. I kept telling him my name was Mickey—Mickey Rooney—but he was in his cups and he couldn't remember. Then, after dinner, he pulled me away from the table and tried to force me over to the piano.

"Hey," I said. "What's going on?"

"It's time," he said, "for you to do your act. C'mon, Charlie."

"What act?"

"We want you to sing and dance for us."

"Hey, pal, thanks. But I don't feel up to that right now." Nobody had said anything about my performing. And I'd just about had it with these people, obviously the kind of rich folks who think their money can buy anything.

This Pillsbury heir confirmed that suspicion when he put in his two cents' worth. "What do you mean, you don't feel up to it? We own you."

I bellowed at him. "You don't own anybody, pal." Then I turned to Duke and said, loud enough for the entire dinner party to hear me, "Let's go, Duke. I can't stand this bunch of crows for another minute."

Pillsbury dropped the series, and *Hey, Mulligan* ended on Saturday night, June 7, 1955.

Now I had an even harder time getting to sleep.

☆ 31 ☆
Discovered Again

At the beginning of 1956, I was thirty-five years old. I'd divorced three women, and was now married to a fourth, and spent weekends visiting my three children. I'd been in show business thirty-three years. I'd made 152 films. I'd earned more than $600 million (for others, not for me) and I had managed to save $2,345.33. And I was still only five feet, three inches tall.

In that year, I made three turkeys, *The Bold and the Brave, Francis in the Haunted House,* and *Magnificent Roughnecks.* Nobody remembers them. I hardly remember them. But I was nominated for an Oscar for my work in *The Bold and the Brave*— mainly on the strength of a crap game sequence which, they tell me, I made up as I went along.

What I do remember is trying, like Judy, to escape from myself, more and more frequently, by downing huge doses of pills. Nembutals, Seconals, Tuinals—a whole family of barbiturates took up residence in my medicine cabinet, prescribed for me by well-meaning, but star-struck (that is to say, stupid), doctors.

The pills helped me sleep at night. They helped get me going again in the morning. Like any addiction, they took over my life, destroyed my freedom, and my sense of self. I'd make the most profoundly sincere resolutions to quit them, then be plunged into the depths of despair when, despite my good intentions, I needed to take more. From being psychologically addicted, I progressed to a physical addiction. My body cried out for them, in every nerve, and I'd try to resist, but didn't know how. Maurice Duke knew me better than I knew myself. His antidote for me was more work. So I compromised by using both pills and work.

And Duke, God bless him, Duke made things happen for me. He did so, not by kissing ass at the major studios, but by mounting projects for me on his own. He made me the producer (as well as the star) of *The Twinkle in God's Eye* at Republic. For that one, I signed Hugh O'Brian in his first movie role. He also had me producing (but not appearing in) a picture called *Jaguar* starring Sabu, who had made a splash almost twenty years before with *Elephant Boy*.

But damn. *Twinkle* and *Jaguar* didn't make any money (at least, I didn't see any of it), and I was still going nowhere in the movies.

I must have been lousy company for Elaine, but she had enough spunk not to let my depression drag her down. She took up horseback riding again, bought a home at Lake Arrowhead and a speedboat to cruise around the lake. Sure, Elaine spent a lot of money. But she also tried to get all my old bills paid, including a tax bill from the IRS for thirty-two thousand dollars. One day, she gave me a look of triumph. She had an envelope in one hand. "Look," she said, "empty."

"Huh?"

"No more debts," she said. "They're all gone. Isn't it a great feeling?"

Yeah, it was. I couldn't stand it. Two weeks later, I flew to Vegas to play a club date and lost fifty thousand dollars on the crap table. Elaine went crazy when I told her that. "That's it," she said. "No more. You can take care of your own bills now."

I think I was feeling pretty good at the time. I'd just done

"The Comedian" on *Playhouse 90*. CBS paid me only ten thousand dollars for doing it, but the part won me more critical acclaim than anything I'd done recently in the movies. Rod Serling, one of TV's top writers, did the adaptation of Ernest Lehman's novel, about a comic who was a combination of Ernie Kovacs, Sid Caesar, Milton Berle, Phil Silvers, and maybe eleven other jokers. He was vicious, greedy, selfish, untrustworthy, a lecher, and an all-around son of a bitch.

The producers of *Playhouse 90* passed this script all over Hollywood. Jackie Gleason, Red Skelton, Bob Hope, Milton Berle, Donald O'Connor, and Jerry Lewis turned it down; none of America's leading comedians wanted to get near it. Then it landed on the desk of my new press agent, Red Doff, who told me I had to do it. I did it, under the direction of a young man named John Frankenheimer.

Now everybody was writing about Mickey Rooney again. "Hey, this Rooney knows how to act!" said Marie Torre of the *New York Herald-Tribune*. Hal Humphrey, then writing for the *Los Angeles Mirror*, did a whole series of columns about me. And Pete Martin came out West to do a profile for *The Saturday Evening Post*. With Martin I tried to correct my image as a brat. I told him, "Hey, I'm not an angel and certainly I've made a million mistakes, you know. And I hope I'm around long enough to make a million more." The *Post* ran Martin's upbeat story (but titled it "Hollywood's Fabulous Brat"). Maurice Duke's phones started ringing. Every producer in television now had a deal for me.

I did a movie instead, *Baby Face Nelson*, a pretty good gangster movie directed by Don Siegel that you may still see on late-night TV, costarring Cedric Hardwicke and Carolyn Jones. Producer Al Zimbalist gave me 25 percent of the profits on it, which I felt really good about until I had to sell my percentage a couple years later, when I really needed the money.

.   .   .

Owning a piece of that film, I was more than normally interested in helping to promote it. So I went to New York for a series of press interviews, trying to hype the film, and had the pleasure, then, of running into a tall, handsome U.S. senator from Massachusetts in the elevator at the Waldorf Towers.

He looked down at me. "You're Mickey Rooney, aren't you?" he asked pleasantly.

"I am, Mr. Senator." I'd seen him on TV during the 1956 conventions, and I had already tapped him a comer in politics. And I heard on the Hollywood grapevine that he was a chip off the old block, his dad, Joe Kennedy, who always seemed to have a thing going with this or that movie queen. The latest rumor had Jack Kennedy linked with Marilyn Monroe.

He said, "I am one of your biggest fans." I could almost see the wheels turning in his head. I suspected he was saying, "I wonder if this little bastard knows I'm fucking Marilyn Monroe?"

I said, "I'm one of your fans, too, but you have been on TV so much, Mr. Senator, that you're stealing all of our stardom." I wanted to add, "And screwing one of our loveliest stars."

And he probably knew that's just exactly what I was thinking. He laughed.

And I knew that he knew. I laughed.

When the elevator reached the main floor, he turned and shook my hand. "Well, Mick, I'll be seeing more of you, I suspect?" I believe he was hoping that wouldn't happen this evening. He was heading, I was sure, to a tryst somewhere up on Park Avenue.

"Anything I can do to help," I said. "Just let me know." I knew I wouldn't be campaigning for him (I was a Republican), but I knew I had some phone numbers for him, when Marilyn wasn't around.

"I'm sure you can help," he said. I don't think he was thinking of anything more than phone numbers either.

When Jack Kennedy became President, he invited me to the White House a number of times, maybe because I was a friend of Judy Garland, who had campaigned like hell for him, and of Peter Lawford, his brother-in-law. Sometimes, I responded. I remember the first occasion, when President Kennedy was addressing a Spanish delegation in the Rose Garden. I stood in the back of the crowd, and couldn't help noticing a beautiful blonde wearing sunglasses way over on the other side of the garden. It was Marilyn. "Jeez!" I wondered. "Does he do it with Marilyn in the White House?"

When the ceremony was over, I wanted to go over and pay my respects to Marilyn. But then a Secret Service man came up to me and said, "Mr. Rooney?"

"Yes?"

"The President would like to speak with you."

So I walked up to the podium, and he leaned over and shook my hand and smiled that fabulous smile and he said, "It's good to see you, Mick." He glanced back over my shoulder, checking out the departing crowd, and, I was sure, the retreating form of Miss Monroe, and wondering if I'd seen her, or talked to her. At least, that's what I read in his mirthful eyes. But all he said was, "It's been a long time since that elevator ride."

I grinned and said, "Mr. President, you got off at the right floor." I was not at all sure I was, then, getting off on the right floor.

Understanding my need to work (and my ongoing need for dollars), Maurice Duke helped by booking me as often as he could in Las Vegas, which was just starting to become the ninth wonder of the world with its glittering casinos and star-studded, sometimes even topless, shows that outstripped the Lido de Paris and the Folies-Bergère. I was a smash hit at the Riviera, where I drew $17,500 a week—and lost twice that on the crap table. I was so angry that I told the audience at my midnight show I was retiring from show business. I had the audience crying and shouting, "No! No!"

I was adamant. "I'm going to retire to a farm and just take care of my cows and chickens and horses," I told them. Then I walked off to a standing, weeping ovation.

ROONEY RETIRES, said the morning papers in Vegas.

But I had no sooner returned to LA than Maurice Duke was trying to persuade me to un-retire. "Wally Cox just bombed at the Dunes," he said, "and the Dunes was wondering if you—"

"Naw," I said. "Didn't you hear? I'm retired."

"Mick," he said. "How much cash you have?"

"Nothing," I said. "Not a cent."

"That's too bad," Duke said. "You know, I'm only your manager, and I'm pretty well fixed. I have a home in Beverly Hills and money in the bank. And you have nothing. And you're retiring."

"That's right," I said. "I'm fed up."

"Too fed up," he said, "to open tonight at the Dunes for seventeen thousand five hundred a week?"

"For how many weeks?" I said.

"Four."

I grinned. "Duke, you son of a gun."

I complain about agents all the time, but I don't know why I waste my energy. It's like complaining because the sun comes up in the East instead of over the Pacific. I tell stories about the times when I couldn't get an agent to return a simple phone call. I recall the time that I phoned Abe Lastfogel at William Morris and told him, "Abe, I'm broke and I need a job," only to have him say, "Mick, I can't help you." And then hang up.

Well, at least he was there to take my call. But that was some time ago. Nowadays, it is fashionable for agents to be out. When you call them, they're always "out." It's in, you see, to be out.

If they're in, they're out. So, they're always out. That way, they'll be in.

And rich. If an agent owns 10 percent of me and 10 percent of fifty-nine other guys, then he automatically has 600 percent. Neat. And if I ever complain to an agent about anything, he always has a pained look on his face, like, "How can you be so ungrateful? Why, Mick, I just named my yacht after you!"

Agents always seem to have so much aplomb. Nothing ever seems to bother them. Why should it? They're rich. Reminds me of my favorite agent story. I meet this agent at Chasen's, older than God, maybe he's the agent for Mel Brooks's character, The Thousand Year Old Man, but he's looking fabulous. I ask him who he books.

"Oh," he says, "I booked Amelia Earhart's tour in the South Pacific."

"Uh-huh."

"I booked the dance team on the *Titanic.*"

"Yeah?"

"I booked General Custer into Little Big Horn."

I say, "Wait a minute, General Custer and all his men were scalped at Little Big Horn."

He says, "Hey, I just book 'em. I don't tell 'em how to wear their hair."

But if it weren't for agents, I wouldn't work. They seem to keep everything glued together—at least in my world.

In Las Vegas, I tried to stay away from the tables, but I guess I was addicted to more than Seconals. Unfortunately, I won real big one night. It happened like this. After my midnight show one night, I joined up with Nick the Greek (real name: Nicholas Dandolos). We started at the Dunes, didn't do too well, then took a cab to the Sahara. I was playing right along with the Greek. He'd put ten five-hundred-dollar chips on the come line, and I'd lay five right alongside him. He'd let the winnings ride, and so would I. Well, we couldn't lose. He'd slap ten thousand dollars on the hard six and eight, I'd plunk down five thousand, and we'd win. We had an incredible streak, something that every crap shooter dreams about. By four-thirtyA.M., the Greek had won more than a million and I was up almost half a million.

At five A.M., we were still going strong. The Greek had almost two million and I was up a mill. A lady with blue hair was about to come out. The Greek whispered to me, "Put ten thousand on the 'don't come' line." The lady rolled an eleven—a winner for her, a loser for us.

"That's it," said the Greek. "There's always a little old lady." What he meant was, every hot streak must come to an end.

So I won almost a million. But that didn't satisfy me. Gambling winnings never satisfy. They just make me want more. More money? No, it's not the money, it's the emotional high— what addicts call "a rush." In fact, I could never hope to duplicate that kind of evening again.

But that episode taught me one thing: it wasn't really money I was after or security. (Security? Hah! My whole life tells me that was the one thing I *never* wanted.) I wanted to keep going on. I needed an audience. I needed acclaim. The Sahara incident proved one thing: I could have retired on a million bucks. But I didn't want to retire. I still wanted to be the toast of the world. And I wasn't. How, I asked myself, could I be Andy Hardy again?

I tried the simplest solution. Fresh off my triumph on *Playhouse 90*, I went to MGM and asked the brass to bring Andy Hardy back as a young man. I was to be a young judge myself, married to my high school sweetheart, Polly Benedict. Ann Rutherford was supposed to play Polly, but she nixed that. She was happily married to a very successful studio head, Bill Dozier, and she had no wish to do films again.

In the end I came back as an attorney for an aircraft company and my wife was a girl I met at work. I had a son, too, played by none other than my real son by Mart Vickers, Teddy, then eight years old. Teddy was following in my footsteps as a kid actor, and he was already an old pro. He'd appeared in a *Playhouse 90* with his mom, starred in a TV adaptation of O. Henry's "Ransom of Red Chief," and appeared with Doris Day in *It Happened to Jane.* Teddy had my sandy hair, my freckles, and my smile. Who else would play the son of Andy Hardy?

So I came back to Carvel in *Andy Hardy Comes Home,* but the trouble was, nobody noticed. The public simply didn't care what had happened to Andy Hardy.

☆ *32* ☆
Barbara

By *now, you* probably know this much about me: I adore beautiful women, and my adoration sometimes makes me do crazy things. When a man adores a woman, he goes too far, makes her the be-all and end-all of his existence, and becomes seven kinds of fool himself.

I adored Barbara Ann Thomason. To begin with, she was the most beautiful woman I'd ever seen. I met her one night at the Horn in Santa Monica. I was smitten.

She spoke with the trace of a British accent, and, when I asked her why, she explained that her father had been an officer in the air force. She grew up where his assignments took him—mostly in England, then later in Phoenix. She said she was in LA to get into the movies. "And why not?" I said, looking into her deep blue eyes, wanting to reach up and touch her blond hair. "You're absolutely gorgeous."

I backed away to size her up. She was slightly shorter than I with a figure that would stop a train. Most short girls with a good figure tend to look chunky, but Barbara was slim, like an Eileen Ford model. She looked tall, but she was just my size.

"Hey," I said, getting close to her as she stood at the bar, "we can see things eye to eye."

She grinned, moved even closer to me, so that the tips of her breasts touched my chest, and looked into the windows of my soul, "eye to eye." Barbara was using the professional name of Caroline Mitchell, and she had won seventeen beauty contests, the last one at Venice's Muscle Beach. We talked until they threw us out of the place.

"No," she said, "I don't mind that you're thirty-seven and I'm only twenty-one." I noted, when I walked her to her little open MG, that she didn't so much walk as glide, like a goddess.

Word got back to Elaine that I was squiring a young blond beauty around Hollywood, a town where the sex life of the stars is never a secret for long. Elaine soon found a young man of her own, and she was ready to call it splits. I should have agreed, but I begged Elaine not to file for a divorce.

So did my psychiatrist, who believed that yet another divorce was not going to be good for my self-image. I knew that was poppycock. I knew in my heart of hearts that Barbara was good for my self-image. But now a four-time loser, I convinced myself that I knew nothing and my doctor knew everything. So I stayed married and played musical girls for a while. I bought Barbara an expensive fur coat. Then, to make things even, I bought Elaine the same kind of coat.

Finally, I stopped being a schiz. On June 15, 1958, I moved out of the house on Fryman Road in Sherman Oaks, and Barbara and I got a place of our own. Now, without benefit of clergy, Barbara and I were living together as man and wife.

On May 21, 1959, Elaine was awarded her interlocutory decree, along with the home in Studio City, the house at Lake Arrowhead, the furniture, a boat, a car, the horses, assorted jewelry, fifty thousand dollars in cash, and twenty-one thousand dollars a year for ten years. The headline in the *Los Angeles Times* read: WIFE DUMPS ROONEY FOR $381,750.

By then, Barbara was five months pregnant, and, technically, she and I couldn't get married in California until May. For the benefit of the press and the public, I announced that I'd divorced Elaine in Mexico in May of 1958 and married Barbara in December. The New York *Daily News* had fun with that. Their headline read: HALF PINT TAKES A FIFTH.

On Friday, September 13, 1959, at St. John's Hospital in Santa Monica, Barbara gave birth to our first child (and my first daughter), Kelly Ann. She was six pounds, ten ounces, and she had blue eyes, just like her mom, and she was beautiful.

Who was I to get such a gift? In my heart of hearts, I knew Kelly Ann came from God. But I wasn't paying much attention to God in those days. Whatever I got, I thought, I earned for myself, with hard work.

In fact, my work wasn't giving me much to cheer about. From 1959 to 1979, I did very few movies I could be proud of. There were twenty-nine in all, and most of them were crap. The only thing I took away from them was the friendship of some of the people who made them with me.

I was downright ashamed of my role in *Breakfast at Tiffany's*, produced by Paramount in 1961, and I don't think the director, Blake Edwards, was very proud of it either. I was too cute as, get this, an eccentric Japanese fashion photographer living in a posh New York apartment, and the whole damn movie was just too too precious. Audrey Hepburn played a high-priced hooker. You had to read Truman Capote's story to know that; you wouldn't have known it from watching the movie.

Requiem for a Heavyweight won a lot of critical acclaim, and I enjoyed playing with Anthony Quinn, the dumb, hulking fighter being used, then cast aside, by everyone. Quinn was (and is) the actor's actor and one of the most consummate gentlemen in Hollywood. Jackie Gleason was in *Requiem,* too, so we had a chance to renew our friendship. Gleason was a lot like me: he didn't know how to wear his money. He was too busy being fat, eating too much, and drinking too much to be a complete human being.

Stanley Kramer was supposed to be some kind of cinematic genius, but he left his genius at home during the shooting of *It's a Mad Mad Mad Mad World*. It had too many comedians—Buster Keaton, Jimmy Durante, Milton Berle, Sid Caesar, Ethel Merman, Dorothy Provine, Buddy Hackett, Dick Shawn, Phil Silvers, Terry-Thomas, Jonathan Winters, Edie Adams, Eddie "Rochester" Anderson, Jim Backus, William Demarest, Peter Falk, Paul Ford, Leo Gorcey, Ben Blue, Edward Everett Horton, Joe E. Brown, Carl Reiner, the Three Stooges, ZaSu Pitts, Sterling Holloway, Jack Benny, and Jerry Lewis—and not really enough story.

You'd think there'd have been a lot happening on the set, with all these great comedians sitting around, but there wasn't. I think that, put together in one place, comedians are the saddest bunch of people I know. What do you get when you put twenty-nine comedians together? Insecurity to the twenty-ninth power. Only Jonathan Winters had the guts to try some things, trying to entertain us with some of his impromptu comedy. I think he was one of the first guys to do really good improvisational stuff, and he had a lot of nerve doing it with this tough audience.

Right after *Mad World* was released, Selig Seligman hired two good comedy writers, Robert Fisher and Arthur Marx, the son of Groucho, to create something that ABC could sell. They ended up with *Mickey*, a sitcom about a Midwesterner who had pulled up roots in the Midwest to run a motel he had inherited at Newport Beach. We made a good pilot in the spring of 1964, under the direction of Richard Whorf, one of the directors of *The Beverly Hillbillies*.

Everybody at ABC seemed to love it—until they tried to sell it. Madison Avenue wasn't buying, it was said, because I had two things going against me: I had been married five times and I had had a fight with Jack Paar on the air during his *Tonight Show*. But ABC told us to go ahead anyway and shoot eighteen episodes. They'd pick up a sponsor later for *Mickey* because they had a great time slot for it, eight P.M. on Friday nights, with no significant opposition on the other networks. That was too good to be true, I thought. And my fears were confirmed when that time slot went to another series. *Mickey* ended up opposite CBS's *The Dick Van Dyke Show*, then the number-one show on TV, and NBC's *Movie of the Week*.

I thought Marx and Fisher had done a great job. In our first show, they had me trapped on the yacht of an heiress full of lust for me (played by a real heiress named Dina Merrill). When I finally escape her clutches, I am wearing nothing but her mink coat, prompting my motel manager, Sammy Ling (played by Sammee Tong), to come out with a bit of Oriental wisdom: "Old Chinese saying: 'Never lend money to man in mink.'"

The ABC executives in New York said they hated the last two shows that had aired but allowed they might stay with *Mickey* if we could play up the role of Sammy Ling. You see, the polls said Sammy was hot. The trouble was, Sammee Tong, an incurable gambler in mighty hock to the mob, committed suicide on October 27. That did it. ABC canned our show after seven episodes.

Once again, I had to do my traditional bounce-off-the-canvas routine. "A right to the jaw by Louis and Rooney is down. He's hurt. He's hurt bad. Seven, eight, nine. He's—no, by God, he's getting up. Rooney's on his feet again, folks. *Unbelievable!*"

Friends helped. Judy Garland had landed a multimillion dollar series on CBS television, her own weekly special, *The Judy Garland Show*, and she wanted me to help her kick it off. "There isn't anyone but Mickey to do this first show with me," Judy told the executives at CBS. At the time, Judy and I may have both been addicted to our own special drugs, but we were also addicted to each other, and anyone who observed our first meeting for rehearsals there on Stage 43 at CBS's Television City could see that.

George Schlatter, the director, eased us toward the bright lights of our set to rehearse. Mel Tormé, the show's musical director, had written a duet for us, a parody of "All I Need Is the Girl/Boy." We felt our way through that, and then through some banter the show's writers had done for us about our old days at MGM. We proceeded to rewrite the script on the spot. "Hey," said Schlatter. "This is going to be just great, just great."

The plan was that we'd rehearse several days, then tape four shows, kind of like dress rehearsals, before live audiences at Television City, two on Thursday evening and two on Friday afternoon. Then, although the show was billed as live, the show that actually went out on the nationwide feed Friday night was an amalgam of the best takes from all four "rehearsals." The show would look live, and the nationwide TV audience wouldn't be any the wiser.

But who was talking wisdom? What the audience wanted was laughter and tears, and that's what Judy was giving them here, the laughter and tears that came when we heard her do all those great songs of hers, and it didn't matter how many times she did them, we still smiled and wept when we heard them.

Only trouble was, Judy was awfully tight in those days, as tight as an E string, and it didn't take much to set her off. On the night of our first dress rehearsal we were all ready for the opening number: Judy at one end of a runway, a big camera on a dolly at the other. The camera was supposed to move in on her, from an extremely long shot to a big close-up, with Judy singing a special upbeat arrangement (done by Mel Tormé) of "Sunny Side Up."

John Harlan, the show's announcer, tells the audience we're ready to roll, and then a voice from the control booth says we have thirty seconds. A hush comes over the crowd. Judy is a sudden apparition, beautifully coiffed, beautifully gowned, eyes sparkling, slim like a fashion model. A voice on a loudspeaker counts down: "Five, four, three, two, one. Roll tape!"

Judy starts to belt out the song, the camera slides up the runway, closer, closer, then—

"Goddamn it!" shouts one of the cameramen.

Someone had failed to secure the electrical cord, and the camera movement has yanked it out of the socket. The video goes black. Judy goes white. George Schlatter tries to take over. "Okay, okay," he says to the audience. "Sorry, folks, everybody out till we get back on track here."

I can see that Judy is absolutely appalled. Her current boyfriend, André Philippe, is right there at her side, lighting a cigarette for her. She accepts the cigarette, but pushes him away. Everyone is watching Judy, and I imagine everyone is saying, "God, what's she gonna do?"

"Hey," I say to Schlatter, but with one eye half cocked at Judy, "no need to get the folks out of here." I grab an assistant director's headset, put it on backward, move halfway up the runway, and start to do what I do best. I put on an impromptu show for the people, a collection of the best things I ever did in vaudeville, the best things I could remember from my old movies, one bit after another. The audience is fascinated, but it isn't the audience that I am trying to fascinate.

It is Judy I am aiming at. And I am hitting my mark. Judy draws closer, stops puffing so furiously on her cigarette, and becomes a little girl again, in love with a clown, this clown. Now, instead of focusing on herself or raging at the production crew, she is going outside herself, watching me do my shtick, laughing at me.

Needless to say, the show did go on. The crew fixed the cables, the cameramen stopped cursing, everybody got in his and her places again, Mort Lindsey's thirty-three piece orchestra sat poised for the downbeat of their leader's baton, and Judy was back on the same page with us once more.

On Friday night, June 24, 1964, the nation was glued to *The Judy Garland Show*. By most accounts, if Judy and her crew of writers and directors could have sustained the level of that first show, they'd still be in business today. The writers weren't afraid to let us have fun, even to make fun of ourselves. They had me singing "Thank Heaven for Little Girls"—surrounded by a dozen six-foot chorus girls. They had me and Judy reminiscing about our musicals at Metro. We re-created one of our all-time numbers from *Girl Crazy*.

And then, in the finale, Judy took her place in front of an old theater trunk, sang a few bars from "Born in a Trunk," then, fingering some memorabilia from the trunk, did "Too Late Now," "Who Cares?" and her own blockbusting version of "Old Man River." Bedlam in the studio. A standing ovation. The show—well, it was one of those memorable moments in show biz, made more memorable because it wasn't just a theater full of people who shared in it, but millions across the land.

Afterward, at a party for the cast, crew, and invited guests, I was standing next to Tormé when Judy made her way over to us. With a wink at me, she said to Tormé, who had spent weeks and weeks helping her get ready for this. "Well?"

"What can I tell you, Sadie?" he said. "You were nothing short of magnificent."

"Yes," she said, preening herself like a peacock. (She *did* look fabulous, all bejeweled and sleek in a couturier gown.) "Yes, I was good, wasn't I?"

Tormé seemed taken aback at first, then laughed when he saw Judy wink at me again. He realized Judy was play-acting— playing the part of a grande dame in the British theater, perhaps.

As I said, it was too bad that Judy couldn't sustain the show's high pitch. If she'd been in the pink, and drugless, maybe she could have. Maybe. Network TV, where almost no one knows what's good, but only what other people say is good, has killed off stronger people than Judy. Judy, stressed out herself, could make everyone around her crazy by insisting, for example, that they drive over and have a drink with her—at four in the morning. (She didn't call me. I'd already made it clear to Judy that I was allergic to alcohol, something I'd discovered at age eighteen when I went weightless in the back of my limousine after celebrating a friend's wedding with a couple bottles of champagne.) Those who did take turns dancing attendance on Judy during *The Judy Garland Show* called their duty "the Dawn Patrol." Few of her friends at this period *ever* saw her sleep.

After my guest shot on Judy's show, I bounced again, this time to do a picture in the Middle East with Lex Barker called *24 Hours to Kill*. Soon, I was in a jet to Beirut. *24 Hours* was low-budget, but my salary was good, thanks to my new agent, Bullets Durgom, a short, bald, ebullient fellow who had represented Frank Sinatra and Jackie Gleason. Bullets got his nickname from his days as a band boy for Tommy Dorsey. He used to sweat so much during his exertions that they started calling him "Bullets." Now, of course, he'd come up in the world. As an agent, he helped Jackie Gleason get an $11 million contract with CBS in 1961. Now, as my agent, his first order of business was to persuade me to stop selling myself so cheap. "I can't get any real money for you if you go off and do a beach picture for two grand a week," he said.

I promised him I wouldn't sell myself short, and he was able to demonstrate the wisdom of his plan by making a deal for me with Stanley Kramer for $125,000 in *Mad World*, a sum that I hadn't seen in some time. But, in March of 1965, I was tempted beyond my strength (the IRS was dunning me for $91,000 in back taxes), and I took a cheap assignment from American International Pictures, which wanted to show me and Brian Donlevy *How to Stuff a Wild Bikini*. I don't know *why* Donlevy took the job. I did it to pay some bills.

My lawyer at the time, Dermot Long, persuaded a superior-court judge in Los Angeles to free up most of the money in my trust fund (it was supposed to stay there until I'd reached the age of sixty) so I could pay my tax bill—on the grounds that the interest I was getting from the principal was less than the penalty being charged by the federal government for nonpayment. If I kept on like this, Long told the court, my principal would all be gone by age sixty.

All of it? How much did I have? Hold your cries of surprise, folks: my trust fund amounted to approximately $126,000. Did you hear what I said? One hundred and twenty-six thousand. Why so little? Well, for one thing, my mom and I had been allowed to withdraw the interest through the years, which we did. And so the dollars that had been deposited in the 1930s didn't have a chance to grow with inflation. As a matter of fact, they shrunk. A 1938 dollar was, in 1965, worth about fifteen cents.

Wild Bikini featured Frankie Avalon and Annette Funicello, and it was one of the worst of the beach-blanket pictures ever. In fact, Bosley Crowther of *The New York Times* called it "the worst film of the last two years—and maybe the next two years." I couldn't argue with that.

Bullets Durgom, of course, was disappointed that I had taken the assignment at all. "How much they give you, Mickey," he said.

"Five grand."

"Mick," he said. "It's no use. I can't keep working to keep your price up when you're taking these lousy little beach pictures."

"Bullets," I said. "I need the dough.

He said, "I'd rather loan it to you."

He thought I didn't understand. But it was he who didn't understand. It wasn't that I needed the money. I needed to work, even if I had to work for next to nothing. That was the long and the short of it. Sure, I was working for a pittance. But, what else would I do with my life? Retire to a farm? Hah! I'd go nuts on a farm.

At home I was already running a farm, a baby farm. Barbara was as fertile as I, and she turned out to be some kind of mother.

From 1959 to 1963, we had one child almost every year. We named the kids Kelly Ann, Kerry Yule, Michael Kyle (after one of my favorite football players of all time, Kyle Rote), and Kimmy Sue. We traded in our home in Beverly Hills for another great place in Brentwood. We had a guest house for Barbara's folks when they came to visit and lots of quarters for the servants, which we started to acquire in bunches. I didn't mind. If Barbara wanted more servants, she got more servants. It was the least I could do for her, especially since I wasn't home for weeks at a time. And when I was home, I wasn't much fun. I was becoming more and more dependent on barbiturates.

I'd had a couple of brief affairs, nothing serious, during my years with Barbara. Beautiful women made me horny, and I hadn't learned to curb my libido, most especially not when a woman came on to me. (Dick Quine used to say women wanted me because of my energy. I doubt that. Women liked me because I made them laugh. What is an orgasm, after all, except laughter of the loins?) But I never imagined that Barbara would play around on me. I am sure, if I was ever sure of anything, that I drove her to it—after she'd tried, and failed, to make me stay faithful.

Barbara knew I was most tempted when I was on the road. And so, she always frowned whenever I came home to announce I was going off on a trip. Sometimes she insisted on going with me, even if that meant leaving the kids with a nanny. When I told her a couple years before that I was going to Yugoslavia to shoot a picture for Roger Corman called *The Secret Invasion,* she insisted on going along to Dubrovnik, even though she was eight months pregnant. This woman really loved me, really loved me with children. But I was too dumb, too selfish to notice.

When I went off to shoot *24 Hours to Kill,* Barbara didn't even ask to go to Beirut with me. It turns out that while I was killing my hours there, she was having a thing with an aspiring actor, Milos Milocevic, a tall guy with dark good looks who had worked as a stand-in for Alain Delon in Paris, then married a Chicago socialite living in LA in order to gain American citizenship. By the time Delon had introduced us to Milos, he was divorced from the socialite and trying to get work in Hollywood. I had tried to get Milos some acting jobs and invited him over from time to time, never suspecting that there was some chemistry between Barbara and him. The cuckolded husband, they say, is always the last to know.

I was probably distracted by my own recent success on the legitimate stage. On September 1, 1965, I opened in a three-week revival of *A Funny Thing Happened on the Way to the Forum* at the Valley Music Theater in Woodland Hills. I played the role that Zero Mostel had made famous, and I didn't just copy the great Mostel. I was my own man.

Charles Champlin's review in the *Los Angeles Times* acknowledged that: under the headline, A ROMAN ROMP FOR ROONEY, Champlin wrote, "Rooney leers, chortles, giggles, struts, runs, dances, sings like a laryngical foghorn, and ad-libs all manner of regional and topical asides. The evening remains a largely personal triumph for Rooney."

I choked up when the audience in Woodland Hills rose to give me a standing ovation. Gosh, that took me back, back to my beginnings. I had forgotten what a rush a real audience could give me—a live, appreciative, clapping, roaring, laughing audience. Audiences, I knew then, as I had never known before, were my real addiction. Hell, I thought, I shouldn't be in the movies. I should be on Broadway.

But Bullets Durgom kept getting me work in pictures. Next job: *Ambush Bay*, to be shot in the Philippines, the one trip in my life I wish I'd never taken. Barbara herself wanted to drive me to the airport the day I left LA for Manila. Milos was at the house. He came up to wish me luck. I shook his hand and said, "Take good care of my wife while I'm gone."

He smiled and assured me he would. I didn't remember, until later, how nervous Barbara was that day and how erratically she drove. Sig Frolich, my friend and stand-in who was sitting in the backseat, reminded me later. Well, Milos did take care of Barbara. In fact, he took her with him to Fort Bragg, a town up the coast of California that looks more like Cape Cod than California, where he had a small part as a submarine crewman in Norman Jewison's *The Russians Are Coming, The Russians Are Coming*. She stayed there with him for two weeks. Then they returned to LA. He spent most of his nights with Barbara, and, by the time I returned at the end of November, they were in the middle of a very torrid love affair.

I had hated my time in the Philippines. The plot of *Ambush Bay* had us hacking our way through the worst kind of jungles on the island, fighting mosquitoes and drinking the local water.

And now, back home, I knew I shouldn't have gone to the Philippines. I began picking up clues of her infidelity as soon as I arrived home. Barbara and Milos were both there at the airport to meet me. Barbara greeted me cooly—while Milos hugged me like a long lost brother and kissed me on the cheek, like a Judas. I found some socks in our family laundry room that weren't mine.

I confronted her. She denied she was having an affair. We fought for a while, and then I went in and took a shower. When I emerged, Barbara was sitting on the bed with a drink in her hand. When the ice cubes tinkled in the glass, I realized her hand was shaking. She announced, in a voice that was full of bravado, "Mick, I need some space. You'd better pack up and leave."

"And go where?" I said.

"I don't care," she said with a smile I had never seen on her face before, defiant and a little scared. "Just give me some space—space and time. We need to be apart for a while."

"How long?" I asked.

She just shrugged.

Now *I* was scared. I just wanted to sleep. I downed a big handful of Seconals and rolled into bed.

When I came to, almost twenty-four hours later, Sig Frolich was at my side to tell me Barbara was gone. "She said she doesn't want to see you here when she gets back."

I was too exhausted to do anything but agree. Sig helped me pack, I checked into the Bel Air Hotel, and Barbara and I separated officially two days before Christmas. I flew to New York on December 28 for a three-week engagement with Bobby Van at the Latin Quarter. I don't know how I got through the three weeks. I was depressed. I was also physically ill, though I didn't know that until I returned to LA.

Sig drove me straight from the airport to the hospital. I felt like a sack of spoiled potatoes. Sig practically had to carry me in. I had lost a lot of weight, down to 116 pounds from 145. My white blood cell count was down. At first, they thought I had leukemia. Finally, they issued a verdict: I had contracted some "exotic Oriental disease" in the Philippines.

As I lay in my hospital bed recuperating, I learned that Barbara was planning to file for divorce. I beat her to it by filing myself, asking for custody of my four children because Barbara was "an unfit mother." I also asked for a court order restraining Milos from setting foot in our home.

Marge Lane, Barbara's best friend, later told me that move had scared Barbara. Afraid she would lose the kids, she asked Milos to leave. Milos flew into a rage, but he packed his things and left, after telling another of Barbara's friends, "If Barbara even looks at another man, I'll shoot her *and* myself."

One Sunday afternoon Barbara visited me in the hospital. We talked for perhaps an hour, and Barbara ended up in tears, promising that we'd get back together no matter what. She still wouldn't admit that there'd been anything improper between her and Milos, but she conceded, "If it makes you unhappy, I won't even see Milos as a friend." Almost immediately, the phone rang in my room. She rushed over and answered it. "Yes," she said, "I'll be right out." It was Milos, telling her to get her ass out. I could see the fear in her eyes as she hurried out the door, but I called after her, "We can make it together, honey. We can make it together."

I was overjoyed about Barbara's promise. I didn't care what Barbara had done. I just wanted her back. Could I forgive her? How could I, a sinner seven times seventy times, *not* forgive?

Barbara left the hospital and returned home with Milos. They met friends for dinner at the Daisy, and sometime during the evening Barbara and Marge Lane had a tête-à-tête in the ladies' room. Barbara told Marge, "I want Milos to leave. Otherwise, I'm going to lose the kids. But he won't go." Marge returned to Brentwood with them and promised to phone Barbara in the morning so that they could hatch a plan.

Barbara would never have a chance to do that. At one-thirty the next afternoon, the police arrived at our home in Brentwood, called by Wilma Catania, a friend of Barbara's who had been staying in the guest house. Shortly after noon, Wilma told Detective Sergeant Newstetter of the Los Angeles Police Department that she and the maid had jimmied open the door of the master bedroom suite and found Milos's body slumped over Barbara's in the master bath.

The police found the bodies, obviously dead, with bullets to their brains. My own .38 revolver lay next to them, a revolver that Barbara had kept in her nightstand "because she was afraid of prowlers."

The kids never saw their mother's body. Apparently, they were asleep in their rooms in another wing of the house during the horror. They never even heard the shots.

Sig Frolich couldn't tell me. He told my doctor, Dr. Buckley. "You'll know how to tell Mick," he said. Then he called my son Timmy, then nineteen, who'd been living with me in some new digs in Benedict Canyon, and my friend Red Barry, and my press agent, Red Doff. He thought they ought to be with me when I got the news.

How does the wisest, most compassionate man in the world tell one of his best friends something like this? Dr. Buckley chose an indirect way. He walked into my room, nodded at me and at my visitors, and was looking at my chart when the phone rang (by prearrangement).

"What? What?" he said. "Both dead? Both of them? Yes. Yes. I understand."

He hung up the phone and looked at me, very sadly.

"What's the matter, Bob?" I mumbled.

"Barbara's had an accident, Mick."

I started to climb out of bed. "Lemme get dressed and go to her."

He wrapped both of his arms around me, looked straight into my eyes, and said, "Barbara is dead, Mickey, and so is the man who killed her."

I didn't have to ask who the man was. I knew. I wanted to know about my children.

Once I knew they were all right, I began to sob, as much in relief for my kids as in sorrow for Barbara. I asked Red Barry to go "get my babies and bring them to me." Then I began to keen. "Oh, poor Barbara," I said over and over. "Oh, poor Barbara." And then: "My poor babies. My poor babies." I died, too, right there in Bob Buckley's arms that night. Something like a steel band seemed to encircle my chest. And I didn't take a full breath for three years.

I was a sparrow, not a man, during the final services, conducted by the same minister who made our marriage legal in 1960, the same man who had baptized Kelly, Kerry, Kyle, and Kimmy Sue. Timmy stayed close to me. So did Dr. Buckley and a few other of my closest friends. They told me later that my weight had dropped below one hundred pounds, that my skin was sagging off my bones, that my eyes were two deep black holes.

Milos Milocevic? His body was lying in the Los Angeles

morgue, waiting to be shipped back to his mother in Belgrade, where she was telling the press that I had plotted to have her son killed.

I was in a close to catatonic state for days, but I was aware enough to care about my kids. As soon as I was released from St. John's, I rented a home in Beverly Hills, then gathered the kids together and kept them close to me—until my attorney, Dermot Long, phoned ten days after Barbara's death.

"Mickey," he said. "You sitting down?"

"Yes. Why?"

"Your mother has just passed away."

"Ahh, God," I prayed. "When will the sorrow end?" It would only end, I would learn, when I stopped fleeing Him. I had been fleeing Him down the days, down the labyrinthine ways, and He kept pursuing me. And I still did not know what He was doing.

Nell had told me not to cry for her, and I didn't. Tearless, I listened to the brief service in her honor in a temple dedicated to Christian Science, and watched, wordless, as they cremated her remains behind a lace curtain. I knew her new life, with God, had to be better than it was with me. When I had fallen, she had fallen, too, and she found consolation only in the bottle. And it wasn't long before Fred Pankey drank himself to death in a cheap motel on Sepulveda Boulevard.

I beat myself when they told me that. I'd lost track of Fred, been trying to find him, and couldn't. But how the hell could I find out where he was, when I didn't even know where I was?

And, then, I really didn't know.

☆ *33* ☆
Visions

I *wasn't quite* ready for a grave marker, not just yet. Oh, I had many more setbacks during the next dozen years, but I would survive them as I survived those holding me back now, with the vestiges of a faith that I'd almost forgotten. I got added help from a visitation.

It came in an unlikely place: the coffee shop of a casino on the shores of Lake Tahoe. I had taken the booking as a last-minute fill-in for Judy Garland, who was too sick to make it herself. I was having breakfast at Harrah's with Bobby Van, Sig Frolich, and a few other people after our show, kind of half listening to a lot of aimless talk, when a busboy came up behind me and whispered, "Mr. Rooney?"

"Yes?" I said. I started to get out of my chair, thinking someone was paging me on the phone. He leaned over, put his lips to my ear, and said, "Mr. Rooney, Jesus Christ loves you very much."

For a moment, I couldn't quite believe what I'd heard. I turned to look at him. He was wearing a white jacket, had blond curls, a white-rose complexion, and shining teeth. He smiled at me. Then he disappeared into the kitchen.

I turned back to my breakfast and tried to finish my coffee and rolls. I finally strode over to the hostess.

"Say," I said, very casually, "I'd like to talk to that busboy who was working our table."

"Which busboy is that?" she asked.

"The one with the light-blond curls," I said. "Sort of surrounded his head like a helmet?"

"Hmmm," she said. "We don't have a busboy like that. No boy here with blond hair."

"Naw," I said, a little impatient with her. "He was just talking to me."

"Well," she said, "you can certainly go back in the kitchen and look."

I was already on my way. But there was no boy back there whose hair was like a—a halo. All of a sudden my flesh crawled, and the hair stood up on my arms. I knew I'd been visited by an angel.

"God," I said, "who am I that you should send an angel to me? I, who have been paying so little attention?"

Marge Lane, Barbara's best friend, felt sorry for me. She saw that I really couldn't cope with four little ones all alone. And she thought I needed a surrogate for Barbara. I guess I thought so, too. At any rate, we married only a few months after Barbara was gone, and we lived together for a while on Rexford Drive. I don't remember much about those days. I was completely incapacitated; all I can recall is telling the judge I couldn't understand why Marge Lane was asking for half of my estate when we'd only been married one hundred days. The judge agreed with me, and he sent my sixth wife packing with small change: $350 a month for twelve months.

Then I was free, free to be alone with my misery.

On November 22, 1967, Julijana Stamenkovic filed charges with the U.S. government demanding it investigate the murder, at my hands, of her son, Milos Milocevic. She asserted that an autopsy would show that her son's arm had been broken before he was killed (proving that he'd been in some sort of struggle with my paid agents) and that he was killed with a rifle bullet, not my .38 revolver. The feds, God bless 'em, told her, through the Yugoslavian consul general in Los Angeles, that they'd stick with the official police report. There was not a scintilla of evidence to support her assertions. I think she just made them up—something a mother in her circumstances had to do. Anything rather than accept the truth of what really happened.

After Marge and I split, Barbara's parents took charge of the kids: Kelly Ann, who was then seven, Kerry Yule, six, Kyle, five, and Kimmy Sue, only four. I saw them from time to time, but I couldn't really be a father to them. I was still hooked on barbiturates, and there didn't seem to be anything anybody could do for me. There wasn't such a thing as a Betty Ford Clinic then. If there had been, I'd have been the first one to sign in. Then, quite unconsciously, Judy Garland helped with an object lesson of her own.

I phoned Judy one day at her home in Brentwood. I'd tried to keep in touch with her, phoned her when she was down, phoned her when she was up. I was careful to avoid the mornings, unless it was shortly before dawn, when she seemed at her best. Most of the time, she wasn't doing well at all. For one thing, she had an agent named David Begelman, who not only failed to get her work but couldn't even recover her most important possession, her musical arrangements, which had been confiscated at the Hotel Pierre for nonpayment of a bill.

On this particular day, in 1967, I kept phoning Judy, but getting no answer, either at four in the morning or four in the afternoon. I had a hunch I'd better go by and see if she was all right. Brothers and sisters sometimes have that sixth sense about each other, and Judy and I were like that, brother and sister.

I phoned Dr. Buckley and asked him to meet me at Judy's place. "Something tells me Judy needs help," I said.

We both hit the place simultaneously. I was grateful for this man's friendship. Dr. Buckley is an internist who has also had considerable training in psychiatry, and because of that he enjoyed (and still enjoys) a fine reputation among his peers. In fact, during the early 1970s, my old friend Howard Hughes heard so many good things about Dr. Buckley that he persuaded the doctor to pull up stakes in Los Angeles and move his practice (and his family) to Las Vegas, where he could be close to Hughes. It was my recollection that Hughes gave Buckley twenty million reasons to make the move. But Bob says that's an exaggeration. "At the time," he says, "it seemed like twenty million." The story gets even better for its ending: despite the $20 million payoff (or whatever), Howard Hughes never saw Dr. Buckley.

When Dr. Buckley and I found the front doors locked, we crawled over a wall, but we couldn't get in the back door, either. I put a handkerchief around my hand and punched in a window-pane—just like in the movies.

We found Judy naked and unconscious, facedown on the bed. "It's okay," Dr. Buckley said, feeling her pulse. "She's not, uh, she's alive." He phoned for an ambulance, then said, "Mick, help me find out what she's on."

We searched the house. I was more experienced in hiding pills than Dr. Buckley, and after looking through the likeliest places, I came up with a cache of pills at the bottom of one of Judy's boots. "Bingo!" I cried.

Dr. Buckley took them from me, cracked one, and tasted it. "Percodan, I think," he said.

As we dressed Judy, I asked Dr. Buckley to tell me about Percodan.

"It's an upper," he said.

"Powerful?"

"I'll tell you how powerful," he said. "If you want to haul a Steinway over the Andes, you take two Percodans. Then you put the Steinway on your back and walk right on over the mountains."

I nodded, but I didn't say anything. I was already starting to pray. This view—of Judy, of myself—pushed me to utter a cry of the heart.

In answer to those prayers, maybe, Jeri Greene appeared on my doorstep. She was the ex-wife of comedian Shecky Greene and a long-standing friend, someone who wanted to help me. She made a start by consulting a mutual friend of ours, Leo Popkin, a movie producer. The two of them decided they had to find a specialist for me. I remember Jeri driving me down from my house in Coldwater Canyon early one winter morning to the corner of Wilshire and Robertson, where Leo Popkin was waiting for us, and for someone else who drove up right after we did. We waited in my car and watched in the rearview mirror while Leo and this man talked. Out in front of his car lights, their breath created visible puffs in the glare of the lights.

Finally, this man came up to my side of my car. When I rolled down the window, he said, "Do you want to get well?"

He said this with such authority that I knew he was a doctor. I said, "Yes, I do, doctor. I don't want to live like this any longer."

He didn't say another word. He just walked away.

Two days later, I was on a plane to San Francisco with Jeri. She helped me check into a hospital there under an assumed name. I was going to get well.

It wasn't easy. Doctors didn't really understand addictions as well then as they do now. They didn't have all the support groups they have today, meetings of Alcoholics Anonymous and other twelve-step programs. These doctors took a very basic, common-sense approach: "You don't want to be a drug addict? Well, then, first of all, you have to stop taking drugs." The doctors kept me in bed, made sure I was eating right, and ordered the nurses to give me back rubs. But, after that, they didn't know what to do. Then, finally, one night I found my own breakthrough. I looked to a Power higher than myself. "Father," I prayed. "Come into my life. I have sinned. I cannot make it without you. Please help! Please help!"

He did help. From that day on, I was a well man.

I didn't pass from sick to well in one day. I spent the next ten years or so working my way from sick to *really* well. But that prayer marked a turning point for me.

Having helped myself, I thought I might be able to help Judy. She was sinking deeper and deeper into the hell that only serious drug abusers ever know. I called her and asked if she had some time to see an old friend.

We went out for a drive in my new Cadillac convertible, so we could talk without anybody else around. I had a destination in mind, but I didn't want to tell Judy what it was. I had to prepare her first. We drove out Sunset, all the way to the beach, then north on Pacific Coast Highway, almost to Oxnard, then doubled back toward Santa Monica.

I spent a good deal of the trip telling her about Dr. Buckley and about how he had helped me get her to the hospital not many months before. I think I also told her that, as a member of the staff of St. John's, he had also tried to help Montgomery Clift and James Dean. (Why I thought that was a recommendation, I don't know. Both Clift and Dean ended up their great, truncated careers in self-destruction.)

When we parked in front of Dr. Buckley's office in Santa Monica, Judy didn't resist going in with me "just to say hello." We said hello. Judy seemed to like him. In fact, she warmed up to him rather quickly. When she started to get down to the specifics of her problem, I excused myself; this was between Judy and the wonderful doctor. She emerged a half hour later, looking a little dazed but smiling bravely.

In the car, on the way home, Judy told me she liked Buckley, but she was puzzled by the doctor's probing into her recent suicide attempt. She said, "He didn't quite buy my story that I was really serious about doing myself in."

"What, Judy? What didn't he believe?"

"Well," she said, "he asked why I'd slashed my wrists. I didn't exactly understand. He said, 'I mean, you could have slashed your ankles just as well.'"

Judy told the doctor she couldn't have done that.

"And why not?" he asked.

"Because," she told him, "I'm a dancer."

Judy looked at me and giggled. "I think he's a pretty wise doctor," she said.

I nodded. "He's got your number."

"Uh-huh," she said, and then, after quite a long pause, "I don't think I want to die. It's just that no one will listen to me. I'm hurting, Mick, and no one will pay any attention."

"I'll listen, Judy," I said. "I'll pay attention."

But I didn't. I wanted to, but I didn't know how. Once I got her home, I was back out in my convertible in no time flat, racing back down Sunset with the wind blowing in my hair.

☆ *34* ☆
More Judy

Poor *Judy. I* had to call her to see if she'd consider working with me on one of my latest dreams—the Mickey and Judy Schools of Musical Comedy. I wanted to start a chain of such schools around the nation to provide training for thousands of youngsters who had talent. I figured Judy and I could help them do that, maybe help open some doors for the best of them.

This must have been 1968, just after I'd finished making a picture called *The Comic,* about the success, downfall, and old age of a silent-film star, obviously based on the life of Buster Keaton. The film wasn't a commercial success, but I was happy with my work and I just knew it would lead to other things.

Anyway, I phoned around and finally found out where Judy was staying. She was in New York, living in a Park Avenue apartment with Johnny Meyer, a songwriter. But when I found Meyer, he told me she was in a hospital, the Leroy on 61st Street. He told me it was nothing serious. She'd only injured her foot.

I found her at the Leroy and asked her what was wrong.

Judy never gave anyone a straight answer when she could think of a crooked one. "I've got leprosy," she said.

I told her she was going into partnership with me in a chain of acting schools. "But we need you out here, so I'm gonna arrange everything, transportation, a place to stay if you need one." I even mentioned my hospital in San Francisco, where they were making some progress in treating people with pill problems. "You don't have to worry about the bills. I'm taking care of everything."

She tried to interrupt me, but when I am spouting off, it's not easy to stop me.

"Because this beautiful idea is going to change your life, Judy. I don't have to tell you, you probably heard, but I've been asleep for the past six months, just wouldn't come out of the house, wouldn't get out of bed, just wouldn't face things, Judy. But it's all changed now. You and I have to open a school. We're going to be together again, just like in the old days, hoofin' it side by side, all across the country."

I told her I'd be sending her a ticket in tomorrow's mail, all I needed was her address. She said she wanted a couple of days to think about it.

Clearly she didn't buy my idea because it was weeks before I heard from her. She called me at my hotel on Long Island where I was doing summer stock, playing George M. Cohan in *George M.* It was about three in the morning and the operator said she was reluctant to disturb me, but she thought it was Judy Garland on the line. "It really does sound like her," said the operator.

I was not wild about being awakened at three A.M., but, for Judy, anything. "Put her on," I said.

"Hi, darlin'," said the voice. It *was* Judy, and she was *up*. "I just wanted to hear your voice."

"Judy," I said, "you all right?"

"Ummm," she said. "Yeah. I'm with friends in Boston. Hey, I had a hell of a time trying to find you."

"Anytime, Judy. You call, and I'll be here for you. It's always been that way. You remember when we arrived in Grand Central and fourteen thousand people were there waiting to see us and I did the blocking for you and away we'd go—"

"Ummm, Mick, it isn't that way anymore. We were the toast of the town then. Now I can't get *arrested.*" She started telling me about her current troubles. The Hotel Pierre was holding all her arrangements, even a lot of her clothes, too, because she had this outstanding *bill.* And she couldn't work because she didn't have her arrangements. And, because she couldn't work, she couldn't pay her bill at the Pierre. And, even if she did work, the boys from the IRS would be there to take her money.

I made a snap judgment. If she was calling me at three A.M., she was in real trouble. She had to know that, at this time in my life, I wasn't the toast of New York either. I wanted to do something for her, right away. "Judy," I said. "I want you to stop singing for a couple of years. You need money? I'll get you money. We'll make it, together." For a moment there, I was using the same words, the same energy I'd used in *Babes in Arms:* "*Say, that's not a bad idea. We can put on our own show. That'd be different. First of all, we're gonna use a barn.*"

But I wasn't acting now. I was serious. "I just want you to get off whatever you're on, Judy. I just want you to be well, my angel. I know you can make it."

She didn't say anything. I waited, six or seven seconds, a long time for me to wait for anything. Finally, I heard this very small voice, not her acting voice but the voice of the real Judy, and it was rising up from her well of despair. She said, "Mick, do you—really—think—I can—make it?"

That broke my heart. Obviously, she had serious doubts that she could. She'd tried to pick herself up off the canvas, had done so, and fallen back again and again and again. Something told me that she didn't have the strength to do it anymore, not on her own.

I said, "I know you can make it, Judy. We'll both make it— with God's help." At that, she was silent. I'd never mentioned

God to Judy before, and I think she was puzzled that I was doing so now. It is a mystery to me why I got the gift of faith and Judy didn't. But I couldn't get too ecclesiastical with her now. I went on: "Judy, I'm going to get Ray Pearson—you remember my friend Ray Pearson, the fullback from UCLA?—I'm going to have Ray Pearson fly out to Boston and get you and bring you back to California. You can live with me and I'll work for us both."

She said, still in that thin, small voice, "Ray Pearson? Yeah, I remember him. Redhead? Okay, Mickey. Okay."

By the time Ray arrived in Boston, Judy was gone. Three days later, I read that she had married Mickey Deans, the manager of Arthur's, a fashionable discotheque in Manhattan and that they had jetted off to London, where Judy had an engagement to play the Palladium. God, wasn't that the story of her life? Judy always had a lot of takers around her and few givers. "Are you still alive, Judy? Are you still breathing, Judy? Just sign this contract. Now sing."

And now, too sick to work, she was working anyway—in London. And London was a disaster for her. I read in the papers that the crowds in the Palladium, angry at Judy for keeping them waiting, started pelting her with tomatoes and celery. Poor Judy.

Months passed with no word from Judy. Then, one morning, I was playing golf at the Downingtown Inn in Pennsylvania, just holing out on the sixth green, when I saw a golf cart with a single passenger in it, heading for us. I had a feeling it was a piece of bad news. It was.

"Mr. Rooney?"

"Yes?"

"Mr. Rooney, Miss Garland has died. We just heard it on the radio."

I felt a sudden chill, deep in my bones. Then I walked over to the edge of the green, dropped to my knees, and pounded the ground with my fist. "Why, Judy? Why?" I hit the ground as hard as I could, maybe thirty or forty times, with my right hand. Then I did the same thing with my left hand. What the hell? My heart was broken. Why not my hands, too?

I drove to New York City for her funeral. Her kids thought about asking me to give the eulogy, but they guessed, quite correctly, that I couldn't handle it. I spent only a few minutes in back of the chapel at Campbell's Funeral Home, then ducked out. I didn't want to look at Judy, to see her like that. To me, Judy was still alive. She's still alive to thousands, maybe millions, of others, too, I know. I have no monopoly on Judy. Others who knew her as well as I still love her. Sid Luft, her husband and my friend, loved her. I wish he'd loved her enough to get her into a good hospital. Liza Minnelli and Lorna Luft, her daughters, and Joey Luft, her son, loved her, but they couldn't help her either.

Ahhh, well, I thought. Judy's not in pain anymore. But I was still sad about her leaving. There will never be another talent like Judy Garland's, never anyone who could sing with such heart. Other singers sing the words. Judy never lost the thought behind the words, never lost the poetry.

Judy turned to drugs because she was in pain and because the drugs made her feel good (or at least a little better) for a time. As one of the MGM kids, of course, she'd been treated for most of her life to magical, instant, solutions to everything. Did Judy have a pimple? A studio magician would make it vanish. Were her breasts too big or too small? The magician would flatten them or pump them up. She never had a normal adolescence, where kids learn to cope with life's problems, test their equipment, learn what works and what doesn't. Cast loose from MGM, she bobbed up and down on stormy seas, never quite sure how to stay afloat. She could never accept herself, so she was always on the run, trying to escape, always turning away from an acceptance of her individuality.

She'd always idolized her own charming father—only to learn, after she'd grown up, that he was a homosexual. She couldn't accept that in him. And then, she had an even harder time accepting a trace of that in herself. She had an affair with a female singer and, caught up in guilt, couldn't accept herself. So she tried to lose herself in a never-never land where reality faded and her dreams drifted, just out of reach.

I still think I could have helped Judy, but she kept dodging me. I guess she felt guilty about her addiction. She should have known that being hooked on barbiturates didn't mean a damn thing to me: after all, I had been there. I understood what she was feeling. So, in fact, did many of her fans. They, too, would have understood. And they would have been far more loving with her than she was to herself.

☆ 35 ☆
Three Goats, a Blanket, and Me

I *have to* consult film indexes to remember the movies I did in the late 1960s and early 1970s: *Skidoo*, which was directed by Otto Preminger; *The Comic*, directed by Carl Reiner; *The Extraordinary Seaman*, with Faye Dunaway and David Niven and directed by John Frankenheimer; and a soft-porn documentary about Hollywood called *Hollywood Blue*.

I wasn't happy with my film work. No actor, no matter how good he is, transcends crap, and that's what I was reduced to accepting. I was so ashamed of myself for my little part in *Hollywood Blue* (I supplied the voice-over) that I got the hell out of town, for good. I moved to Florida, determined I would have nothing more to do with Hollywood, but not before I met and married my seventh wife. Seven is supposed to be lucky, and with Carolyn Hockett I thought I was. She wasn't in show business, and she had no show-business ambitions. I met her in Miami when I'd accepted an invitation to play in a celebrity golf tournament down there, and she had a job in customer relations with *The Miami Herald*. A friend in the sports department introduced me to her.

She was a very pretty blonde, who bore a mighty resemblance

to Barbara, and, like Barbara, she was a lot younger than I. She was very intelligent, as I learned when we met over a glass of wine. She was, moreover, a Catholic, and I am sure the thought crossed my mind: if she's a Catholic, she probably doesn't believe in divorce. "Well," she said, "I *don't* believe in divorce. But I had one myself. I have a son, Jimmy. He's only three."

I told Carolyn and Jimmy about Barbara, and about my four babies, now living with Barbara's folks in Inglewood. If we got married, what would Carolyn think about my trying to get custody of Kelly, Kerry, Kyle, and Kimmy Sue? I showed her their pictures. She didn't even gulp. She loved kids.

Even up close, she loved them. I took Carolyn and Jimmy back to LA with me, and everyone got along famously. "Look, Carolyn, we both love God, and we both love each other. Let's have children. Let's get married." She said yes. I chartered a plane to Las Vegas for the wedding and braced myself for the newspaper stories about this half-pint actor who was setting new records in the marriage game.

I did shtick for the reporters. I told them I was like a welterweight who'd had too many bouts: "My heart has been broken so many times, it has cauliflower valves." I told them I had a marriage license that I kept with me at all times. It was made out to "To Whom It May Concern." I told them I was going to march in the Rose Bowl Parade in Pasadena come New Year's: "Mickey Rooney and His All-Wife Marching Band." I told them that when I said to the minister at the wedding chapel, "I do, I do," he said, "I know, I know."

I foundered around for some months, without work. Without work. It's the worst thing anybody can say about an actor in Hollywood.

"Shoot," I told Carolyn, "I'm washed up for good now. Let's get out of this town."

She hadn't married me because of my show-business connections anyway. "Heck, yes," she said. "Let's go to Florida." So we moved to Fort Lauderdale and bought a little house on Forty-fifth Street, right across the street from the Coral Ridge Country Club. I don't know how we qualified for a mortgage. I think the banker remembered Andy Hardy and figured that with a judge for a father, I was worth the risk.

We moved in without a stick of furniture, just our clothes. I can remember the three of us, Carolyn, Jimmy, and I, sitting on the carpeted floor about seven o'clock one evening. Carolyn said, "Honey, what do you think we're going to do now?"

I said, "Don't worry, Carolyn, God will take care of us."

He did, but He took his time about it. It was touch-and-go for quite a while. For a time I made appearances at cocktail parties in Florida for five hundred dollars a pop, pretending to be an old friend of the host, circulating around for an hour, pretending to smile, pretending, in fact, to be Mickey Rooney.

Word about my plight must have drifted down to Miami, where my old friend Eddie Bracken was a principal in something called the Coconut Grove Theater. One night, Bracken, who had made *A Slight Case of Larceny* with me in 1953, came knocking on our door in Fort Lauderdale. He wanted to introduce me to his partner. They wondered if I'd be interested in doing a play down there called *Three Goats and a Blanket.*

"We can't pay you what you're worth, Mick," said Bracken, "but we'd love for you to do it. It's going to start in about ten days, and we'd like to go into rehearsal in the next two or three days. Would you read this play?"

I wanted to kiss him on the lips. I didn't have so much as one hundred dollars in my pocket. I said, "Certainly, I'll read it."

I liked it. The authors, Woody Kling and Robert J. Hilliard, might well have written it with me in mind. It was a comedy about alimony, a modern spin on the ancient legal custom of awarding a wife who was no longer wanted "three goats and a blanket." Ex-wives got more demanding, however, explained one of the characters in the play. "And now look what's happened! Alimony is a big business! It's bigger than the A and

P! Bigger than the Mafia! It's the fastest-growing business in America!"

They wanted me to play the lead, a TV producer in New York who is out of work and stuck with paying five hundred dollars a week alimony while living on twenty-eight dollars a week himself. His beautiful, if somewhat flighty, ex-wife, rather than help him out by taking a penny less than five hundred dollars, invites him to sleep on a cot in her living room until he can sell another show to the network. He hates the idea, mainly because he cannot bring himself to tell his even-more-beautiful girl-friend that he is living in his ex-wife's apartment. That leads to a number of farcical situations involving his ex-wife, his attor-ney, a local cop, and, of course, his girlfriend.

Bracken and I ended up playing *Three Goats and a Blanket* all over the country, mostly in dinner theaters. It was my meal ticket for more than a decade, and Bracken's too, when he had time to accept a booking with me.

In 1972, Carolyn and I went back to LA and asked the court to give me custody of my kids. There was some considerable advance publicity on that, and quite a crowd in the Santa Monica superior courtroom was gathered when Carolyn and I arrived with our attorney, Robert Neeb, and some witnesses who could testify to my worth as a parent.

Each of us made a case. The Thomasons said I was an unfit parent and that the children would do better living with them. I didn't think I was an unfit parent and told the judge I wanted the kids.

The judge reminded me that I'd been in LA on four separate occasions in 1971. "Why didn't you even phone the kids?"

"Because, Your Honor, at the time, I was dying. I was dying. But now I am alive and I want my children. I love my children."

Carolyn was on the stand for two days, telling the judge that she loved them, too, and could care for them. "I am the eldest of six children, Your Honor," she said.

But His Honor ended up giving custody to the Thomasons. He said he thought the kids would do better with their grandparents. In truth, the kids did very well with the Thomasons. They grew up in Palos Verdes, a posh suburb right on the Pacific Ocean, and they turned out very well.

Kelly Ann is now happily married, with a cute little daughter named Lacy, now six. Kerry Yule is also married and the mother of twins. Kyle is a professional dancer, dance instructor, and choreographer in Hollywood. And Kimmy Sue, who works as a dental assistant, was married two years ago to a fine young man, a master mechanic. We are all a lot closer now than we were during the 1970s. I talk to them on the phone a lot. They seem to have forgiven me. For everything.

Carolyn and I lost the court battle, but we got a consolation prize. On January 11, 1970, I was with Carolyn when she gave birth to our daughter, Jonell. My last-born was like an angel to me, all pink and white. Maybe it was just a proud father's imagination, but I think she smiled at me when I first tickled her under the chin and kissed her good night.

It was Ruth Webb, I later learned, who had told Eddie Bracken that I might be available to do *Three Goats*. Ruth was a Hollywood talent agent who was not too greedy to work hard for a has-been who was hardly commanding big dollars in the movie business. She settled for less because she knew that I was willing to settle for less.

So Ruth, a former actress herself, tall and beautiful, continued to get me work, mostly doing *Three Goats* at every dinner theater in the land. I thanked God for Ruth, and I thanked Him, too, for all the theater managers who kept asking me back. The fact is, my name still had drawing power. Why? People knew me, and they wanted to see more of me. Someone did a poll in the mid-1970s showing respondents pictures of people appearing on the covers of a new magazine called *People* to see who were the most recognizable faces in the land. I came in number three behind President Richard Nixon and Muhammad Ali.

But my celebrity didn't make me rich. It didn't even make me well off. I began to think that it never would. What I had to do, I thought, was start using my fertile imagination on a series of business schemes, invest my modest earnings in them, get others to invest in them if I could, and then relax in my new affluence. I was inspired by Joel McCrea, who invested in ranch land, and Joan Crawford, who took a big stock position in Pepsi Cola.

Over the years I've come up with dozens of moneymaking schemes. I remember inventing something called Rip Offs, disposable shorts and panties for men and women who traveled and couldn't be bothered doing laundry. I also invented disposable bras and called them, naturally, Tip Offs. The people at Fruit of the Loom, who have made millions on cotton underwear, seemed quite interested at first, but the idea people frowned on it. It wasn't their idea.

I went to see the Ralston Purina people and told them they were missing an opportunity to serve pet owners by producing some pet drinks. "You make great dog and cat food," I said, "but you don't market anything for our pets to drink. You could make a lot of money with doggie drink, puppy pop, kitty cola. I'm not suggesting anything with sugar in it—that wouldn't be good for them. I mean some drinks that contain vitamins and minerals that would help make better coats, give them stronger teeth."

"Oh," they said. "We tried that. It didn't work."

I paid a visit to the Franklin Mint, the company that makes commemorative coins. I asked them, "Why don't you mint coins with Mickey Rooney's face on them—with Clark Gable's, Spencer Tracy's, Jimmy Cagney's and—"

"Hey," they said, "we did it. It didn't work."

I doubted that.

One of my ideas did bring forth fruit, but not for me. When I was living in Florida, broke as hell, I phoned Jack Haley, Jr., then sitting in the president's chair at MGM. (This was when they were playing musical presidents. They had Kirk Kerkorian for a while, then James Aubrey, then Haley.) I'd been trying to do a Mickey Rooney documentary, something that would start out with me on the Brooklyn Bridge, where I began, and end up on the lot at MGM. We wanted to do a kind of Mickey Rooney travelogue, for TV. I told him, "I'd be strolling along, see? And then I'd say, 'This is Stage Twenty-seven. Listen, can you hear the music? That's Judy and me in there. We're doing a movie called *Girl Crazy.*' Then the viewers would see a few bits of footage from *Girl Crazy.* Then I'd walk down the street to another stage and say, 'Gee, I can hear Busby Berkeley saying, "Roll 'em now." ' And we'd see some footage from *Babes in Arms.* And I'd move on down the street and say, 'I can still see George Seitz in here. He was my director on most of the Andy Hardy movies.' And we'd see a clip from *Love Finds Andy Hardy.* Then I'd move on, stop in front of another stage, reminisce about Wally Beery, and show a few feet of film from *Stablemates.* "

"No."

"What?" I said.

"No."

"Hey, Jack Junior, I only want a few feet of film. I'll be glad to pay you for it."

"No," he said, "we can't sell you any footage of your pictures, and we can't give you any footage of your pictures." Jack Jr. wasn't very friendly.

I hung up on him, angry as hell because he couldn't or wouldn't give me three or four feet of an old film. I'd helped MGM gross $2 billion dollars and he couldn't even let me borrow a few clips?

Four months later, I got a phone call from MGM. It was Mr. Haley's secretary. Could I take a call from Mr. Haley? I could. Seems he wanted to do a picture called *That's Entertainment*— clips from some of the great MGM musicals of the past, and he wanted me to do some of the voice-over.

"Hey," I said to him. "Great idea. Where'd you get it?"

"If you do this for us," Haley said, ignoring my question, "we'll pay you well. And I'll give you some of your films, too. You can do whatever you want with them."

So I got a round-trip ticket from Fort Lauderdale to LA and I spent a day on *That's Entertainment*. The movie came out in 1974, and it grossed millions for a studio that was then making more money on its hotel-casinos in Las Vegas and Reno than it was on its movies. I got $385, the minimum Screen Actors Guild wage for a day's work. No film.

I had other ideas. I invented a new golf club and an indoor golf course on Astroturf, open twenty-four hours. You hit a Wiffle Ball off the tee and a regular golf ball on the green. I wanted to franchise the idea, set up a chain of indoor facilities called Mickey Rooney's Two Ball Golf. But I couldn't get the financing.

To try and raise my own financing, I took a flyer in oil. Wildcat drilling—the riskiest end of the "awl bidness," as they say in Texas—didn't give me much of a yield. Reports from my partners in Throckmorton County were always full of hope, though. They cheered when their salty mud turned to "good, freshwater mud."

I started up a company called Lovely Lady Cosmetics and developed a women's cologne called Me. My slogan: "Put Me Next to Him." Or an essence called Trapeze. Slogan: "There's Danger in Every Drop." I also thought up some poetic perfumes: Midsummer Night's Dream, Taming the Shrew, Twelfth Night. I don't mind sharing the ideas with you now. Go ahead, steal 'em. (In fact, somebody already stole Me. Just the other day, I saw it on sale at a perfume counter in Marshall Field's in Chicago.)

I put hair in an aerosol can. It wasn't hair, but it looked like hair. I called it Complete, for the Man Who Wants to Be. It was something like cotton candy. You just sprayed it on your bald top and it stuck there till you washed it off. Or until you were caught out in the rain.

I set up Elim, a pharmaceutical company. I invented Elim-N-Ache, for headaches, Elim-N-Ate, a laxative, Elim-A-Weight, for dieting; and Elim-N-Itch, a foot powder.

I invented a round hot dog with a hole in the middle that you could put on a hamburger bun. I called it a Weenie Whirl and set up a Mickey Rooney's Weenie World franchise deal, with my first two stores in New Jersey and Long Island. The Weenie Whirls had mustard in the middle of the O. And I had variations, different stuff to put in the middle of the dog: cheese (called a Yankee Doodle), relish (a Micklish), sauerkraut (an Eric von Weenie), chili (a Pancho Weenie), onions (a Marco Weenie), and raisins and pineapple (a Surfboard Weenie).

The Canfields of Chicago developed my idea for a new, melon-flavored soft drink called Mickey Melon. I developed a Sambuca-flavored drink called Thirst. Slogan: "Thirst Come, Thirst Served." And a carbonated tea (before Lipton ever thought of it) called Thirst-T. I think I have a knack for writing slogans. I wrote Anheuser-Busch and suggested "Be Beer Wiser, Bud. Drink Budweiser." You've heard that one. You haven't? Oh.

Somebody once suggested that I'd missed my calling. "You should have gone to work on Madison Avenue," he said. "Become an advertising executive."

"Naw," I said.

"Why not?"

"Because I don't drink martinis. And I don't take eleven months to come up with an ad campaign."

If I'd been at all smart investment-wise (as they say on Madison Avenue), I would have invested, early on, in Santa Anita stock. I had a chance to do it in 1940, to buy five shares at $5,000 a share. Mom said no. Too bad. Those five shares would be worth $3,050,000 today.

But when I had a chance to buy some of Santa Anita in 1980, I jumped at it. Now I own maybe a million dollars' worth of stock in Santa Anita.

No, the snack bars at Santa Anita don't carry Weenie Whirls. Not yet. But I'm going to phone Bob Strub, the CEO at Santa Anita, and see if he might want to introduce them at our track.

I have to try.

My get-rich-quick schemes were hard on Carolyn. Eventually, I think, she got more and more anxious about our future. In real life, I was playing the part of Micawber in *David Copperfield*, who always kept telling his family that "something will turn up." In Dickens's novel, something did turn up for Micawber at the end. He took his family to Australia and made more than a go of it.

But Carolyn didn't feel like playing a part in a Dickens novel. I was traipsing around the country as a king—"King of the Dinner Theaters," that is—and Carolyn remained a commoner, mired down and doing the dishes back in Fort Lauderdale.

Still and all, I thought we had a pretty good marriage. I loved Carolyn and thought she was the best wife I ever had. She was a great mother, too. I was loyal to Carolyn—having finally learned to control my libido.

Then, one day in 1974, Carolyn picked me up at the airport in Fort Lauderdale, kissed me hello, and said she'd found a new home for us. Would I mind if we stopped by the lawyer's office to sign some papers?

"Well, no," I said. "I didn't know we were that close to finding the new home we wanted. But if you've found a nice place . . . ."

We pulled into a shopping center, got out of the car, and went up to the office of this lawyer, who said, "You Mr. Rooney?" I said I was. Then he served me with divorce papers, already signed by Carolyn.

She didn't want to discuss it. She was just through, and that was that.

I'm still friends with Carolyn, still send money to help her and the kids. Only recently have I learned why she called it quits. She couldn't stand the insecurity of living with me. I was always surrounded with hangers-on and deal makers, who kept cutting off such big chunks of my earnings that she never had enough money to run the household. I never seemed to wise up or grow up. Financially, I was (and still am) an infant, letting others run my life. It was no surprise that I later turned to a whole succession of agents, business managers, and deal makers who robbed me in ways that were both legal and illegal. Sometimes, an agent who is also a lawyer can be the worst. In 1971, one of my agents (who was also a lawyer) went to jail for embezzling ten thousand dollars on a contract, but he was a piker compared to others supposedly working for me who have not gone to jail.

I have never cared for lawyers. I guess they are a necessary evil. If you need a lawyer, my advice is hunt around, ask about him, make a rational choice. You'll find a good one, I'm sure. Then, hire another lawyer to watch him.

When Carolyn had seen me about to sign yet another dubious deal, she begged me not to. I got my back up and told her, "I'm gonna sign it. If you don't like it, you can get out." I didn't really mean that. I explode like that all the time, and those around me know I am just letting off steam. But Carolyn was only twenty-three. She took me literally. Soon she was talking to a divorce lawyer—and no longer to me.

At the lawyer's office, I pleaded with her. "Why, Carolyn, why?" She just shook her head no and drove us both home. I stumbled into the house, gave the children a teary kiss, and lay down on our king-sized bed. Jeez, I said to myself, what do I do now?

☆ *36* ☆
Ruth Webb,
Super-Agent

L*ike a* punch-drunk fighter who keeps coming out for the next bell no matter how battered he is, I was off two days later for a week's run in Houston of *Three Goats and a Blanket*, which we had changed to *The Laugh's on Me*. But I was in a daze, delivering my lines like a robot, and I kept asking myself, "What's wrong with you, Rooney? What's wrong with you, Rooney?"

Rather than run toward life, I ran away. I tried to escape, again, into drugs. This time, it was Quaaludes, fashionable new little pills that could put you on a mountain peak, then drop you just as quickly to the desert floor.

Thanks to Quaaludes, I collapsed on the stage right in the middle of a performance in the spring of 1974. I'd never done that before. I go on, no matter what. I have appeared on stage with a temperature of 104. I have gone on with bad wheels (show-biz parlance for legs almost too weak to stand on). Once, in Chicago at the Arie Crown Theater to do *Three Goats*, I ate stewed prunes late one morning before a matinee and ended up walking right off the stage five minutes into the first act, tossing off a line that gave me a hint of an excuse to leave: "I have to go, uh, to, the phone," filling my drawers as I hustled offstage, to the puzzlement of the fifteen hundred people sitting there.

The actor and the actress left onstage did their best to stall the audience. "Where's he going?" said the actor who was playing the cop.

"Oh," said the actress who was playing my ex-wife, "he has several places to go."

"Does he, uh, always leave like this?"

"Oh, not usually. But then—he usually does."

"He left, like, he was, uh, going someplace."

"Well, when he leaves me, he usually does go—somewhere. Uh, why don't you sit down?"

"Thank you. After walking the beat, it does feel good to sit down."

Believe it or not, they went on like that for ten minutes until I reappeared, after a quick shower and a change of drawers, a little breathless but ready to take it from where we left off.

In Houston, I was lucky I didn't die. I was a basket case. They put me in the hospital and phoned Mickey, Jr., Timmy, and Ruth Webb to give them the bad news. They all rushed to my side. Later, Ruth told me what a state I'd been in. For the first couple of days, I couldn't even talk, and then, when I could, I babbled on deliriously. Ruth stayed right beside me for ten days, sleeping in a twin bed right next to mine, while I suffered all the hallucinations of the damned. I saw bugs and bats and spiders. I saw stars and suns and moons. I heard weird music and the cries of ghosts and banshees. I walked right up the sides of the walls that surrounded me.

All this time, Ruth was nursing me, rubbing my back, bathing me, saying she loved me—like a sister, of course. Finally, she said she had to get back home, but added, on the way out the door, *"Mi casa es su casa"*: "My house is your house."

I took her literally. Five days later I showed up at her home in the Hollywood Hills with my road manager, Jack Krieg, a wonderful, dapper guy with a goatee whom I had met on a golf course in Cleveland a couple years back. "Hey, Ruth," I said, "I'm ready to put my life back together. I've got some great ideas for a show."

Ruth already had a houseful of people and assorted other critters: Jamie, her live-in lover, her son, Mike, her ninety-six-year-old mother (who was a painter), an actor named Dean Dittman, two live raccoons (who lived in a wire cage just outside the library window), an alley cat named K, a mutt named Tippie, and a big, scarlet macaw named Sidney.

I think Ruth guessed that I had had a little talk with God, told Him that I'd slipped—again—but that I didn't want to slip anymore. Maybe that's why she kept her promise. I made her house my house. I slept on the living-room sofa, not far from the babbling fountain in the foyer, and Jack slept on the floor. I took over Ruth's desk and her telephone, and Ruth transferred her activities to her dining-room table.

I enjoyed all the action around Ruth's home—she had a lot of parties and people around all the time I could talk to, including some of her other clients: Martha Ray, Virginia Mayo, Joan Fontaine, Shelley Berman, Peter Lupus, Ann Miller, Mamie Van Doren, Gene Barry, Judy Carne, John Carradine, Jaye P. Morgan, Richard Egan, and Donald O'Connor.

When there weren't any people around, I could always talk to Sidney the parrot. I remember coming home from a golf game late one afternoon to find Ruth and her ménage and a few early arrivals in the throes of preparing for a party. Finding an audience, I proceeded to outline a new idea of mine—maybe it was my spray-on hair or maybe it was Weenie Whirls, I can't really remember. I had five people in a circle around me. They were fascinated by my idea at first, but then as I went on with my spiel, they gradually drifted away, one by one, until no one was left—except the scarlet macaw. That didn't bother me. For ten more minutes I went on to explain to Sidney how we were going to syndicate the idea.

Agents should all take lessons from Ruth Webb. She always

gave more than even I expected, even introduced me to a Christian Science healer, who helped me. I have been doing my Christian Science "lessons" every week ever since. I am a member of Christian Science—in my heart.

I also tithe to Dr. Frederick K. C. Price's Crenshaw Christian Center in Los Angeles. Dr. Price is only one of a large group of televangelists I watch and admire: Robert Schuller, Oral and Richard Roberts, Pat Robertson, Gloria and Kenneth Copeland, Kenneth Hagen, Jan and Paul Crouch, and Jerry Falwell.

And, yes, I even admire Jimmy Swaggart and Jim and Tammy Bakker. God brought these evangelists along to help explain His Good News. Insofar as they do that, insofar as they help people, I supported them, and do support them. When they slip and fall, I, who have slipped and fallen many times myself, feel bad for them. But I also believe they can come back. I mistrust preachers who love humanity but know nothing about people. I prefer teachers who understand how human beings can fail because they have fallen themselves.

Am I a fundamentalist, then? Please do not try to pigeonhole me in a neat category. I am also a spiritual member of various Catholic and Jewish congregations around the country. I am the universal believer, believing in an all-loving God who wants us close to Him, no matter how wandering the route we take to get there. I don't think it really matters to God.

God made man (and all there is in this world) to be. That's all. To be. We're the ones who make life difficult for ourselves by thinking that God wants us to be this or that—a great pianist or a great pitcher, a great dancer or a great race-car driver, or a straight-A student or the world's greatest grandmother. In God's sight, it's good enough for us to just be. Most of us, however, don't know that. We strive to be more. Striving is what makes us such interesting creatures. Striving is what makes stories. Striving is what makes history.

And Ruth Webb was a real striver. In fact, she turned into something of a dynamo, an energy source that pumped away day and night on my behalf. She sent forth streams of notes to casting directors in New York and Hollywood. She booked me on *Hollywood Squares*. She persuaded Merv Griffin to put me on his talk show, again and again. She made it impossible for people to forget me.

"Hey," they'd say, "there's Rooney, working again." Ruth started turning out a periodic newsletter, gossiping about all of her clients, that she sent to every producer in the land. She always led with news about Mickey Rooney. For eight straight years, on September 23, she bought space on the electronic billboard in Times Square to wish me a happy birthday.

Soon, I was getting some modest movie offers. In 1975, I did *Find the Lady* for John Trent and *Bon Baisers de Hong Kong* (sometimes called *From Hong Kong with Love*), a kind of spoof on James Bond, for Yvan Chiffre. Neither of these pictures raised my stock very high, but they and Ruth's PR kept me in the public eye. So I wasn't too surprised to get a phone call one day from Stanley Kramer, who wanted me to play in a prison picture, *The Domino Principle*, with Gene Hackman.

Then the people at Disney took a fancy to me. I did *Rachel's Man* for them in late 1976, *Pete's Dragon* in 1977, and *The Magic of Lassie* in 1978. Then Francis Ford Coppola got on the horn to tell me he'd purchased the rights to a children's classic called *The Black Stallion*. He had a part in it for me, a former jockey called out of retirement by a little boy with a beautiful black Arabian horse and a dream about winning a race. Did I think I could play a former jockey?

"Gee," I said, "I don't know. I never played a jockey before."

The call from Coppola, one of the finest filmmakers in the land, rejuvenated me, so it was time for another wedding. (There *was* a time when I wasn't married. I forget when. Fifteen or twenty minutes, I think, in 1968. Marriage was my M.O., as Jack Webb used to say in *Dragnet*.)

This time, the lady in question was Jan Chamberlin, a country and western singer who had come over to visit Ruth Webb when I was still a camper-in-residence. Jan had not been dating Mickey Rooney, Jr., at the time (as some believe). My son just liked her singing, and he wanted me to meet her. She was a little reluctant to meet me, but then, one day, she and Mickey, Jr., dropped by. Ruth wasn't home, but I was. I invited them in, and, wouldn't you know it, I was thoroughly charmed by Jan. (She looked like Barbara and Carolyn: very attractive, very blond, very warm.)

So Jan and I became an item. I moved in with her and her two boys, Chris and Mark Aber, then about nine and ten. Ten months later, I asked her if she'd go along with me to Hong Kong. She was hesitant. She wasn't sure she wanted to go public with our relationship.

"Sure," I said, "I know I'm a high-risk guy. But I'm not talking marriage. You can walk, anytime you want." Jan left her two boys with her sister, Ronna, and we were off—via Paris—to the Orient. Jack Krieg, my agent, went along to referee. Yes, ever since I started going with Jan, it's been one big, joyous fight. The reason we don't part: the fight isn't over yet. What do we fight about? Whatever. Jan was upset early in 1991 when one of the supermarket tabloids printed some lies and filth about my making a pass at another woman, but no tabloid can ever break the bonds between me and Jan, who is my holiday kid. We wrote a song together, pressed a record called "My Holiday Kid."

> *You holiday kid.*
> *You're my holiday kid.*
> *Didn't we live more?*
> *Didn't we give more?*
> *Than anyone did?*
> *You're my holiday kid.*

When we returned home, Jan found the home she was renting had been sold out from under her. So I bought a place for us in

Sherman Oaks, then, later, another one in a development called Red Sail, an island home in Westlake Village, out in the Conejo Valley, about thirty miles northwest of Hollywood.

Finally, Jan and I were married on July 28, 1978, in the Conejo Valley Church of Religious Science. I was fifty-seven, she was thirty-nine. This time, I told myself, it's for keeps.

In many ways, I haven't changed a bit. I am still the same self-absorbed guy I was when I married Ava. I like to do what I want, when I want, where I want, without much thought for the wants of others. The people around me fare best when they do not challenge me. But Jan challenged me then and she's still doing it, fifteen years later. The challenge is good for me.

Jan's my life, my world, my friend. She has her faults. (I, of course, am perfect.) Sometimes I mistreat her. She mistreats me, too. Jan spends too much money, but so do I. We have come to the point where we try to work things out, day by day.

When I am not working, I spend my time as many of you do, watching television, particularly television sports. I still play the ponies, and I have my own small stable of thoroughbreds because I not only like to bet on horses, I like to think I am also helping improve the breed. It's a delusion, I know, but a relatively harmless one. And I still love going to the track, where I thrill to the sights (the green of the infield, the varied hues of the ladies' hats, the jockeys in their silks), the smells (fine cigars and cheap peanuts), and the sounds, particularly the sounds: the trill of the trumpet before the horses come out for their parade around the track, the buzz of the crowd getting louder as post time nears, and the rasping voice of the trackman shouting, "And they're off!" Then the throaty roar from the grandstand as the thoroughbreds careen around the final turn and race up the stretch, and the sudden silence just before the man in the booth intones, "Results of the eighth race are . . . official."

Going to the track? There is nothing like being there.

I still play a lot of golf. But I am glad I wasn't out on the links in the early spring of 1979 when a fateful phone call came in from some people in the East who wanted me to make my first attempt on Broadway.

"Oh, Mickey," cried Jan. "You've got to do it."

"No," I growled. "I don't gotta do it. It's a dumb idea. You haven't even heard what the idea is. It's a dumb idea."

"What is it?" she asked.

"It's burlesque," I said. "And burlesque is dead."

☆ *37* ☆
Sugar Babies

T*he story of* my resurrection begins with a straitlaced college professor named Ralph Allen, who had an unusual hobby for a college professor: he was hooked on burlesque. Allen went to college at Amherst, then to Yale for graduate work. As an assistant professor, he translated plays by a sixteenth-century Spanish dramatist and served for years as an officer in the American Society for Theatre Research. By the time he landed his third teaching job at the University of Tennessee, he'd become fascinated by the history of burlesque.

In 1971, he produced an old-fashioned burlesque show at a college theater in Pittsburgh, and in 1977 he delivered a learned paper at a theater history conference at Lincoln Center in New York. The paper, "At My Mother's Knee, and Other Low Joints," was scholarly, but it was also funny. The academics were howling by the time Allen had finished. So was a Broadway producer named Harry Rigby, whose curiosity had taken him to hear Allen.

Rigby had been thinking he could do an old-fashioned burlesque show for Broadway, and he'd gone so far as to talk about the project with a TV director in LA named Norman Abbott, a nephew of Bud Abbott, Lou Costello's straight man. Norman Abbott had a collection of his uncle's sketches himself, and he wanted a chance to direct a show if Rigby could ever put one together. Now Rigby was telling himself maybe this guy Allen could help make the idea work. He told himself, "If Allen can get these professor guys laughing, maybe there's a show here."

Rigby didn't need to list his credits for Allen. He'd made a name for himself by putting on revivals—*No, No, Nanette, Hello, Dolly!* And now he was telling Allen that he thought he could do another revival, this time of burlesque itself. He wondered if Allen had any more of the same kind of material.

Allen told Rigby, "I've collected almost three thousand burlesque skits."

That pleased Rigby. Getting the material would be no problem. The only problem was what to leave out. The two men shook hands on a deal there and then, after Rigby promised Allen 2 percent of the profits from his show—if there ever were any profits.

Rigby listened hard when Allen said that what made burlesque soar was the right top banana. "You say, 'The comic was king.' Well, who can we get to be the comic?" Rigby asked.

Allen didn't hesitate a moment. "There's one guy in America who can put it over, and he's Joe Yule, Jr., the son of a great top banana. Mickey Rooney."

"Uh-huh," said Rigby. "Uh-huh. But how do we get Rooney?"

Allen said he thought some significant bucks would do the trick.

To get those bucks, Rigby paid a call on Terry Allen Kramer, who'd been a backer of *Nanette*. She was the daughter of a rather wealthy New York financier, Charles A. Allen, and she'd been enjoying Broadway as an angel. Terry liked the idea and gave Rigby a tentative yes. "It might be fun," she said.

But *I* didn't think burlesque would be fun at all. When Rigby phoned me (I think I may have been doing a revival of *George M* at a dinner theater somewhere) I told him it was a bullshit idea. I only remembered the burlesque of the late 1930s and early 1940s, when burlesque had come on bad times, when every man who went to the shows wore a raincoat—whether it was raining or not.

Rigby said, "Hey, not so fast, Mickey. I think Broadway might be ready for this. We're thinking of kind of an idealized burlesque, a memory that flatters the original burlesque, seen through rose-colored glasses."

"Hmmmm," I said.

"We're thinking of some funny sketches, risqué but not dirty, plenty of good-looking dancers in great costumes, and lots of good music from the twenties and thirties. And the comic. He has to be king."

That caught my attention. "What have you got to show me?" I asked.

"Nothing yet," he said. "I'll get back to you."

For some months in 1978, I hardly ever gave Allen, Rigby, or burlesque another thought, but Jan did. Jan gave it lots of thought. And every chance she could get, she tried to convince me that I'd be crazy to turn this down.

"Oh, Jan," I said. "If I go to work on Broadway, it'll kill our marriage."

"Kill?" she said. "How?"

"I'll be away."

"Yeah," she said. "And I'll be right there with you."

"You mean," I said, "you'll travel with me? If this goes ahead, we'll have tryouts in some cities before we ever get to New York. Have you ever spent any time in Philadelphia? Did you see that game show on TV the other day? First prize was a week in Philadelphia. Second prize was two weeks in Philadelphia."

"It'll be okay," she said. "I love you, and I want to be with you." She smiled. "Even in Philadelphia."

I had another reason to hold back. I didn't think Broadway would accept me. During another argument, I said, "I'm not in the club, Jan."

Jan couldn't buy that excuse either. As my number-one fan, she had ten times more esteem for me than I had for myself. And, as you will soon see, I was wrong. To succeed in New York, you don't need to belong to "the club." New York is an open society; it's the Hollywood crowd that's closed and cliquish. New Yorkers have the biggest, softest hearts in the world. Entertain them and they go nuts.

Next thing I knew, I had Professor Allen's script in hand. It was called *The New Majestic Follies and Lyceum Gardens Review*. Finally, I had a really good reason to turn the project down: a lousy title! Even more important, the script was no good: no book, no story, just a bunch of old schtick. I passed.

Then one day I am in Albany, Kentucky, doing *The Laugh's on Me* at a dinner theater and a guy with a Dick Nixon five o'clock shadow shows up in my dressing room. He says he is Ralph Allen, the professor from the University of Tennessee.

Allen is far from professorial. In fact, he has me laughing till my sides hurt—delivering joke after joke after joke from the burlesque I knew when I was just a little kid. He has a skit for me where I am dressed in drag and playing an aging chorus girl named Hortense who has been used and abused. "Is that Hortense?" asks one straight man. "No," says another comic, "she's as relaxed as I've seen her."

Allen had some other news for me. Rigby had decided on the lady who would be my costar: Ann Miller.

"Ann Miller?" I said. It was an inspired choice. She could dance. Wow, could she dance! She was more or less my age (though a helluva lot more well preserved). And she could sing—beautifully. "Hmmm. Ann Miller. Gee, I haven't married *her* yet."

Allen laughed at my joke. We talked some more, and I began to get a better feel for this project. But I had a problem with the title, _The New Majestic Follies,_ etc. As gently as I could, I told him, "Your title stinks."

"Not to worry," he said. "Harry Rigby's got a much better title." He paused, enjoying my anticipation. "It's _Sugar Babies._"

"_Sugar Babies?_" I said.

"Yeah," said Allen. "That's what they called the candies sold in the aisles in the old burlesque shows. 'Sugar Babies.'"

"But isn't that what they used to call the chorus girls? 'Sugar Babies?'"

"Right," said Allen. "That's what makes it a good title. Couple different meanings here. _Sugar Babies_ will feature some real cuties. Fourteen, count 'em, fourteen chorus girls."

I liked that. I have always liked chorus girls—from the time they first hugged me to their bare bosoms when I was just a babe myself. I told Allen I'd do it.

The next day, when he phoned back, I said I _wouldn't_ do it. You know how comics are—insecure. That's because comedy isn't easy. You never know what gags will work, or when they'll work, or even if they'll work. Frankly, I wasn't a damn bit sure if any of this would work in 1979. And what Rigby and Allen wanted me to do represented a big investment in time. During our tryouts on the road, we'd only break even at best. And on Broadway, we could bomb out in a week.

I went back to LA, thinking I'd hear no more from either of them, but these cusses wouldn't give up. Both of them came out to talk some more. Allen made me laugh some more by doing every gag in the show. Rigby made me laugh even harder by promising me five thousand dollars a week, guaranteed, no matter what happened, for twenty-six weeks, even if we closed in Philadelphia. Hell, I'd earned better, but not recently. And I had nothing else.

"Okay," I said, "let's give _Sugar Babies_ a try."

It was March 1979 when I first met our director, Norman Abbott, in our tryout studio in Lower Manhattan. Abbott was a nice guy who had directed many a fine television show, and he had a special feel for comedy. But I wasn't sure he knew anything about burlesque, and I saw nothing there in the Michael Bennett Studio to make me believe otherwise.

On the other hand, I took an immediate liking to Ernie Flatt, the show's choreographer, and to the dancers he'd assembled. I was less than happy, however, with the director's wish to put me on roller skates for one of the numbers. Hell, I hadn't skated since 1950, almost thirty years and thirty pounds ago. I might be taking my life in my hands. Somebody suggested that if the show lost me, it was all over. "No, no," said Abbott. "Roller skating is in right now. Rooney's got to learn it."

I learned it, but I wasn't happy about it. Another thing I wasn't thrilled with was the script. Many of the sketches may have read well, but they didn't *play*. We hadn't put them, as they say, "on their feet." The main problem was that Abbott hadn't found a good straight man for me. For the first week of rehearsals, Abbott himself was playing the straight man while he scurried around trying to find a second banana.

When a whole week had gone by without a straight man, I balked. "I love ya, baby, but this isn't going to work out." Frankly, I was beginning to think that Abbott didn't know a damn thing about burlesque. And, as someone who had grown up with it, literally from the cradle, I thought I was qualified to make a judgment. At my request, Rigby fired Abbott.

But Abbott wasn't the real problem. The real problem, we began to realize, even after our new director, Rudy Tronto, came aboard, was this: the sketches weren't coming across. History was fine, but we were on the brink of the 1980s. We had to do things that modern audiences would dig. For days, instead of rehearsing, Rudy and Ralph and I worked together, sifting through old sketches, writing new ones that sounded old, rearranging things, pruning things down, and always, always trying to end every sketch with a big bang.

When I fell with a bang, roller skating during a tryout in San Francisco, Rigby and Tronto took out the roller-skating number and replaced it with a medley of songs by Jimmy McHugh, arranged by Arthur Malvin, to be sung by me and Ann Miller.

I didn't want to do that either. I wasn't proud of my singing. I have a voice like a bullfrog. Tronto pleaded with me, "Won't you just go up and see Malvin?"

So I went up to Arthur Malvin's room at the Clift Hotel, but I told him I didn't even want to listen to his medley. I gave him all the arguments I could think of. Then I gave him what I thought would be the clincher—coming from the star of the show. "I don't want to have to learn all this stuff," I said. "So why bother?"

"Because Rigby wants it in," said Malvin.

"Then let Rigby sing it," I said.

"Look," said Malvin, "just do me a favor. Listen to the medley. If you don't like it, you can tell Rigby. But at least I'm off the hook. I told him I'd play it for you."

So Malvin's arranger, Stan Freedman, played the medley for me, and Malvin sang the lyrics. They started with "I Hear a Song Coming On," segued into "I Can't Give You Anything but Love, Baby" and ended with "On the Sunny Side of the Street." When they were finished, I sat there, filled with all sorts of good vibrations. I luxuriated in them for a few moments while Malvin and Freedman waited to hear what I thought. "It's good," I said, my voice almost a whisper. "It's very good. Let's do it."

They laughed and clapped each other on the back. I said I wanted to do the medley that very night on the stage of the Curran. Malvin phoned Rigby. "First the good news, Harry. Mick loves the medley. Now the bad news: he wants to do it tonight."

Rigby asked to talk to me. "You don't want to do it tonight," he said. "We have to get some costumes for you and Ann. We have to write some orchestrations."

"Bullshit," I said. "The orchestra can fake it. Ann and I will find something to wear."

Rigby gave in. What the hell? This was just a tryout. So we

went ahead. That night, Ann and I and the orchestra felt our way through the medley and the audience flipped for all these great nostalgic songs.

Nostalgia worked in San Francisco, but it didn't work in LA, where we staged our next tryout. Los Angeles, the land of instant everything, where if a building is ten years old they tear it down? Forget it. Furthermore, the *Los Angeles Times* sent a woman to see the play who was offended by the whole thing. Sylvie Drake wrote the haughtiest review I've ever seen: "It's so bad, it's awesome . . . abysmally reactionary . . . may find its audience . . . maybe the Magic Mountain crowd."

Chicago's Irv Kupcinet, one of the best columnists in the nation, didn't feel that way. When we arrived at the Windy City, our next stop, Kup said, "Sugar Babies at the Arie Crown Theater slipped Our Town a Mickey, and the effect was effulgence." Not only that, he liked the gags.

We kept polishing the show—in Chicago, then Detroit, then Philadelphia. Somewhere along the line, I redid Allen's skit about Hortense, the aging chorine, and renamed her Francine, a girl with a very sad tale to tell. She had an abused childhood, in a large family. "Fifteen in the family. All children. My father used to say to me, 'Listen, stupid.' (He always called me Listen.) 'Why don't you get a job, so at least we'll always know what kind of work you're out of.' I joined a dance troupe. Well, I did. I danced on my right leg. I danced on my left leg. And between the two of them I made a lot of money."

Gotten up as I was, with big, false boobs and a red fright wig, I knew we had just the right combination—of corn and raunch—to make Francine a hit.

By the time we reached New York, we were ready, but we wondered whether New York was ready for us. We had twenty-nine good sketches, great music, and some beautiful dancers. We had Ann Miller, 56, but still in top form. And we had me. I'd just turned 59, but I was feeling 159 because I was sure they would not love me in New York City. I tried to cover up my dread—even sent congratulatory flowers to Ann and every woman in the cast—and went around backstage making jokes with the director and the crew.

God, did I read New York wrong! After the overture, when the curtain went up at the Mark Hellinger on October 8, 1979, the audience saw the back of a huge old brown overcoat in the spotlight, marked with brightly colored patches on the shoulders and elbows, and a battered top hat. The face beneath the hat slowly turned. It was Mickey Rooney, grinning his rubbery grin. Then the applause began, light at first, then louder and louder and louder, until the whole theater was on its feet, clapping its damn head off.

The applause went on for twenty-four minutes (Rudy Tronto had a stopwatch on it), and during that ovation I cried with joy. Now I knew something about the reservoir of goodwill that had been stored in the hearts of these New Yorkers.

After the applause died, I proceeded to give the people who had come to a burlesque show something of what they expected (though certainly not from me): I stripped slowly, very slowly, to the strains of a Jimmy McHugh melody, "A Good Old Burlesque Show," until I was down to my bright-red long johns, laughing a laugh that began when I was Puck.

We raced through our twenty-nine sketches, giving this Broadway crowd the kind of entertainment it had obviously hungered for. We took eight curtain calls, Ann and I, four chorus boys, fourteen, count 'em, fourteen dancers, a belly dancer, a fan dancer, ten white doves, and one little dog who didn't know how to do anything.

And then we scurried down to our dressing rooms to get ready for an after-theater party at a disco called New York New York. It took us quite some time to get there. Folks crowded into our dressing rooms to give us hugs and kisses. Barbara Sinatra was the first one to reach mine (explaining that Frank had been busy rehearsing for his own opening the next night at the Waldorf). Then came songwriter Ralph Blane, who reminded me that he'd been a singer in the group that backed me and Judy in our personal appearances at the Capitol Theater in 1939, forty years ago. Then came Harry Rigby, wearing a yellow rose in his lapel, and Ruth Webb, my all-believing agent, and Jack Krieg, my faithful Kato, and about one hundred autograph seekers wanting a little piece of Broadway history.

When Jan and I finally arrived at the disco, Terry Allen Kramer had already come and gone—back to her office to wait for the reviews (which were coming in not only from the papers but from the critics on television's late news shows). But Rita Hayworth was there, with her daughter Yasmin, Barbara Walters, Eartha Kitt, Joan Bennett, Shirley MacLaine, Diana Rigg, Arlene Dahl, Gloria Vanderbilt, Earl Wilson—and a fey little blond guy with a camera in his hand: Andy Warhol.

I circulated around with Jan at my side, drinking a Coke and thanking everyone for coming. I tried to sound sage to reporters. "A comedian," I said, "is someone who says funny things. A comic is someone who does funny things. But in burlesque you have to be a comedian and a comic."

Another reporter asked me if I learned this art from my father.

"No," I said. "I am my father. I am Joe Yule."

About midnight, Terry Allen Kramer was back in the club and at the microphone with some notes in her hand and a copy of *The New York Times*. She said, "I have some early returns here." She laughed—an indication that her news was good—and the crowd roared its approval. "First, NBC. Pia Lindstrom loved it." Cheers from the crowd. "On CBS, Dennis Cunningham—he said, 'Ann Miller is irresistible. And Mickey Rooney is not just a scream but several hundred screams.'" Bigger cheers.

Someone cried out, "What about *The Times*?"

"Oh, yes," said Terry. "*The Times. The Times*"—she was milking the suspense—"the *Times* sent their first-string reviewer, Walter Kerr. And Walter Kerr"—she paused again, grinning mischievously. "Walter Kerr said he had a good time, thank you." Bedlam.

Later that night, after Jan and I had gotten back to our rented digs in Englewood Cliffs, New Jersey, across the Hudson from Manhattan, Jack Krieg presented us with a copy of *The Times* and the *Post* and the *Daily News*. Kerr wrote a very stylish review:

"The occasion is essentially a Rooney occasion (it seems to me extremely unlikely that anyone would have stolen the mothballs out of 60-year-old burlesque routines and done them, throttle open, all flags flying, without him), and the indefatigable Rooney is exactly as energetic and exactly as talented as he was when, at the age of 3 or 4, he rammed a cigar into his mouth, raked a derby over his brow, and made a star out of himself."

Clive Barnes said in the *Post* that Rooney was "Broadway's most promising newcomer . . . the true icing on 'Sugar Babies,' a Top Banana if we ever had one."

Rex Reed wrote in the *Daily News*, "If burlesque or even vaudeville was ever this good, then we were dumb losers to let it go."

Time magazine, which had me typecast as a brat for four decades, suddenly decided I was venerable. It talked about me as a veteran with assured versatility, about my "lungs of iron and feet that skitter like a sandpiper's" and my leers as "the naughtiest boy in the class."

Not to be outdone, *Newsweek* said *Sugar Babies* was "a welcome attempt to restore some of the simple virtues of good, not-so-clean fun to the over-intellectualized spirit of the Broadway musical" and that I was "the heart and soul and body of the enterprise."

Brendan Gill of *The New Yorker* said I was "among the three or four greatest men of the Twentieth Century" right after Einstein and Freud and promised he'd keep coming back to see the show again and again.

Well, needless to say, *Sugar Babies* became the hottest ticket in New York, standing room only at every one of our eight performances a week, against some pretty good competition: *Evita, Sweeney Todd, The Best Little Whorehouse in Texas,* and *Annie.* When the guy who had rented us our home in New Jersey phoned to find out how long he should plan on staying in Miami, I told him, "This show'll have a longer run than five of my marriages." The show recovered half of its nut by mid-February and was making a profit of seventy-thousand dollars a week by mid-April.

God, I loved it. I'd been the toast of Broadway forty years before with Judy. Now, after all my setbacks, I appreciated my celebrity much more the second time around. I also appreciated the dough. I'd signed a contract for ten thousand dollars a week. Soon, the producers gave me a raise—fifteen thousand a week, then twenty thousand. Then, after the show went into the black, I signed a new contract giving me 10 percent of the gross, and I was knocking down thirty thousand a week. I also ended up getting 1 percent of the producer's share forever, no matter where *Sugar Babies* was produced.

I loved that time in New York—the vitality, the people, the acclaim, and the money I was making. The beat went on, and it was all *up* beat. One morning in late February, I got a phone call from my son Timmy whose first words were, "Congratulations, Dad!"

"Oh," I said. "You've seen *Life* magazine?" My *Sugar Babies* face was grinning out at America on six million *Life* covers, issue of March 1980.

"No, Dad," he said. "The Academy Award nomination! You're up for an Oscar for *The Black Stallion.* "

I was speechless. A scene flashed before me: of me and Martha Vickers, sitting slumped over our kitchen table, feeling soiled (though we were dressed in our best formal wear) because the Academy had just phoned to dis-invite us to the ceremonies.

"Ahh, Timmy," I said, "thanks a lot for that news. That's good news."

I wasn't too surprised to find out that folks liked me in *The Black Stallion*. Vincent Canby had tipped me off with his *Times* review back in December. Canby said the movie's "chief claim on our attention . . . is the appearance of Mr. Rooney in the film's second half as a race-horse trainer. He's very funny, crotchety, and almost as wide as he is high, and he serves the film in two important ways. He's completely authentic as the tough old guy who's supposed to be in the story, and he acts as a link between this not so stirring horse movie and the still vividly remembered 'National Velvet.'"

I didn't end up winning the Oscar for *The Black Stallion*. The Academy members gave it to Melvyn Douglas for his role in *Being There*, and I applauded that as hard as anybody from my seat in the LA Music Center. I had to take a day off from *Sugar Babies* to jet back for the Awards night, but I wouldn't have missed the ceremony to save my soul. Correction: I went there to *heal* the deep wounds in my soul.

☆ 38 ☆
You Ain't Seen Nothin' Yet

Heated, *I didn't* sit back and bask in my own glory. No. I did what I'd done all my life: I signed up to do some more work. TV producer Alan Landsburg came to me with a script about a retarded old guy named Bill Sackter who'd spent forty-six years in an insane asylum in Minnesota and survived it all, until the state welfare department had him released, with apologies. I was currently on everyone's lips as Mr. Top Banana, but Landsburg had faith in me as an actor, an actor who could do anything.

I didn't let him down. We shot *Bill* in Westchester County during the day while I was doing *Sugar Babies* at night, and I gave one of the best performances of my life. CBS ran *Bill* on the night of December 22, 1981, and many of my fans think it is the best thing I ever did on TV. I got terrific reviews, won a Golden Globe Award (from the Hollywood Foreign Press Association), and received a Peabody Award. Then the TV industry gave me my first Emmy.

While *Sugar Babies* continued to pack in the Broadway crowds, I did another TV movie for CBS, a true story about a Chicagoan named Jack Thum, who cared for dozens of homeless children while he struggled to make a living himself—as a clown. It was called *Leave 'Em Laughing*. My old friend Jackie Cooper directed this show, which also starred Anne Jackson and Red Buttons, and it ran that season and got fine reviews.

I also signed with NBC to do another series, *One of the Boys*, a cute story about an unconventional old guy who moves in on campus with his grandson, who always worries about his gramp's shenanigans. The producers, Saul Turtletaub, Bernie Ornstein, and Bud Yorkin, shot it at Drew University in New Jersey to accommodate me. Some thirty-five million viewers watched *One of the Boys* when it premiered in the fall of 1981, and Tom Shales, America's best TV critic, liked it. But the network canceled it in April. Who knows why? That same spring, the networks also canceled shows starring Angie Dickinson, James Arness, Mike Connors, Lorne Greene, Robert Stack, and James Garner.

I had too many good things happening to me to shed more than a single tear over the cancellation of a TV series. I got an invitation that spring to attend the biggest, swingingest, most exclusive party on Derby Day in Kentucky at the home of Preston and Anita Madden at their horse farm in Lexington. I even received some invitations to a few Hollywood parties, including Danny Thomas's every-other-year affair, a fund-raiser for his St. Jude's Hospital in Tennessee. I hadn't seen Thomas since he'd snubbed me on the set at RKO years before (he'd kept me waiting for hours, then said, "Sorry, I don't have time to see you," and walked right by me), so I was surprised, one day during a visit to Hollywood, to get a phone call in my booth at the Brown Derby from none other than Thomas. "Hey, Mick," he said. "I just saw you come in. All I can say is, 'Excuse me for being an asshole.' "

I am, I think, a forgiving man. I am also an unforgiving man. I am a loud, quiet man. I'm a public, private man. I'm a nonreligious, religious man. I'm a very impatient, patient man. I'm an angry, peaceful man. In other words, I am a man of many contradictions. But now I was ready to forgive. "Gee, Danny," I said, "it's okay. I'm glad we're still friends." Heck, I was ready to forgive everybody.

Well, almost everybody. With some extra dollars in my jeans, I decided that I would try to right an old wrong. I hired the Philadelphia firm of Berger and Montague to file a class-action suit against eight major Hollywood studios for not paying me and about nine hundred other actors and actresses for our TV residuals on movies we'd done before February 1960. I thought that David Berger and H. Laddie Montague made a pretty good case for *Rooney* v. *Columbia Pictures* before the U.S. District Court for the Southern District of New York. They argued that the studios had rights to show my movies in movie theaters, but no rights to exhibit my movies in "alternative markets," that is, on TV and videocassette.

Judge Conner didn't agree. He agreed with the lawyers for the studios, who contended that I'd signed all my rights away—in fourteen different contracts with MGM and in a number of contracts with the other studios—and he dismissed the case in April of 1982. David Berger took it to the U.S. Supreme Court, which wouldn't hear the case, noting, with the New York court, that we'd all signed the same basic contract in those pre-1960 flicks, one that gave all subsidiary rights to the studios that hired us.

I have an answer to that, and I don't have to get into any subtle legalities to make my case. It is simply this: *we didn't know what we were doing.* We had no idea when we signed our contracts, in the 1930s and 1940s, what a bonanza television would be in the 1970s, or 1980s, or how much money the studios would make by selling the likes of *Babes in Arms* and *National Velvet* to television.

But the studios knew. Television was already proven by 1937; the smart guys at the studios only had to wait a few years before they could start selling off their treasure for megabucks. And I think the studios might have been willing to listen to a reasonable presentation by the outfit we'd delegated to represent us, the Screen Actors Guild. Trouble was, the Guild sold us down the river in 1960, when my friend Ronald Reagan was president of SAG.

It happened this way. In 1960, actors' unions on both coasts, the American Federation of Television and Radio Artists in the East and SAG in the West, were competing for network television jobs. In an effort to bring network production to the West, SAG said it would only take 6 percent of all future residuals (as opposed to AFTRA, which had already struck a deal for 100 percent). Furthermore, SAG traded the actors' rights to all pre-1960 residuals if the studios would pay a chunk of money, $2.65 million, into the SAG pension fund. After that, the studios could sell the TV and videocassette rights to any pre-1960 movies without paying the actors and actresses a red cent.

Why do you think the Sony Corporation recently paid billions for Columbia Pictures? For its real estate? No, for what they called its "software." Hey, to me, that's not software. Those are my pictures and Cary Grant's and Jimmy Cagney's and Jimmy Stewart's and Frank Capra's. And that's why Sony coughed up billions for Columbia Pictures.

SAG presented the plan to its members. They voted for it. They were battling for work now and in the future. The broken-down old actors? Well, said the SAG leadership, that's why they were setting up the pension fund.

I still think I have a case, but SAG doesn't even want to talk about it. SAG is more concerned with now than then. Sometimes I wonder if SAG doesn't agree with Lew Wasserman, president and board chairman of MCA-Universal, who was once quoted as saying that paying residuals to an actor was like coughing up a fee to the plumber every time you flushed the toilet.

That really set me off. When I read that, I phoned Howard Koch, now a Hollywood big shot whom I had given a start in this business, and told him I wanted to know how Lew Wasserman fit into this business. "Can he act?" I asked.

Koch said, "No."

"Can he sing?"

"No."

"Can he dance?"

"No."

"Can he direct?"

"No."

"Can he write?"

"No."

"Can he do makeup?"

"No."

"Can he design costumes?"

"No."

"Well, does he know anything about the camera, lighting, special effects?"

"No."

"Well," I said, "just what in the hell does he do for this business?"

Koch laughed—out of embarrassment.

Leon Ames, the SAG president when I was pushing my class-action suit, wrote me a note telling me to stop fighting for the residuals. He said I was beating a dead horse. I told Ames, "Yeah? Well, watch his ass move when I hit him again!"

I believe in justice. And I believe in the court system. Someday, somehow, I am going to find a lawyer who will make a case that proves the injustice of all this. It's too late, you say, because the statute of limitations has passed? I don't think so. Every time Ted Turner shows one of my movies on his TV station or sells one of my movies to another network or to another cable TV station, he's committing the same crime all over again. He's got the smoking gun right in his hand.

On August 30, 1982, we closed *Sugar Babies* in New York. Our run had lasted three years and two months on Broadway—1,208 performances. At the party that night in Manhattan, I thanked all the folks who had made my resurrection possible.

"It takes somebody to make a somebody," I said, "and in this case it was everyone from Terry Allen Kramer, Harry Rigby, and Columbia Pictures to the entire backstage crew, wardrobe department, gofers, and the entire marvelous company. Thanks to all of them, my career has been resurrected." Rigby has passed on, and Sony has bought Columbia Pictures. But Terry Allen Kramer is still a bright particular star in my firmament, still active, still on the lookout for a show we can do together. I don't want to get too syruptitious here, don't want to give any of my readers an attack of diabetes, but I do want to tell the world how marvelous this woman has been. There's never been a male producer, in my experience, who can compare with her.

On April 11, 1983, the Academy surprised me again, with a special Oscar for Lifelong Career Achievement. It was another teary evening for me. Clips from all my old films were shown and then I was dragged up onto the stage at the Music Center (I'm joking, folks; I *ran* up there) in my white tie and tux to get my second Oscar (not a miniature this time). Bob Hope, a guy who was just breaking into show business the year I landed on the top of Hollywood's heap, handed it to me, calling me "the kid who illuminated all our yesterdays and the man who brightens all our todays."

After we closed in New York, everybody else in the country was clamoring for *Sugar Babies,* so we took it on the road and played for another five years. I could hardly afford not to go on the road. In some cities, like Chicago, I was knocking down fifty thousand dollars a week.

In 1988 and 1989, we did four months in London, mostly SRO, and Ann Miller was right there alongside me. I think we were as strong as ever. Somehow, we had as many fans in London as we had in New York or Chicago. Margaret Thatcher invited us over to 10 Downing Street for lunch.

While I was in London, I resolved to see how Ava Gardner

was doing. I knew she'd retired there, so I found someone who could give me her phone number. I let her number lie on my nightstand for a few days, then finally rang her. She answered herself, and, though the voice was a little croaky, it was Ava all right, and she seemed happy to hear from me. I closed my eyes as we talked. I could still see that beautiful dimpled chin and that sultry smile. But my reverie stopped when she told me she'd had two strokes and wasn't feeling all that swift these days. "Don't be surprised," she said, "if someday soon you hear that I've blown my fuckin' brains out."

"Awww, Ava," I said. I'd had too many friends who'd turned out suicides; over the last few years I'd lost Red Barry and Dick Quine that way. And now, here was Ava, not only a friend, but one of my wives, telling me she wanted to end her own life.

That stopped her for some long moments. Then she said, haltingly, "I—don't—know—God."

I said, "Fortunately, Ava, God knows you."

That took her aback and kind of melted any reserve she may have had. She ended up inviting me over for dinner at her place near Hyde Park on Sunday evening.

"Ava," I said, "I'd love to have dinner with you."

But I stood her up. I heard later that she'd gotten all dolled up for my visit and that she was furious when I turned out to be a no-show. I don't blame her. But I just couldn't go—I was afraid to. I had had fantasies—that I might fall in love with her again, and she with me—and, shoot, I was married to Jan. I'd heard that she was just as beautiful as she'd ever been, and I knew she was twice as salty. After Frank Sinatra married Mia Farrow, Ava's comment was priceless: "I always thought that Frank would end up sleeping with a boy."

If I'd gone over there, what would have really happened? To think that after all these years, and all the tears, me and Ava together again, each of us older and wiser—who knows?

But I stayed with Jan. In Jan, I have a loving wife who takes care of me, puts up with my rudeness and my unthinking behav-

ior, my pie-in-the-sky ideas and my get-rich-quick schemes, ago-
nizes with me over this or that TV series that hasn't panned out,
reads to me in bed, even gives me water massages in our blue-
bottomed pool and backyard spa.

Jan helps make a comfortable home for me, a nice place in the
Conejo Valley surrounded by tall cypress trees. I have a den I
can retreat to, watch my games there, surrounded by the photos
of my closest friends, old and new: Katharine Hepburn, Barbra
Streisand, Brooke Shields, Dick Shawn, Charles Chaplin, John
McEnroe, Ben Hogan, Tom Watson, Jack Nicklaus, Woody
Hayes, Chris Evert, Bjorn Borg, Sean Penn, Faye Dunaway,
Kirk Douglas, Burt Lancaster, Bette Davis, Cary Grant, Lau-
rence Olivier, Burt Reynolds, James Mason, Anthony Quinn,
Fred Astaire, Richard Nixon. As you can see, they span several
generations, and they come from different worlds.

But my major comfort these days comes from Jan, and she
needs me, too, to take care of her, to produce candlelight and
good conversation. I think that many marriages die because
couples get flabby in the head. They need to exercise their
brains, read books, perform mental aerobics—daily. Otherwise,
they have nothing to talk about. We sometimes share a room at
Camarillo State Hospital, where, you will not be surprised to
learn, we bounce off those rubber walls, with no bruises to
anybody. We can never part, Jan and I. Christ, who'd feed the
dogs? Just Kidding, of course.

I thank God for Jan. I also thank Him for my bunch of loving
children—all nine of them—and for our menagerie of pets:
Holly, a little black poodle we found abandoned in a gas station
around Christmastime. Angel, half boxer, half Airedale, a brave
bitch with a sweet heart. McGee, a loving, brown and white
water spaniel. And five Yorkies. Get this: they're named Charlie
Chaplin, Gloria Swanson, Theda Bara, Judy Garland, and Andy
Hardy.

To these pets, I add all the other assorted crawling and flying
things who make their way into our home in Westlake Village—

ants, spiders, crickets, moths, and the like—whom I like to think of as little people. "What are you little people doing in here?" I say. "Go on now, get back outside." Then I try to usher them out as gently as I can.

Truth is, I like animals. They're more dependable, much more dependable, than most humans I know.

☆ 39 ☆
Retire? Sheee-it!

I *still explode* with ideas.

I have plans to start my own studio, try to resurrect the studio system again with something I choose to call Sunrise Pictures, a re-creation, on my own terms, of MGM. The best, first way to make it happen is to visualize it as if it has already become a reality. Sunrise Pictures produces clean, wonderful entertainment. And on modest, intelligent budgets, too. Sunrise does ten pictures a year for, maybe, as little as $1.5 million each, certainly no more than $10 million. Of course, I do not have any Steven Spielbergs who get $15 million off the top. But I have some young film geniuses working with me, cameramen and sound men and editors and directors, young men and women who are only too glad to do their stuff for $200,000 a picture, plus a percentage of the profits—for life.

Actors and actresses, too. I am giving them a chance to do two or three pictures a year, instead of one every three years, so that they are now becoming household words. We don't do the kind of pictures that too many others are doing these days, what I call "suckin' and fuckin' pictures" like *All Dressed Up and No Place to Blow*.

Nothing makes me angrier these days than to think how far Hollywood has fallen.

Understand me. I have nothing but love and respect for this great motion picture business, and I give thanks that I've been allowed to be a passing part of it. It's been a wonderful gift. But I couldn't end this book without saying this:

What was then is not now. This isn't sour grapes. It just gripes me to know that Hollywood is no longer Tinseltown, no longer the Tiffany of the world. It pains me to realize that the lion does not roar any longer at MGM. It annoys me to think that Harry Cohn is not yelling at someone over on the lot at Columbia to get things done. It outrages me to read that David Begelman can forge a check for $10,000, then blackball the actor that blew the whistle on him, Cliff Robertson, while he, Begelman, gets a fifteen-picture deal. It kills me to find out that Paramount stole an idea from Art Buchwald, then made $365 million on *Coming to America* and still had the guts to say they weren't "into profit." I want to throw up when I read that William Morris and MCA and CAA can each boast four hundred or more clients in the business and extract their 10 percent from each of them.

How, you ask, do these people get away with this? Here's my answer: they're paying someone off. Someday, it will all come out. Remember, I told you first.

The guys with the power in Hollywood today, the guys with their names above the title, are thieves. They don't make movies, they make deals. Their major function is to cut themselves in for 10 percent of the gross—off the top, of course—which is why they make movies that cost $50 million.

I know I'm in the middle of what my friend Kevin Pawley calls one of my diatribes, but since I am up on my soapbox now, let me add one more lament for Hollywood before I climb down.

It's about the Boulevard. Hollywood Boulevard, once the symbol of dreams, is now a sick dream. Yes, it literally makes me sick to drive up the street these days. It not only looks like Skid Row, teeming with bums and drunks and derelicts. It looks like the Reeperbahn in Hamburg, crawling with sex addicts, pimps with their little painted teenyboppers in tow, some of them looking no older than fourteen, spitting on the names of the stars like Gable and Garland. (Even those names on the sidewalk have been devalued: almost anyone in the business can arrange to have his or her name planted there by paying $3,600.)

Hollywood itself was once a fair lady under a pink parasol who blushed when a suitor approached. Now she's a painted old whore who can't wait for the gangbang to begin. Hollywood, to me, has to be more than a tour through Universal Studios to look at a fake shark and a rubber monkey, more than a film library for the Ted Turners and the Sony Corporations of this world. My heart breaks when I think of all the young, creative talent that wants to work like we did in the old days and cannot because there is no more studio system that will put people to work.

I believe that Hollywood will rise again, even if (maybe because) it has to start from scratch again.

Every now and then somebody asks me when I'm going to retire. *Retire?* I give it the same serious consideration that the French general gave the Germans' invitation to surrender: *Merde.* Retire? Sheee-it. I will always be leading the cheers for life, and I hope that's the way people will always see me and remember me, as a cheerleader for life, out there in front of the crowd with a megaphone in my hand, crying out, "Gimme an L! Gimme an I! Gimme an F! Gimme an E! LIFE! LIFE! LIFE!"

But if I energize people, people in turn energize me. Applause got me started, it kept me going through my bad days, and it keeps me going still.

I figure I'll be working for a long time to come. As I write this, George Burns is still going strong, and he's ninety-four. If George can do it, so can I. And I may beat him by quite a few lengths because George, you see, is a widower who was only married once. Since actuaries have proven that married men live longer, and I've been married eight times, I should live at least eight times longer than George Burns. I should still be around in 2672. No matter how long I'm around, I'm going to make the most of it.

I dare to joke about death? Hey, why not—if I can get a laugh? That's what I do. I make people laugh. I make people feel. It's as holy (and as human) an occupation as any other. Maybe more holy (and human) than most. And that's the way I have always lived, for the laughs—today. N-O-W. No Other Way.

And I thank God for sending so many people to help me do this—producers, directors, writers, musicians, cameramen, sound men, set designers, costumers, makeup people—all my fellow actors and actresses and all those extras and all those people (starting with my mom) who helped me be me and gave me to believe that it was always okay to express my individuality.

This, too, is my wish for you, for everyone. Be. Live. And don't worry too much about the troubles you have that seem to loom so large today. They will pass. They are what I like to call small stuff.

W. H. Auden put it just right.

> *Thou shalt not live within thy means,*
> *Nor on plain water and raw greens.*
> *If thou must choose*
> *Between the chances, choose the odd,*
> *Read* The New Yorker, *trust in God,*
> *And take short views.*

That's pretty much the life I've led. Never within my means, never on raw greens, choosing the odd (filly or colt), reading *The New Yorker*, trusting in God.

And as Mr. Auden advised, I always took the short view, in more ways than one. What else could I do? I've been short all my life. And if anyone wonders what my dying wish will be, they can stop wondering. That will be easy.

I'll just tell them, "I'll have a short bier."

The Feature Films of Mickey Rooney

1. ORCHIDS AND ERMINE. First National, '27. Original screenplay: Carey Wilson. Comedy construction: Mervyn LeRoy. *Alfred Santell.* Colleen Moore, Jack Mulhall, Sam Hardy, Gwen Lee, Jack Duffy, Hedda Hopper, Fred Kelsey, Frank Hagney, Kate Price. Cinderella story of the flapper era with six-year-old MR playing a swaggering, cigar-smoking midget who makes a pass at hotel switchboard operator Moore. 69 m.

2. EMMA. MGM, '32. Sp: Frances Marion. *Clarence Brown.* Marie Dressler, Jean Hersholt, Richard Cromwell, Myrna Loy, John Miljan, Purnell B. Pratt, Leila Bennett, Barbara Kent, Kathryn Crawford, Geo. Meeker. 73 m.

3. THE BEAST OF THE CITY. MGM, '32. Sp: John Lee Mahin from a story by W. R. Burnett. *Chas. Brabin.* Walter Huston, Jean Harlow, Wallace Ford, Jean Hersholt, Dorothy Peterson, John Miljan, Emmett Corrigan, J. Carrol Naish. Police chief Huston's war against hood Hersholt is stymied when chief's detective brother Ford falls for the gangster's mistress Harlow. MR, unbilled, is seen briefly as Huston's son. 87 m.

4. SIN'S PAY DAY. Mayfair, '32. Sp: Gene Morgan and Betty Burbridge. *Geo. B. Seitz.* Dorothy Revier, Forrest Stanley, Harry Semels,

Sp=Screenplay.

Directors' names are in italics.

Hal Price, Alfred Cross, Lloyd Whitlock, Bess Flowers. Underworld attorney Stanley hits skids after his wife leaves him when he refuses to abandon his practice, and is befriended by slum kid MR (billed as Mickey McGuire). When kid is killed by gangster's stray bullet, lawyer vows revenge, works way back to DA, regains wife. Reissued as *Slums of New York* in 1938. 61 m.

5. HIGH SPEED. Columbia, '32. Sp: Adele Buffington from a story by Harold Shumate. *D. Ross Lederman.* Buck Jones, Loretta Sayers, Wallace MacDonald, Dick Dickinson, Wm. Walling, Ed. Le Saint, Ward Bond, Pat O'Malley. Auto racer Jones, disqualified through crooked gang's schemes, stages comeback, uncovers gang leader, saves girl, wins race. MR (billed as Mickey McGuire) is hero's crippled pal, son of his dead racing companion. 63 m.

6. OFFICER THIRTEEN. Allied. '32. Sp: Frances Hyland from a story by Paul Edwards. *Geo. Melford.* Monte Blue, Lila Lee, Seena Owen, Chas. Delaney, Florence Roberts, Jackie Searle. Motorcycle cop Blue vows to avenge death of his partner Delaney by motorist who forced both to crash and then was acquitted because of his influence. MR (billed as Mickey McGuire) is the son of the dead cop. 62 m.

7. FAST COMPANIONS (also called THE INFORMATION KID). Universal, '32. Sp: Earl Snell from a story by Gerald Beaumont. *Kurt Neumann.* Tom Brown, Jas. Gleason, Maureen O'Sullivan, Andy Devine, Berton Churchill, Morgan Wallace. Race track programmer with orphan MR living with bookie Gleason. 71 m.

8. MY PAL, THE KING. Universal, '32. Sp: Jack Natteford and Tom Crizer from a story by Richard Schayer. *Kurt Neumann.* Tom Mix, Tony the Wonder Horse, Paul Hurst, Noel Francis, Stuart Holmes, Jas. Kirkwood, Jim Thorpe. On rodeo tour of Balkans, cowboy Mix saves boy king MR from evil regent Holmes. 60 m.

9. THE BIG CAGE. Universal '33. Sp: Ed. Anthony and Ferdinand Reyher from a book by Anthony and Clyde Beatty. *Kurt Neumann.* Clyde Beatty, Anita Page, Andy Devine, Vince Barnett, Raymond Hatton, Wallace Ford. Showcase for Beatty playing a circus lion tamer. Noted *The New York Times*: "MR is very clever as Jimmy O'Hara, the orphan who aspires to be an animal trainer." Subplot deals with love affair between aerialist Page and lion tamer Ford who has lost his nerve after a mauling. 76 m.

10. THE LIFE OF JIMMY DOLAN. Warners, '33. Sp: David Boehm and

Erwin Gelsey from the play *The Sucker* by Bertram Milhauser and Beulah Marie Dix. *Archie Mayo.* Douglas Fairbanks, Jr., Loretta Young, Aline MacMahon, Guy Kibbee, Lyle Talbot, Fifi Dorsay, Harold Huber, Shirley Grey, Geo. Meeker, Farina, John Wayne. Prize fighter Fairbanks, fleeing from crime committed while drunk, hides out on farm for underprivileged children, one of whom is MR. Remade as *They Made Me a Criminal* ('39). 89 m.

11. THE BIG CHANCE. Eagle Pictures, '33. Sp: Mauri Grashin. *Albert Herman.* John Darrow, Merna Kennedy, Natalie Moorhead, Mathew Betz, Hank Mann, J. Carrol Naish, Eleanor Boardman. Boxer Darrow doublecrosses his crooked manager by winning a fixed fight. MR is kid brother of boxer's girlfriend Kennedy. 62 m.

12. BROADWAY TO HOLLYWOOD. MGM, '33. Sp: Willard Mack and Edgar Allan Woolf. *Willard Mack and Harry Rapf.* Alice Brady, Frank Morgan, Madge Evans, Russell Hardie, Una Merkel, Jackie Cooper, Eddie Quillan, Ed. Brophy, Jimmy Durante, May Robson, Fay Templeton, Nelson Eddy. MR is third generation vaudevillian in forty-year saga of show business family. 88 m.

13. THE WORLD CHANGES. Warners, '33. Sp: Ed. Chodorov from the novel *America Kneels* by Sheridan Gibney. *Mervyn LeRoy.* Paul Muni, Mary Astor, Aline MacMahon, Donald Cook, Alan Dinehart, Guy Kibbee, Margaret Lindsay, Henry O'Neill, Jean Muir, Anna Q. Nilsson, Patricia Ellis, Willard Robertson, Douglass Dumbrille, Sidney Toler, Alan Mowbray, Marjorie Gateson, Jackie Searle. Panorama of seven decades from Dakotas of pioneer times to Wall Street of '29. MR (billed 27th in cast) plays son of pioneers Nilsson and Robertson. 91 m.

14. THE CHIEF. MGM, '33. Sp: Arthur Caesar and Robert E. Hopkins. *Chas. F. Riesner.* Ed Wynn, Chas. 'Chic' Sale, Dorothy Mackaill, Wm. (Stage) Boyd, Effie Ellsler, Geo. Givot, C. Henry Gordon, Purnell B. Pratt, Bradley Page, Nat Pendleton, Jackie Searle. Wynn, son of dead fire hero on old Bowery, becomes honorary fire chief through series of accidental heroic deeds. MR is a local youth named Willie, but despite 7th billing, he has no dialogue and is in only one scene. 80 m.

15. BELOVED. Universal, '34. Sp: Paul Gangelin and Geo. O'Neill from a story by Gangelin. *Victor Schertzinger.* John Boles, Gloria Stuart, Albert Conti, Morgan Farley, Dorothy Peterson, Lucile Gleason, Mae Busch. Musician Boles devotes life to writing symphonic portrait of

America. MR plays him as child prodigy in epic spanning ninety years. 78 m.

16. I LIKE IT THAT WAY. Universal, '34. Sp: Chandler Sprague and Jos. Santley from a story by Harry Sauber. *Harry Lachman.* Roger Pryor, Gloria Stuart, Marian Marsh, Shirley Grey, Lucile Gleason, Noel Madison, Gloria Shea, Mae Busch, Merna Kennedy, John Darrow, Onslow Stevens. Programmer about insurance agent (Pryor) who falls for nightclub singer (Stuart) whose background his sister (Marsh) is leery of. MR is a Western Union messenger boy. 66 m.

17. LOVE BIRDS. Universal, '34. Sp: Doris Anderson from a story by Clarence Marks and Dale Van Every. *Wm. A. Seiter.* Slim Summerville, ZaSu Pitts, Frederick Burton, Emmer Vogan, Dorothy Christy, Maude Eburne, Hugh Enfield. Rural enemies Summerville and Pitts are each duped into buying the same shack miles from nowhere but it turns out to be located in center of gold rush. MR is Pitts's nephew. 62 m.

18. HALF A SINNER. Universal, '34. Sp: Earle Snell and Clarence Marks from the play *The Deacon* by John B. Hymer and LeRoy Clemens. *Kurt Neumann.* Sally Blane, Joel McCrea, Berton Churchill, Alexandra Carlisle, Guinn Williams, Walter Brennan. Card shark Churchill (recreating the role he originated on Broadway in '25) posing as deacon is exposed by pair (Blane and McCrea) who met him while riding the rails. She has since settled down in small town working in hotel where MR is owner's son. McCrea is now garage mechanic and coach of MR's football team. Filmed previously as *Alias the Deacon* ('27) with Jean Hersholt in the title role, and remade in '40 with Bob Burns. 78 m.

19. THE LOST JUNGLE. Mascot, '34. Sp: Sherman Lowe and Al Martin. *Armand Schaefer and Dave Howard.* Clyde Beatty, Cecilia Parker, Syd Saylor, Warner Richmond, Wheeler Oakman, Lloyd Ingraham, Maston Williams, J. Craufurd Kent, Lloyd Whitlock. Feature version of Beatty serial about wild animal expedition and search for lost treasure on tropic isle. MR is last billed as "Mickey." (Rooney also was in the serial.) 70 m.

20. MANHATTAN MELODRAMA. MGM, '34. Sp: Oliver H. P. Garrett and Jos. L. Mankiewicz from a story by Arthur Caesar. *W. S. Van Dyke.* Clark Gable, Myrna Loy, Wm. Powell, Leo Carrillo, Nat Pendleton, Geo. Sidney, Isabel Jewell, Frank Conroy, Shirley Ross, Jimmy

Butler. Orphans MR and Butler grow up together to become a bigtime gambler (Gable) and DA (Powell) respectively. 93 m.

21. UPPERWORLD. Warners, '34. Sp: Ben Markson from a story by Ben Hecht. *Roy Del Ruth.* Warren William, Mary Astor, Ginger Rogers, Andy Devine, Dickie Moore, Ferdinand Gottschalk, Robert Barrat, J. Carrol Naish, Sidney Toler, Henry O'Neill. Love triangle involving a railroad magnate, his social climbing wife and a chorus girl. Twelfth billed MR is a youngster named Jerry McDonald, although the role seems to be missing from the release print and probably ended on the cutting-room floor. 75 m.

22. HIDE-OUT. MGM, '34. Sp: Frances Goodrich and Albert Hackett from a story by Mauri Grashin. *W. S. Van Dyke.* Robert Montgomery, Maureen O'Sullivan, Ed. Arnold, Eliz. Patterson, C. Henry Gordon, Ed. Brophy, Herman Bing, Louise Henry, Harold Huber. Racketeer Montgomery hides out on Catskills farm where he falls for MR's school-teacher sister O'Sullivan. Noted *Variety:* "Rooney wellnigh steals the picture." 80 m.

23. CHAINED. MGM, '34. Sp: John Lee Mahin from a story by Edgar Selwyn. *Clarence Brown.* Clark Gable, Joan Crawford, Otto Kruger, Stuart Erwin, Marjorie Gateson, Una O'Connor, Akim Tamiroff. Wealthy shipping magnate Kruger loses girlfriend Crawford to South American rancher Gable. MR turns up briefly poolside aboard a luxury liner. 76 m.

24. BLIND DATE. Columbia, '34. Sp: Ethel Hill. *Roy Wm. Neill.* Ann Sothern, Paul Kelly, Neil Hamilton, Spencer Charters, Jane Darwell, Joan Gale, Geneva Mitchell. Neglected by auto mechanic boyfriend Kelly, secretary Sothern goes on blind date with her boss's son Hamilton. MR is her kid brother. 76 m.

25. DEATH ON THE DIAMOND. MGM, '34. Sp: Harvey Thew, Jos. Sherman and Ralph Spence from the book by Courtland Fitzsimmons. *Ed. Sedgwick.* Rob't Young, Madge Evans, Nat Pendleton, Ted Healy, C. Henry Gordon, Paul Kelly, Ed. Brophy, Willard Robertson, Robert Livingston, David Landau. Baseball team is plagued by snipers in the bleachers, stranglers in the locker room, poisoners in the commissary, booby-trapped spitballs, but overcomes odds to win the pennant, thanks to upstanding young pitcher Young. MR is the team's batboy. 69 m.

26. THE COUNTY CHAIRMAN. Fox, '35. Sp: Sam Hellman and

Gladys Lehman from the play by Geo. Ade. *John Blystone.* Will Rogers, Evelyn Venable, Kent Taylor, Louise Dresser, Berton Churchill, Frank Melton. Rural county chairman Rogers helps get partner Taylor elected DA, though latter's future father-in-law is rival candidate. MR is a local kid named Freckles. 79 m.

27. RECKLESS. MGM, '35. Sp: P. J. Wolfson from a story by Oliver Jeffries. *Victor Fleming.* Jean Harlow, Wm. Powell, Franchot Tone, May Robson, Rosalind Russell, Nat Pendleton, Ted Healy, Rob't Light, Henry Stephenson, Louise Henry, Allan Jones, Jas. Ellison, Farina, Man Mountain Dean. Sports promotor Powell and millionaire Tone vie for Broadway dancer Harlow in soaper. MR is young pal of Powell whom latter sets up in various youthful enterprises and who offers meager savings to his mentor when trouble arises. 99 m.

28. THE HEALER (also called LITTLE PAL). Monogram, '35. Sp: Jas. Knox Millen and John Goodrich from the novel by Rob't Herrick. *Reginald Barker.* Ralph Bellamy, Karen Morley, Judith Allen, J. Farrell MacDonald, Rob't McWade. Bellamy is doctor whose work with crippled children is jeopardized when society girl Allen starts chasing him. MR is cripple who recovers use of legs by "exercise of supreme faith." 75 m.

29. A MIDSUMMER NIGHT'S DREAM. Warners, '35. Sp: Chas. Kenyon and Mary C. McCall from the play by Wm. Shakespeare. *Max Reinhardt and Wm. Dieterle.* Jas. Cagney, Olivia de Havilland, Joe E. Brown, Hugh Herbert, Dick Powell, Frank McHugh, Victor Jory, Ross Alexander, Grant Mitchell, Nini Theilade, Verree Teasdale, Jean Muir, Ian Hunter, Anita Louise, Hobart Cavanaugh, Arthur Treacher. Said *The New York Times:* "Rooney's remarkable performance as Puck is one of the major delights of the work." 132 m.

30. AH, WILDERNESS! MGM, '35. Sp: Frances Goodrich and Albert Hackett from the Eugene O'Neill play. *Clarence Brown.* Wallace Beery, Lionel Barrymore, Aline MacMahon, Cecilia Parker, Spring Byington, Charley Grapewin, Frank Albertson, Eric Linden, Ed. Nugent, Bonita Granville. Circa 1906 American family portrait about teenager Linden's relationship with his father (Barrymore) and his tippling uncle (Beery). MR is the family's youngest son, Tommy. 98 m.

31. RIFFRAFF. MGM, '35. Sp: Frances Marion, H. W. Hanemann and Anita Loos from a story by Marion. *J. Walter Ruben.* Jean Harlow, Spencer Tracy, Una Merkel, Jos. Calleia, Victor Kilian, J. Farrell

MacDonald, Roger Imhoff, Juanita Quigley, Vince Barnett, Paul Hurst, Geo. Givot. Waterfront belle Harlow becomes involved in fisherman's strike led by Tracy against tuna king Calleia. MR is kid brother of Harlow and Merkel. 93 m.

32. LITTLE LORD FAUNTLEROY. Selznick/United Artists, '36. Sp: Hugh Walpole from the story by Frances Hodgson Burnett. *John Cromwell*. C. Aubrey Smith, Freddie Bartholomew, Dolores Costello Barrymore, Henry Stephenson, Guy Kibbee, Eric Alden, Una O'Connor, Jackie Searle, E. E. Clive. American lad (Bartholomew) inherits lordship and goes to live with English grandfather (Smith) who refuses to receive boy's mother (Costello) because his own son had married against his wishes. MR is lord's Brooklyn pal, bootblack Dick Tipton. Previously filmed in 1914 and 1921, and remade as a TV movie in 1979. 101 m.

33. THE DEVIL IS A SISSY (also called THE DEVIL TAKES THE COUNT). MGM, '36. Sp: John Lee Mahin and Richard Schayer from a story by Rowland Brown. *W. S. Van Dyke*. Freddie Bartholomew, Jackie Cooper, Ian Hunter, Peggy Conklin, Katherine Alexander, Gene Lockhart, Kathleen Lockhart, Jonathan Hale, Grant Mitchell, Harold Huber, Frank Puglia. English lad (Bartholomew) comes to school in America, falls in with local toughs MR and Cooper, helps MR get money for tombstone for latter's executed gangster father. *The New York Times* said of MR: "His is, without question, one of the finest performances of the year." 91 m.

34. DOWN THE STRETCH. Warners, '36. Sp: Wm. Jacobs. *Wm. Clemens*. Patricia Ellis, Dennis Moore, Willie Best, Gordon Hart, Gordon Elliott. Programmer about jockey (MR) who becomes ward of horsewoman Ellis out of pity because his father rode her father's mounts and became involved in her father's racing scandal. 65 m.

35. CAPTAINS COURAGEOUS. MGM, '37. Sp: John Lee Mahin, Marc Connelly, and Dale Van Every from the Rudyard Kipling novel. *Victor Fleming*. Spencer Tracy, Freddie Bartholomew, Lionel Barrymore, Melvyn Douglas, Charley Grapewin, John Carradine, Jack LaRue, Oscar O'Shea. In the screen classic, Douglas's pampered son Bartholomew falls from ocean liner and is picked up by Portuguese fisherman Tracy from Gloucester-based boat of Captain Barrymore. MR is Barrymore's son. Remade as a TV movie in 1977. 116 m.

36. SLAVE SHIP. 20th C-F, '37. Sp: Sam Hellman, Lamar Trotti, and

Gladys Lehman from the Wm. Faulkner story based on the novel *The Last Slaver* by Geo. S. King. *Tay Garnett.* Warner Baxter, Wallace Beery, Eliz. Allen, Geo. Sanders, Jane Darwell, Jos. Schildkraut, Billy Bevan, Francis Ford, J. Farrell MacDonald, Paul Hurst, Miles Mander. MR is cabin boy on slave ship whose captain (Baxter) falls for a woman, abandons black ivory trade, faces mutiny. 91 m.

37. A FAMILY AFFAIR. MGM, '37. Sp: Kay Van Riper from the play *Skidding* by Aurania Rouverol. *Geo. B. Seitz.* Lionel Barrymore, Cecilia Parker, Sara Haden, Eric Linden, Spring Byington, Charley Grapewin, Julie Haydon. In the first of the Hardy movies, the Judge faces election woes when he signs an order halting aqueduct which would be a boon to the county. 68 m.

38. HOOSIER SCHOOLBOY. Monogram, '37. Sp: Rob't Lee Johnson from the novel by Ed. Eggleston. *Wm. Nigh.* Anne Nagel, Frank Shields, Ed. Pawley, Wm. Gould, Bradley Metcalf, Doris Rankin, Helena Grant. Farmboy (MR) who is ridiculed by classmates for his loyalty to his war-wounded dad is helped by pretty teacher whose beau gets the old man a job driving a milk truck. When his father is killed during a strike, the dairy owner adopts MR. 62 m.

39. LIVE, LOVE AND LEARN. MGM, '37. Sp: Chas. Brackett, Cyril Hume, and Richard Maibaum from a story by Marion Parsonnet. *Geo. Fitzmaurice.* Rob't Montgomery, Rosalind Russell, Rob't Benchley, Helen Vinson, E. E. Clive, Monty Woolley (in screen debut). Struggling artist Montgomery weds wealth-weary heiress Russell who finds herself on the Park Avenue she tried to escape after husband reaches the big time through aid of society matron Vinson. MR is a pesky neighborhood kid who keeps bothering the artist at work. 78 m.

40. THOROUGHBREDS DON'T CRY. MGM, '37. Sp: Lawrence Hazard from a story by Eleanore Griffin and J. Walter Ruben. *Alfred E. Green.* Judy Garland, Sophie Tucker, C. Aubrey Smith, Ronald Sinclair, Forrester Harvey, Frankie Darro, Chas. D. Brown. In his first film with Garland, MR is jockey sought by English sportsman Smith to ride latter's champion mount, and is bribed to throw the race by his own crooked father (Brown). Garland (billed ahead of MR) is niece of owner of racetrack boardinghouse. 79 m.

41. YOU'RE ONLY YOUNG ONCE. MGM, '38. Sp: Kay Van Riper. *Geo. B. Seitz.* Lewis Stone, Cecilia Parker, Fay Holden, Sara Haden, Ann Rutherford, Frank Craven, Eleanor Lynn, Ted Pearson. The

Hardys go swordfishing off Catalina during the Judge's vacation and return home so he can meet note signed for publisher friend Craven. 76 m.

42. LOVE IS A HEADACHE. MGM, '38. Sp: Marion Parsonnet, Harry Ruskin, and Wm. R. Lipman. *Richard Thorpe.* Gladys George, Franchot Tone, Ted Healy, Frank Jenks, Virginia Weidler, Fay Holden, Ralph Morgan. Broadway star George adopts two waifs (MR and Weidler) as a publicity stunt and is defended in her "kidnapping" by columnist Tone who loves her. 73 m.

43. JUDGE HARDY'S CHILDREN. MGM, '38. Sp: Kay Van Riper. *Geo. B. Seitz.* Lewis Stone, Cecilia Parker, Fay Holden, Ann Rutherford, Ruth Hussey, Betty Ross Clarke, Jonathan Hale. The Judge heads power commission investigation in Washington and discovers daughter has leaked information to lobbyists, but Andy's innocent actions save the day as usual. 77 m.

44. HOLD THAT KISS. MGM, '38. Sp: Stanley Rauh. *Edwin L. Marin.* Maureen O'Sullivan, Dennis O'Keefe, Geo. Barbier, Jessie Ralph, Fay Holden, Ed. S. Brophy, Frank Albertson, Ruth Hussey, Phillip Terry. MR is brother of O'Sullivan who is pretending to be a debutante to impress a clerk (O'Keefe) while he, to win her, is feigning wealth. 79 m.

45. LORD JEFF. MGM, '38. Sp: Jas. Kevin McGuinness from a story by Bradford Ropes, Val Burton, and Endre Boehm. *Sam Wood.* Freddie Bartholomew, Chas. Coburn, Gale Sondergaard, Peter Lawford, Terry Kilburn, Herbert Mundin, Walter Tetley, Geo. Zucco, Monty Woolley. Bartholomew is a delinquent who is sent to an English naval training school, rebels and runs away. Irish-accented MR is buddy who covers up for him. 85 m.

46. LOVE FINDS ANDY HARDY. MGM, '38. Sp: Wm. Ludwig from a story by Vivien R. Bretherton based on characters created by Aurania Rouverol. *Geo. B. Seitz.* Lewis Stone, Judy Garland, Cecilia Parker, Fay Holden, Ann Rutherford, Lana Turner, Betty Ross Clarke, Marie Blake, Don Castle, Gene Reynolds. When regular girl-friend Rutherford leaves for Christmas visit with grandmother, Andy takes up with new girl next door (Garland). 90 m.

47. BOYS TOWN. MGM, '38. Sp: Dore Schary and John Meehan from a story by Schary and Eleanore Griffin. *Norman Taurog.* Spencer Tracy, Henry Hull, Leslie Fenton, Gene Reynolds, Ed. Norris, Addi-

son Richards, Jonathan Hale, Minor Watson, Victor Kilian. The memorable film of how Father Flanagan (Tracy) started Boys Town with four youngsters, the toughest of whom is MR, whose gangster brother wanted him to have a fresh start. 93 m.

48. STABLEMATES. MGM, '38. Sp: Leonard Praskins and Richard Maibaum from a story by Wm. Thiele and Reginald Owen. *Sam Wood.* Wallace Beery, Arthur Hohl, Margaret Hamilton, Minor Watson, Marjorie Gateson. MR is a homeless jockey (again) who talks drunken veterinarian-turned-tout Beery into operating on foot of prospective race winner. 89 m.

49. OUT WEST WITH THE HARDYS. MGM, '38. Sp: Kay Van Riper, Wm. Ludwig, and Agnes Christine Johnston. *Geo. B. Seitz.* Lewis Stone, Cecilia Parker, Fay Holden, Sara Haden, Ann Rutherford, Virginia Weidler, Don Castle, Ralph Morgan, Tom Neal, Nana Bryant, Gordon Jones. Andy helps the Judge aid latter's old sweetheart and her husband save the water rights on their Arizona ranch. 83 m.

50. THE ADVENTURES OF HUCKLEBERRY FINN. MGM, '39. Sp: Hugo Butler from the story by Mark Twain. *Richard Thorpe.* Walter Connolly, Wm. Frawley, Rex Ingram, Lynne Carver, Jo Ann Sayers, Minor Watson, Victor Kilian. MR plays the title role. 90 m.

51. THE HARDYS RIDE HIGH. MGM, '39. Sp: Kay Van Riper. Wm. Ludwig, and Agnes Christine Johnston. *Geo. B. Seitz.* Lewis Stone, Cecilia Parker, Fay Holden, Sara Haden, Ann Rutherford, Virginia Grey, Marsha Hunt, Minor Watson. The Hardys learn that the Judge is apparently heir to a fortune and go on a spending spree before discovering it is all a mistake. 80 m.

52. ANDY HARDY GETS SPRING FEVER. MGM, '39. Sp: Kay Van Riper. *W. S. Van Dyke.* Lewis Stone, Cecilia Parker, Fay Holden, Sara Haden, Ann Rutherford, Helen Gilbert, Terry Kilburn, Sidney Miller, Addison Richards, Joe Yule, Sr. Andy falls for his high school teacher (Gilbert) and is in the throes of puppy love and the class play simultaneously. 85 m.

53. BABES IN ARMS. MGM, '39. Sp: Kay Van Riper and Jack McGowan from the play by Richard Rodgers and Lorenz Hart. *Busby Berkeley.* Judy Garland, Chas. Winninger, Guy Kibbee, Henry Hull, June Preisser, Geo. "Gabby" Hayes, Margaret Hamilton, John Sheffield, Rand Brooks, Ann Shoemaker. MR and Garland carry on for ex-

vaudevillian parents. In Oscar-nominated tour-de-force, MR plays romantic lead, sings, dances, appears in blackface and false beard and mustache, impersonates Gable, Barrymore, etc. 95 m.

54. JUDGE HARDY AND SON. MGM, '39. Sp: Carey Wilson. *Geo. B. Seitz.* Lewis Stone, Cecilia Parker, Fay Holden, Sara Haden, Ann Rutherford, June Preisser, Maria Ouspenskaya, Henry Hull, Martha O'Driscoll. In less frivolous Hardy outing, an elderly couple facing eviction turns to the Judge for help. 88 m.

55. YOUNG TOM EDISON. MGM, '40. Sp: Bradbury Foote, Dore Schary, and Hugo Butler. *Norman Taurog.* Fay Bainter, Virginia Weidler, Geo. Bancroft, Eugene Pallette, Victor Kilian, Bobby Jordan, Lloyd Corrigan, J. M. Kerrigan, Clem Bevans. MR played the inventor through teen-age. 85 m.

56. ANDY HARDY MEETS DEBUTANTE. MGM, '40. Sp: Thos. Seiler and Annellee Whitmore. *Geo. B. Seitz.* Lewis Stone, Cecilia Parker, Fay Holden, Sara Haden, Ann Rutherford, Judy Garland, Diana Lewis, Addison Richards. Andy falls for NYC socialite Lewis whose newspaper photo he had seen and asks Garland to set up introduction when he goes to the big city. 87 m.

57. STRIKE UP THE BAND. MGM, '40. Sp: John Monks, Jr., and Fred Finklehoffe. *Busby Berkeley.* Judy Garland, Paul Whiteman, June Preisser, Wm. Tracy, Larry Nunn, Ann Shoemaker. MR turns high school band into a swing group and raises money for ensemble to go to Paul Whiteman's Chicago auditions with MR as drummer and Garland as singer. 120 m.

58. ANDY HARDY'S PRIVATE SECRETARY. MGM, '41. Sp: Jane Murfin and Harry Ruskin from a story by Katherine Brush. *Geo. B. Seitz.* Lewis Stone, Fay Holden, Sara Haden, Ann Rutherford, Gene Reynolds, Ian Hunter, Kathryn Grayson (film debut), Todd Karns, Addison Richards. As senior class president and treasurer, Andy accepts bad check from father (Hunter) of pretty coed (Grayson), but the Judge proceeds to help the father and Andy gives the girl job as senior committee secretary. 100 m.

59. MEN OF BOYS TOWN. MGM, '41. Sp: Jas. Kevin McGuinness. *Norman Taurog.* Spencer Tracy, Bobs Watson, Larry Nunn, Darryl Hickman, Henry O'Neill, Anne Revere, Lee J. Cobb, Sidney Miller, Arthur Hohl, Lloyd Corrigan, Addison Richards. MR, now mayor of Boys Town, and Tracy as Father Flanagan prepare to ask money from

pawnbroker Cobb who helped found the city which now faces bank-ruptcy. Sequel to #47. 106 m.

60. LIFE BEGINS FOR ANDY HARDY. MGM, '41. Sp: Agnes Chris-tine Johnston. *Geo. B. Seitz.* Lewis Stone, Fay Holden, Sara Haden, Ann Rutherford, Judy Garland, Ray McDonald, Patricia Dane. Andy spends a month in NYC visiting his 'other' girlfriend Garland after graduating from high school, and gets taken by gold-digger Dane. 100 m.

61. BABES ON BROADWAY. MGM, '41. Sp: Fred Finklehoffe and Elaine Ryan from a story by Finklehoffe. *Busby Berkeley.* Judy Garland, Fay Bainter, Virginia Weidler, Jas. Gleason, Ray McDonald, Richard Quine, Donald Meek,. Alexander Woollcott. MR is member of song-and-dance trio seeking big Broadway break, and who, after meeting young singer (Garland), proceed to produce their own show to gain recognition. 117 m.

62. THE COURTSHIP OF ANDY HARDY. MGM, '42. Sp: Agnes Christine Johnston. *Geo. B. Seitz.* Lewis Stone, Cecilia Parker, Fay Holden, Sara Haden, Ann Rutherford, Donna Reed, Wm. Lundigan, Frieda Inescort, Harvey Stephens. Before leaving for college, Andy has fling with daughter (Reed) of couple seeking divorce through the Judge. 93 m.

63. A YANK AT ETON. MGM, '42. Sp: Geo. Oppenheimer, Lionel Houser, and Thos. Phipps from a story by Oppenheimer. *Norman Taurog.* Freddie Bartholomew, Edmund Gwenn, Ian Hunter, Peter Lawford, Marta Linden, Alan Mowbray, Juanita Quigley, Alan Napier, Terry Kilburn. MR abandons hope of attending Notre Dame when his widowed mother (Linden) weds Englishman (Hunter), and ends up, reluctantly, at Eton. 87 m.

64. ANDY HARDY'S DOUBLE LIFE (also called ANDY HARDY STEPS OUT). MGM, '42. Sp: Agnes Christine Johnston. *Geo. B. Seitz.* Lewis Stone, Cecilia Parker, Fay Holden, Sara Haden, Ann Ruther-ford, Esther Williams, Susan Peters, Wm. Lundigan, Bobby Blake. Andy regrets that his college is not co-educational but manages to juggle dating routine between steady girl Rutherford and new flame, Esther Williams (in screen debut). 91 m.

65. THE HUMAN COMEDY. MGM, '43. Sp: Howard Estabrook from the Wm. Saroyan novel. *Clarence Brown.* Frank Morgan, Jas. Craig, Marsha Hunt, Fay Bainter, Van Johnson, Donna Reed, Jackie 'Butch'

Jenkins, Ray Collins, Dorothy Morris, Ann Ayars, John Craven, Henry O'Neill, Alan Baxter, Darryl Hickman, Barry Nelson, Rob't Mitchum. Eloquent film of rural Americana at start of WWII as seen through the eyes of teenager MR, who received his second Oscar nomination for Best Actor. 116 m.

66. **GIRL CRAZY.** MGM, '43. Sp: Fred Finklehoffe from the play by Guy Boulton and Jack McGowan. *Norman Taurog.* Judy Garland, Gil Stratton, Rob't E. Strickland, Rags Ragland, June Allyson, Nancy Walker, Guy Kibbee, Frances Rafferty, Henry O'Neill, Howard Freeman, Tommy Dorsey and his Orchestra. In remake of the '32 Wheeler and Woolsey film, MR is Yale playboy whose father sends him to isolated boys college in West. He saves the school from foreclosure by staging big jamborees and turns it coed. MGM remade it in '65 as *When the Boys Meet the Girls.* 97 m.

67. **THOUSANDS CHEER.** MGM, '43. Sp: Paul Jarrico and Richard Collins from their story "Private Miss Jones." *Geo Sidney.* Kathryn Grayson, Gene Kelly, Mary Astor, John Boles, Ben Blue, Frances Rafferty, Frank Jenks. Army private Kelly romances concert singer Grayson who happens to be daughter of his colonel (Boles). Film is highlighted by USO show featuring most of MGM's contract players, with MR as emcee. 124 m.

68. **ANDY HARDY'S DOUBLE TROUBLE.** MGM, '44. Sp: Harry Ruskin, Wm. Ludwig, and Agnes Christine Johnston. *Geo. B. Seitz.* Lewis Stone, Fay Holden, Sara Haden, Herbert Marshall, Bonita Granville, Jean Porter, Keye Luke, Lee Wilde, Lyn Wilde. Andy falls for young coed Granville who is attracted to English professor Marshall, so he turns his attention to blond twins. 107 m.

69. **NATIONAL VELVET.** MGM, '44. Sp: Theodore Reeves and Helen Deutsch from the novel by Enid Bagnold. *Clarence Brown.* Donald Crisp, Elizabeth Taylor, Anne Revere, Angela Lansbury, Jackie 'Butch' Jenkins, Arthur Treacher, Reg. Owen, Juanita Quigley, Terry Kilburn. The classic about a young girl (Taylor) who, with help of stable boy MR, trains horse to be jumper and rides it in the Grand National. 125 m.

70. **ZIEGFELD FOLLIES.** MGM, '46. *Vincente Minnelli.* MR had at least two numbers with Judy Garland in this all-star musical: "Will You Love Me in Technicolor As You Do in Black and White?" and "As

Long As I Have My Art." Curiously, for a star of Rooney's caliber (he then was the studio's #1 attraction), both of his songs, and his entire part, ended on the cutting-room floor. 110 m.

71. LOVE LAUGHS AT ANDY HARDY. MGM, '46. Sp: Harry Ruskin and Wm. Ludwig from a story by Howard Dimsdale. *Willis Goldbeck*. Lewis Stone, Fay Holden, Sara Haden, Bonita Granville, Lina Romay, Dorothy Ford, Clinton Sundberg, Addison Richards. End of the line for original Hardy series finds Andy returning from army to resume his schooling and romance with Granville. He becomes despondent when she announces impending marriage to someone else and decides to leave college until he spots a new girl (Romay), so he stays on to romance her, finish school, and get his law degree. 91 m.

72. KILLER McCOY. MGM, '47. Sp: Frederick Hazlitt Brennan from a story by Thos. Lennon, Geo. Bruce, and Geo. Oppenheimer. *Roy Rowland*. Brian Donlevy, Ann Blyth, Jas. Dunn, Sam Levene, Tom Tully, Walter Sande, Mickey Knox, Bob Steele, Gloria Holden, Jas. Bell. MR is a young tough who turns boxer and accidentally kills his mentor in the ring. He then gets mixed up with gangster Donlevy whom he ends up reforming. A remake of *The Crowd Roars* ('38). 104 m.

73. SUMMER HOLIDAY. MGM, '48. Sp: Frances Goodrich and Albert Hackett from the play *Ah, Wilderness!* by Eugene O'Neill. *Rouben Mamoulian*. Gloria DeHaven, Walter Huston, Frank Morgan, Jackie 'Butch' Jenkins, Marilyn Maxwell, Agnes Moorehead, Anne Francis, Selena Royle, Howard Freeman, Ruth Brady. In musical remake of #30, MR is now the eldest son who graduates from college and falls for daughter (DeHaven) of town's leading merchant. 92 m.

74. WORDS AND MUSIC. MGM, '48. Sp: Fred Finklehoffe from a story by Guy Boulton and Jean Holloway. *Norman Taurog*. Perry Como, Ann Sothern, Tom Drake, Betty Garrett, Janet Leigh, Marshall Thompson, Richard Quine, Clinton Sundberg, Emory Parnell, and guests: June Allyson, Judy Garland, Lena Horne, Gene Kelly, Cyd Charisse, Mel Tormé, Vera-Ellen. MR is Lorenz Hart to Tom Drake's Richard Rodgers in laughably distorted biopic of the famed composers. 119 m.

75. THE BIG WHEEL. United Artists, '49. Sp: Rob't Smith. *Ed. Ludwig*. Thos. Mitchell, Michael O'Shea, Spring Byington, Mary Hatcher, Hattie McDaniel, Lina Romay, Steve Brodie, Allen Jenkins, Dick

Lane. MR is racing driver's son who tries to follow in his late father's tracks, beginning with hot rods and midgets and working way up to the Indianapolis Classic. 92 m.

76. QUICKSAND. UA, '50. Sp: Rob't Smith. *Irving Pichel.* Jeanne Cagney, Peter Lorre, Barbara Bates, Taylor Holmes, Art Smith, Wally Cassell, Minerva Urecal, Patsy O'Connor. MR is skirt-chasing auto mechanic who commits a series of crimes to cover his initial mistake of borrowing $20 from the boss's till. 79 m.

77. HE'S A COCKEYED WONDER. Columbia, '50. Sp: Jack Henley. *Peter Godfrey.* Terry Moore, Wm. Demarest, Chas. Arnt, Ross Ford, Ned Glass, Mike Mazurki, Douglas Fowley, Wm. Phillips. MR is magician's nephew who uses tricks to capture a gang of inept thieves. 86 m.

78. THE FIREBALL. 20th C-F, '50. Sp: Tay Garnett and Horace McCoy. *Tay Garnett.* Pat O'Brien, Beverly Tyler, Marilyn Monroe, Jas. Brown, Ralph Dumke, Milburn Stone, Glenn Corbett. With aid of amiable priest O'Brien, embattled orphan MR becomes a professional roller-skating champion. 84 m.

79. MY OUTLAW BROTHER. UA, '51. Sp: Gene Fowler, Jr., from the novel *South of the Rio Grande* by Max Brand. *Elliott Nugent.* Wanda Hendrix, Rob't Preston, Rob't Stack, Carlos Muzquiz, Jose Torvay, Elliott Nugent. MR searches Mexico for his bandit brother Stack who has been sending money home to NYC to support the family. 82 m.

80. THE STRIP. MGM, '51. Sp: Allen Rivkin. *Leslie Kardos.* Sally Forrest, Jas. Craig, Wm. Demarest, Kay Brown, Tommy Rettig, Tom Powers, Myra Dell, Monica Lewis, Vic Damone, Louis Armstrong, Jack Teagarden. Programmer about drummer MR who gets mixed up with bigtime bookie Craig and falls for latter's girlfriend dancer Forrest. Title refers to Hollywood Boulevard. 85 m.

81. SOUND OFF. Columbia, '52. Sp: Blake Edwards and Richard Quine. *Richard Quine.* Anne James, Sammy White, John Archer, Gordon Jones, Wally Cassell, Arthur Space. Military comedy about a nightclub entertainer (MR) who finds himself in the army. 83 m.

82. ALL ASHORE. Columbia, '53. Sp: Blake Edwards and Richard Quine from a story by Edwards and Rob't Wells. *Richard Quine.* Dick Haymes, Peggy Ryan, Ray McDonald, Barbara Bates, Jody Lawrance, Fay Roope, Jean Willes, Patricia Walker, Edwin Parker, Ben Welden,

Joan Shawlee. Three sailors on the town, with MR landing daughter of rich businessman. 80 m.

83. **MICKEY ROONEY, THEN AND NOW.** Columbia, '53. *Ralph Staub.* One-reeler featuring MR commenting on scenes from his films since '30. 10 m.

84. **OFF LIMITS.** Paramount, '53. Sp: Hal Kanter and Jack Sher. *Geo. Marshall.* Bob Hope, Marilyn Maxwell, Eddie Mayehoff, Stanley Clements, Marvin Miller, John Ridgely, Joan Taylor, Carolyn Jones, Mary Murphy, Jack Dempsey. Hope, manager of boxing champ Clements, is hoodwinked into joining army to protect his fighter, who is deferred. He meets and agrees to train soldier MR who wants to become a boxer, and falls for the kid's aunt (Maxwell), who objects to her nephew's ambitions. 89 m.

85. **A SLIGHT CASE OF LARCENY.** MGM, '53. Sp: Jerry Davis from a story by Jas. Poe. *Don Weis.* Eddie Bracken, Elaine Stewart, Marilyn Erskine, Douglas Fowley, Rob't Burton. Army buddies MR and Bracken open a gas station, engage in price war with rival across the street, and tap industrial gas pipe under their own station. 71 m.

86. **DRIVE A CROOKED ROAD.** Columbia, '54. Sp: Blake Edwards from Richard Quine's adaptation of a story by Jas. Benson Nablo. *Richard Quine.* Dianne Foster, Kevin McCarthy, Jack Kelly, Harry Landers, Jerry Paris, Paul Picerni. MR is a race driver who is duped into steering the escape car for three bank robbers. 82 m.

87. **THE ATOMIC KID.** Republic, '54. Sp: Blake Edwards from a story by Benedict Freedman and John Fenton Murray. *Leslie H. Martinson.* Rob't Strauss, Elaine Davis, Bill Goodwin, Whit Bissell, Hal March, Fay Roope, Peter Leeds, Joey Forman, Rob't E. Keane, Stanley Adams. In Rooney production, MR is a schnook who becomes the radioactive survivor of an A-bomb explosion. MR's only film with any of his actress wives. 86 m.

88. **THE BRIDGES AT TOKO-RI.** Paramount, '55. Sp: Valentine Davies from the Jas. Michener novel. *Mark Robson.* Wm. Holden, Grace Kelly, Fredric March, Rob't Strauss, Chas. McGraw, Earl Holliman, Dennis Weaver, Gene Reynolds. MR is a helicopter jockey whose talent is rescuing downed pilots during the Korean War. 103 m.

89. **THE TWINKLE IN GOD'S EYE.** Republic, '55. Sp: P. J. Wolfson. *Geo. Blair.* Coleen Gray, Hugh O'Brian, Joey Forman, Don Barry,

Touch Connors, Jil Jarmyn, Ruta Lee, Raymond Hatton. Fine little film about a young parson (MR) who attempts to bring religion into a rugged frontier community. Rooney also produced it and wrote title song. 73 m.

90. FRANCIS IN THE HAUNTED HOUSE. Universal-International, '56. Sp: Herbert Margolis and Wm. Raynor based on characters created by David Stern. *Chas. Lamont.* Virginia Welles, Paul Cavanagh, David Janssen, Mary Ellen Kaye, Richard Deacon, Jas. Flavin. Belated finale to the silly *Francis* series with MR replacing Donald O'Connor and Paul Frees's voice pinch-dubbing for that of Chill Wills as the mule. In this outing, the mule and MR track down murderer who is stalking medieval castle which has been transplanted stone by stone from Scotland to America. 79 m.

91. THE BOLD AND THE BRAVE. RKO, '56. Sp: Rob't Lewin. *Lewis R. Foster.* Wendell Corey, Don Taylor, Nicole Maurey, John Smith, Race Gentry, Stanley Adams. Good little war film about three GIs in Italy. MR is a happily wed lady killer who dreams of opening a restaurant in New Jersey. His hilarious dice game scene where he risks his $30,000 pot under a blanket during an air raid helped him win a supporting actor Oscar nomination. 90 m.

92. MAGNIFICENT ROUGHNECKS. Allied Artists, '56. Sp: Stephen Kandel. *Sherman A. Rose.* Jack Carson, Nancy Gates, Jeff Donnell, Myron Healey, Willis Bouchey, Eric Feldary, Alan Wells. Roughneck oilmen MR and Carson in South America vie with wildcatter Healey to get government contract by bringing in first producing well. 72 m.

93. OPERATION MAD BALL. Columbia, '57. Sp: Blake Edwards, Jed Harris and Arthur Carter from a play by Carter. *Richard Quine.* Jack Lemmon, Kathryn Grant, Ernie Kovacs, Arthur O'Connell, Jas. Darren, Roger Smith, Dick York, Wm. Leslie. Very funny movie about wheeler-dealer Medical Corps private (Lemmon) who stages an illegal bash for a group of nurses in wartime France. MR does a cameo as a bop-talking master sergeant in charge of transportation for the area. 105 m.

94. BABY FACE NELSON. UA, '57. Sp: Irving Shulman and Daniel Mainwaring from a story by Shulman. *Don Siegel.* Carolyn Jones, Cedric Hardwicke, Leo Gordon, Anthony Caruso, Jack Elam, Ted DeCorsia, John Hoyt, Emile Meyer, Elisha Cook, Jr. MR is the notorious Prohibition-era killer. 85 m.

95. ANDY HARDY COMES HOME. MGM, '58. Sp: Ed. Everett Hutshing and Rob't Morris Donley. *Howard W. Koch.* Patricia Breslin, Fay Holden, Cecilia Parker, Sara Haden, Teddy Rooney, Joey Forman, Jerry Colonna, Donald Barry, Johnny Weissmuller, Jr., Wm. Leslie, Vaughn Taylor, Frank Ferguson. Rooney-produced attempt to revive the Hardy series. Now a West Coast lawyer, Andy returns to Carvel after twelve-year absence with his wife and children to purchase a site for an aircraft plant, and is convinced to stay on and become a judge. Rooney's own son played Andy Hardy, Jr. 80 m.

96. A NICE LITTLE BANK THAT SHOULD BE ROBBED. 20th C-F, '58. Sp: Sydney Boehm from an article by Evan Wylie. *Henry Levin.* Tom Ewell, Mickey Shaughnessy, Dina Merrill, Madge Kennedy, Frances Bavier, Richard Deacon, Stanley Clements. MR and Ewell rob bank of $30,000, set up Saratoga racing stable, lose everything on their horse, pull another robbery, end up in jail, learn that their horse has become a big race winner. 87 m.

97. THE LAST MILE. UA, '59. Sp: Milton Subotsky and Seton I. Miller from the play by John Wexley. *Howard W. Koch.* Alan Bunce, Frank Conroy, Leon Janney, Frank Overton, Clifford David, Harry Millard, Ford Rainey, Johnny Seven, Donald Barry, Michael Constantine. MR is "Killer" John Mears (the career-making Spencer Tracy stage role) in remake of the '32 film about his breakout from death row. 81 m.

98. THE BIG OPERATOR. Albert Zugsmith/MGM, '59. Sp: Rob't Smith and Allen Rivkin from the story by Paul Gallico. *Chas. Haas.* Steve Cochran, Mamie Van Doren, Mel Tormé, Ray Danton, Jim Backus, Ray Anthony, Jackie Coogan, Chas. Chaplin, Jr., Ben Gage, Billy Daniels, Lawrence Dobkin, Jay North, Leo Gordon, Donald Barry, Ziva Rodann, Joey Forman. MR is a crooked union boss who terrorizes Cochran when latter threatens to expose his racket. A remake of *Joe Smith, American* ('42). 90 m.

99. PLATINUM HIGH SCHOOL. Zugsmith/MGM, '60. Sp: Rob't Smith from a story by Howard Breslin. *Chas. Haas.* Terry Moore, Dan Duryea, Yvette Mimieux, Warren Berlinger, Richard Jaeckel, Conway Twitty, Jimmy Boyd, Harold Lloyd, Jr., Elisha Cook, Jr., Mason Alan Dinehart, Cliff Edwards. In loose remake of the '55 *Bad Day at Black Rock*, MR is an engineer who returns from Pakistan to investigate his son's death at a military school on a remote California island. 95 m.

100. THE PRIVATE LIVES OF ADAM AND EVE. Zugsmith/Universal-International, '60. Sp: Rob't Hill. *Albert Zugsmith and Mickey Rooney.* Mamie Van Doren, Fay Spain, Mel Tormé, Tuesday Weld, Martin Milner, Cecil Kellaway, Paul Anka, Ziva Rodann. Stormbound bus passengers take refuge in a church where they share a common dream of the Creation. MR is a chiseling gambler in the group and a puckish devil in the dream. 86 m.

101. BREAKFAST AT TIFFANY'S. Paramount, '61. Sp: Geo. Axelrod from the book by Truman Capote. *Blake Edwards.* Audrey Hepburn, Geo. Peppard, Patricia Neal, Buddy Ebsen, Martin Balsam, Alan Reed, John McGiver, Jose-Luis de Vilallonga, Gil Lamb, Stanley Adams. Story of madcap call-girl Hepburn and her romance with a kept man (Peppard). MR does cameo as a bucktoothed, myopic Japanese photographer who lives in the upstairs apartment. 114 m.

102. KING OF THE ROARING TWENTIES. Allied Artists, '61. Sp: Jo Swerling from the book *The Big Bankroll* by Leo Katcher. *Jos. M. Newman.* David Janssen, Dianne Foster, Jack Carson, Mickey Shaughnessy, Diana Dors, Keenan Wynn, Dan O'Herlihy, Wm. Demarest, Jos. Schildkraut, Murvyn Vye, Regis Toomey, Teddy Rooney. Cheapie biopic of the notorious '20s gambler, Arnold Rothstein (Janssen). MR is his boyhood friend who sells him out to the press and is rubbed out for squealing. 106 m.

103. REQUIEM FOR A HEAVYWEIGHT. Columbia, '62. Sp: Rod Serling from his television play. *Ralph Nelson.* Anthony Quinn, Jackie Gleason, Julie Harris, Stanley Adams, Herbie Faye, Cassius Clay, Jack Dempsey, Madame Spivy. MR is the trainer of washed-up prize fighter Mountain Rivera (Quinn). 85 m.

104. EVERYTHING'S DUCKY. Columbia, '62. Sp: John Fenton Murray and Benedict Freeman. *Don Taylor.* Buddy Hackett, Jackie Cooper, Joanie Sommers, Roland Winters, Elizabeth MacRae, Richard Deacon. MR and Hackett are dim-witted sailors who befriend a talking duck that knows the secret formula vital to the success of the navy's launching program. 80 m.

105. IT'S A MAD MAD MAD MAD WORLD. UA, '63. Sp: Wm. and Tania Rose. *Stanley Kramer.* Spencer Tracy, Milton Berle, Sid Caesar, Buddy Hackett, Ethel Merman, Dick Shawn, Phil Silvers, Terry-Thomas, Jonathan Winters, Edie Adams, Dorothy Provine, Jimmy

Durante, others. Mad dash to locate hidden cache when group of strangers are given clue by dying man (Durante) about site of stolen money. MR and Hackett join race in runaway plane. 190 m.

106. SECRET INVASION. UA, '64. Sp: R. Wright Campbell. *Roger Corman.* Stewart Granger, Raf Vallone, Edd Byrnes, Henry Silva, Mia Massini, Wm. Campbell. British officer Granger forms team of convict specialists for wartime mission in Yugoslavia. MR is a vociferous anti-British Irish Republican. 95 m.

107. TWENTY-FOUR HOURS TO KILL. Assoc. British, '65. Sp: Peter Yeldham and Peter Welbeck. *Peter Bezencenet.* Lex Barker, Walter Slezak, Michael Medwin, Helga Somerfeld, Wolfgang Lukschy, Frank Anglade, Helga Lehner, Maria Rohm. MR is international flight pilot who double-crosses gold smuggling syndicate run by Slezak in Beirut. 83 m.

108. IL DIAVOLO INNAMORATO (In US '68, THE DEVIL IN LOVE). Fair, '66. Sp: Ettore Scola and Ruggero Maccari. *Ettore Scola.* Vittorio Gassman, Claudine Auger, Gabrielle Ferzetti, Ettore Manni, Liana Orfei, Giorgia Moll, Annabella Incontrera. Gassman is the Devil's emissary sent to Florence to reap discord between the Medicis and the Papal State. MR is his invisible (except to Gasman) aide. 97 m.

109. AMBUSH BAY. UA, '66. Sp: Marve Feinberg and Ib Melchior. *Ron Winston.* Hugh O'Brian, Jas. Mitchum, Tisa Chang, Pete Masterson, Harry Lauter, Greg Anderson. Nine marines on Philippines mission contact female spy who has information vital for MacArthur's upcoming invasion. MR is the tough sergeant who stays behind to hold off an enemy patrol. 109 m.

110. HOW TO STUFF A WILD BIKINI. American-International, '66. Sp: Wm. Asher and Leo Townsend. *Wm. Asher.* Annette Funicello, Dwayne Hickman, Brian Donlevy, Buster Keaton, Beverly Adams, Harvey Lembeck, John Ashley, Jody McCrea. In *Beach Party* pap, MR is a fast-talking ad-man named Peachy Keane who is searching for the perfect body for a contest, with the aid of Tahitian witch doctor Keaton and a pelican. 93 m.

111. THE EXTRAORDINARY SEAMAN. MGM, '68. Sp: Philip Rock and Hal Dresner from the novel by Rock. *John Frankenheimer.* David Niven, Faye Dunaway, Alan Alda, Jack Carter, Juano Hernandez, Barry Kelley. Sailors MR, Alda, and Carter, fleeing the Japanese in the

Philippines, come across a ghost (Niven) from the WWI Royal Navy who has been doomed to live on shipboard until he vindicates his family honor. 81 m.

112. SKIDOO. Paramount, '68. Sp: Doran Wm. Cannon. *Otto Preminger.* Jackie Gleason, Carol Channing, Frankie Avalon, Fred Clark, Michael Constantine, John Phillip Law, Peter Lawford, Burgess Meredith, Geo. Raft, Cesar Romero, Groucho Marx. Ex-mobster Gleason is called on by aging syndicate boss Marx to rub out informer MR who is living in luxury in prison. 97 m.

113. THE COMIC. Columbia, '69. Sp: Carl Reiner and Aaron Rubin. *Carl Reiner.* Dick Van Dyke, Michele Lee, Cornel Wilde, Jeannine Riley, Pert Kelton, Jeff Donnell, Steve Allen, Carl Reiner, Nina Wayne, Barbara Heller, Gavin MacLeod, Jay Novello, Fritz Feld, Jerome Cowan. The rise and fall and rise again of a comedy star (Van Dyke) from silent films to contemporary TV. MR is his old vaudeville pal. 94 m.

114. 80 STEPS TO JONAH. MPI-Warners, '69. Sp: Frederic Lewis Fox from a story by Fox and Gerd Oswald. *Gerd Oswald.* Wayne Newton, Jo Van Fleet, Keenan Wynn, Sal Mineo, Diana Ewing, Slim Pickens, R. G. Armstrong, Brandon Cruz, Teddy Quinn, Butch Patrick, Jackie Cahane. MR does a cameo as a drunk whose testimony about a stolen car accident is needed to clear Newton who has been hiding out as a handyman at a school for blind children. 105 m.

115. THE COCKEYED COWBOYS OF CALICO COUNTY. Universal, '70. Sp: Ranald MacDougall. *Tony Leader.* Dan Blocker, Nanette Fabray, Jim Backus, Wally Cox, Jack Elam, Henry Jones, Stubby Kaye, Noah Beery, Marge Champion, Donald Barry, Jack Cassidy, Hamilton Camp, Byron Foulger, Iron Eyes Cody. Comedy-drama of a lonely frontier blacksmith (Blocker) who sends for a mail-order bride. MR is seen briefly as a local cowpoke named Indian Tom. 99 m.

116. HOLLYWOOD BLUE. Sherpix, '70. *Bill Osco.* Tasteless compilation of erotic shorts and newly-filmed hard-core pornography, the "redeeming values" of which are interpolated interviews with MR and June Wilkinson who philosophize on Hollywood's sex life. MR's all-time low in films. 90 m.

117. B. J. LANG PRESENTS. CoBurt Productions/Maron Films, '71. Sp: Yabo Yablonsky from a story by John Durin. *Yabo Yablonsky.* Keenan Wynn, Luana Anders. MR is an insane ex-movie director who

fantasizes about the past and acts out his productions with a terrified girl in a warehouse of film memorabilia. 85 m.

118. EVIL ROY SLADE. Universal, '72. Sp: Garry Marshall and Jerry Belson. *Jerry Paris.* John Astin, Dick Shawn, Henry Gibson, Dom DeLuise, Edie Adams, Pam Austin, Milton Berle, Penny Marshall, John Ritter, Pat Buttram (narrator). Top-billed MR is railroad president Nelson Stool whose nemesis is a rotten outlaw (Astin) whose villainy knows no bounds in this satirical TV-movie western. 105 m.

119. RICHARD. Bertrand Castelli/Aurora City Group, '72. Sp: Lorees Yerby and Harry Hurwitz. *Lorees Yerby and Harry Hurwitz.* Richard M. Dixon (Jas. LaRoe), Dan Resin, Lynn Lipton, John Carradine, Paul Ford, Vivian Blaine, Kevin McCarthy, Hazen Gifford, Hank Garrett, Paul Forest. MR is the guardian angel in a satirical study of Richard Nixon's life from boyhood through the presidency. 83 m.

120. PULP. UA, '72. Sp: Mike Hodges. *Mike Hodges.* Michael Caine, Lizabeth Scott, Lionel Stander, Dennis Price, Nadia Cassini, Al Lettieri, Leopoldo Trieste, Amerigo Tot. MR had his best role in years as a '30s Hollywood star specializing in gangster roles who hires a hack writer (Caine) to "ghost" his revealing memoirs. 95 m.

121. THE GODMOTHERS. Michael Viola Prod., '73. Sp: Mickey Rooney from a story by Woody Kling and Robert Hilliard, based on an idea by Jerry Lester. *Wm. Grefe.* Frank Fontaine, Jerry Lester, Joe E. Ross, Billy Barty, Lou March, Tony Adams, Muriel James. Hoods MR and Lester are on the lam after angering Godfather Fontaine. Rooney wrote not only the screenplay but also the music. 97 m.

122. ACE OF HEARTS. Mundial Film, S. A., '74. Sp: Santiago Moncada. *Tulio DeMicheli.* Chris Robinson, Pilar Velazquez, Teresa Gimpera, Julian Ugarte, Eduardo Fajardo. Big business intrigue that revolves on the turn of a card. MR is Papa Joe, a poker playing gangster.

123. THUNDER COUNTY (aka IT SNOWS IN THE EVERGLADES). Trans-International Films, '74. Sp: K. Gordon Murray. *Chris Robinson.* Chris Robinson, Ted Cassidy. MR is a bartender in a bayou country roadhouse. 92 m.

124. THAT'S ENTERTAINMENT. MGM, '74. Sp: Jack Haley, Jr. *Jack Haley, Jr.* MR was one of eleven stars narrating scenes from MGM's best between '29 and '58 and talked about the movies he did with Garland. 132 m.

125. JOURNEY BACK TO OZ. Filmation, '74. Sp: Fred Ladd and Norm Prescott. *Hal Sutherland.* MR provided the voice of the Scarecrow in this animated feature (made in '63) about Dorothy and Toto's revisit to Oz. Voices: Liza Minnelli (Dorothy), Milton Berle (Cowardly Lion), Danny Thomas (The Tinman), Margaret Hamilton (Aunt Em), Paul Ford (Uncle Henry), Rise Stevens (Glinda, the Good Witch), Ethel Merman (Mombi, the Bad Witch) and Herschel Bernardi, Jack E. Leonard, Mel Blanc, Larry Storch. Songs by Sammy Cahn and James Van Heusen. 90 m.

126. BON BAISERS DE HONG KONG (FROM HONG KONG WITH LOVE). Films Christian Fechner-Renn Productions, '75. Sp: Christian Fechner and Yvan Chiffre. *Yvan Chiffre.* Les Charlots, Huguette Funfrok, David Tomlinson, Clifton James, Jean Manson. James Bond parody showcasing the popular French comedy foursome, looking for mad millionaire MR who has kidnapped the queen of Great Britain. 97 m.

127. RACHEL'S MAN. Afton Films/Hemdale, '75. Sp: Moshe Mizrahi and Rachel Fabien. *Moshe Mizrahi.* Rita Tushingham, Leonard Whiting, Michal Bat-Adam, Rachel Levi, Avner Hiskiyahu, Dahlia Cohen, Sari Shapira, Yair Reuben, Robert Stevens (narrator). Biblical drama about Jacob and Esau. MR is their uncle Laban. 111 m.

128. FIND THE LADY. Quadrant Films, '76. Sp: David Main and John Trent. *John Trent.* Lawrence Dane, John Candy, Dick Emery, Peter Cook, Alexandra Bastedo. Gangster comedy filmed in Canada. MR is an inept, gun-happy hood. 90 m.

129. THE DOMINO PRINCIPLE. Avco-Embassy, '77. Sp: Adam Kennedy, based on his novel. *Stanley Kramer.* Gene Hackman, Candice Bergen, Richard Widmark, Edward Albert, Eli Wallach, Ken Swofford, Neva Patterson. MR is the cell-mate of convict Hackman who's sprung with him to take part in highly secret job for a mysterious organization. 100 m.

130. PETE'S DRAGON. Buena Vista, '77. Sp: Malcolm Marmorstein from a story by Seton I. Miller and S. S. Field. *Don Chaffey.* Helen Reddy, Jim Dale, Red Buttons, Shelley Winters, Sean Marshall, Charlie Callas, Jim Backus, Jeff Conaway, Jane Kean. MR is a grizzled lighthouse keeper in Disney's live action/animated fantasy about a young orphan's adventures with an occasionally visible dragon named Elliott. 127 m.

131. THE MAGIC OF LASSIE. International Picture Show, '78. Sp: Jean Holloway, Rob't B. Sherman and Richard M. Sherman. *Don Chaffey.* Jas. Stewart, Pernell Roberts, Stephanie Zimbalist, Alice Faye, Michael Sharrett, Mike Mazurki, The Mike Curb Congregation, Lassie. MR is down-at-the-heels wrestling manager of Mazurki. 99 m.

132. DONOVAN'S KID. Buena Vista, '79. Sp: Harry Spalding from a story by Peter S. Fischer. *Bernard McEveety.* Darren McGavin, Shelley Fabares, Murray Hamilton, Michael Conrad, Ross Martin, Katy Kurtzman. MR is sidekick to con man McGavin in Disney's made-for-TV turn-of-the-century western. 99 m.

133. THE BLACK STALLION. Zoetrope/UA, '79. Sp: Melissa Mathison, Jeanne Rosenberg and William D. Wittliff, based on the novel by Walter Farley. *Carroll Ballard.* Kelly Reno, Teri Garr, Clarence Muse, Hoyt Axton, Michael Higgins. MR won a supporting actor Oscar nomination as the former jockey who takes in a runaway and his horse and teaches the boy to ride. 118 m.

134. ARABIAN ADVENTURE. Columbia/EMI, '79. Sp: Brian Hayles. *Kevin Connor.* Christopher Lee, Milo O'Shea, Oliver Tobias, Emma Samms, Peter Cushing, Capucine, Shane Rimmer, Puneet Sira, John Ratzenberger. Light-hearted Arabian Nights fantasy with MR as "guardian of the rose" and keeper of three fire-breathing monsters. 98 m.

135. MY KIDNAPPER, MY LOVE. Roger Gimbel Prod./EMI Television, '80. Sp: Louie Elias based on the novel *The Dark Side of Love* by Oscar Saul. *Sam Wanamaker.* Jas. Stacy, Glynnis O'Connor, J. D. Cannon, Jan Sterling, Richard Venture, Ellen Geer, Lonny Stevens. MR is a petty crook who talks his brother, a crippled newspaper vendor, into kidnapping a wealthy, emotionally disturbed runaway in a get-rich-quick scheme. TV movie. 105 m.

136. LEAVE 'EM LAUGHING. Chas. Fries Productions, '81. Sp: Cynthia Mandelberg and Peggy Chantler Dick, based on the life story of Jack Thum. *Jackie Cooper.* Anne Jackson, Allen Goorwitz, Elisha Cook, Red Buttons, Wm. Windom, Michael LeClair. MR plays Jack Thum in this true story of a failed Chicago clown and his devoted wife who become surrogate parents to thirty-seven orphaned and rejected children. TV movie. 105 m.

137. THE FOX AND THE HOUND. Buena Vista, '81. *Art Stevens, Ted Berman, and Richard Rich.* In Disney's animated version of Daniel P.

Mannix's children's classic, MR is the voice of Tod, the fox. Others supplying voices are Kurt Russell, Pearl Bailey, Jack Albertson, Sandy Duncan, Jeanette Nolan, Pat Buttram, John McIntire, John Fiedler, Paul Winchell. 93 m.

138. L'EMPEREUR DU PEROU (THE EMPEROR OF PERU). Cine-Pacific/Babylone Films, '81. Sp: Fernando Arrabal. *Fernando Arrabal.* Monique Mercure, Jean-Louis Roux, Guy Hoffman, Ky Houtuk, Ankk Jonathan Starr. MR is a former railroad engineer living in a wagon near an abandoned railway station who befriends three homeless youngsters. A Canadian/French co-production. 100 m.

139. BILL. Alan Landsburg Productions, '81. Sp: Corey Blechman, based on the story of Bill Sackter by Barry Morrow. *Anthony Page.* Dennis Quaid, Largo Woodruff, Harry Goz, Anna Maria Horsford, Kathleen Maguire, Jenny Dweir. MR won the Golden Globe Award as Best Actor for his playing of a mentally retarded adult who tackles life outside of the mental institution where he spent forty-four years. TV movie. 110 m.

140. SENIOR TRIP. QM/Kenneth Johnson Productions, '81. Sp: Kenneth Johnson and Dan Kibbie. *Kenneth Johnson.* Scott Baio, Fay Grant, Randy Brooks. MR does a cameo as himself in this made-for-TV comedy about a group of Midwestern high school seniors who come to New York City to commemorate their graduation. 105 m.

141. THE BLACK STALLION RETURNS. Zoetrope/UA, '82. Sp: Richard Kletter and Jerome Kass. *Robert Dalva.* Kelly Reno, Teri Garr, Jodi Thelen, Allen Goorwitz. MR recreates his role of ex-jockey/trainer Henry Dailey in this sequel to #133. 93 m.

142. BILL: ON HIS OWN. Alan Landsburg, '83. Sp: Barry Morrow. *Anthony Page.* Helen Hunt, Dennis Quaid, Teresa Wright. Further adventures of Bill Sackter. 100 m.

143. THE CARE BEARS MOVIE. Samuel Goldwyn Jr. '85. Sp: Peter Sauder. *Arna Selznick.* George Engel. Animated feature with MR as Mr. Cherrywood, telling bedtime stories about the Care Bears, who teach one lesson: never stop caring. 75 m.

144. IT CAME UPON A MIDNIGHT CLEAR. Columbia. '84. Sp: George Schenck and Frank Cardia. *Peter H. Hunt.* Scott Grimes, Barrie Youngfellow, Annie Potts, Gary Bayer. MR is a retired NYC detective who persuades his heavenly archangel to let him return to earth and help a wayward angel find the Christmas spirit. 100 m.

145. **BLUEGRASS**. Landsburg. '88. Sp: Mart Crowley. *Simon Wincer*. Cheryl Ladd, Wayne Rogers, Anthony Andrews, Dianne Ladd. Another racetrack picture, done as a four-hour miniseries for CBS. 210 m.

146. **ERIC THE VIKING**. UIP. '89. Sp: Terry Jones. *Terry Jones*. Tim Robbins, Eartha Kitt, Imogene Stubbs, John Cleese. Fantastic voyage of Vikings (including MR) who are sick of rape and pillage, looking for magic end to age of violence. 104 m.

147. **MY HEROES HAVE ALWAYS BEEN COWBOYS**. Martin Poll. '91. Sp: Joel Don Humphreys. *Stuart Rosenberg*. Scott Glenn, Kate Capshaw, Ben Johnson. Okies. 101 m.

Rooney's Two-Reelers

NOT TO BE TRUSTED. Fox, '26. Screenplay: Murray Roth from a story by Mabel Herbert Urner. *Thomas Buckingham*. Supervised by George E. Marshall. MR is a midget.

The Mickey McGuire Shorts

(1927–28, released by F.B.O.; 1929–33, released by Radio Pictures; 1934, released by Columbia Pictures.)

All were produced by Larry Darmour and directed by (variously) Albert Herman, Earl Montgomery and J. A. Duffy.

In the first, Rooney was billed as Mickey Yule. In the others, his billing was Mickey "Himself" McGuire. Beginning with *Mickey's Race* in '33, the billing was "Mickey McGuire, now known as Mickey Rooney."

1927: *Mickey's Circus, Mickey's Pals, Mickey's Battle, Mickey's Eleven.*

1928: *Mickey's Parade, Mickey in School, Mickey's Nine, Mickey's Little Eva, Mickey's Wild West, Mickey in Love, Mickey's Triumph, Mickey's Babies, Mickey's Movies, Mickey's Rivals, Mickey the Detective, Mickey's Athletes, Mickey's Big Game Hunt.*

Mickey Rooney also directed, but did not act in, *My True Story* (Columbia, '51) with Helen Walker, and he produced, but did not act in, *Jaguar* (Republic, '56) with Sabu. (Mickey McGuire also hosted one in the series of Columbia's *Screen Snapshots* in '34, a one-reeler with Lloyd Hughes, Marie Prevost, Mary Pickford, Dolores Del Rio, Douglas Fairbanks, Louis Wolheim, others.)

1929: *Mickey's Great Idea, Mickey's Explorers, Mickey's Menagerie, Mickey's Last Chance, Mickey's Brown Derby* (first in sound), *Mickey's Northwest Mounted, Mickey's Initiation, Mickey's Midnight Follies, Mickey's Surprise, Mickey's Mixup, Mickey's Big Moment.*

1930: *Mickey's Champs, Mickey's Strategy, Mickey's Mastermind, Mickey's Luck, Mickey's Whirlwind, Mickey's Warriors, Mickey the Romeo, Mickey's Merry Men, Mickey's Winners, Mickey's Musketeers, Mickey's Bargain.*

1931: *Mickey's Stampede, Mickey's Crusaders, Mickey's Rebellion, Mickey's Diplomacy, Mickey's Wildcats, Mickey's Thrill Hunters, Mickey's Helping Hand, Mickey's Sideline* (Mickey and the Toonerville Kids get boxing pointers from heavyweight champ Jim Jeffries.)

1932: *Mickey's Travels, Mickey's Holiday, Mickey's Golden Rule, Mickey's Busy Day, Mickey's Charity, Mickey's Big Business.*

1933: *Mickey's Ape Man, Mickey's Race, Mickey's Big Broadcast, Mickey's Disguises, Mickey's Touchdown, Mickey's Tent Show, Mickey's Covered Wagon.*

1934: *Mickey's Minstrels, Mickey's Rescue, Mickey's Medicine Man.*

Some of the shorts were compiled into a feature, *Mickey's Derby Day,* 1936.

Afterword

Someone once told me that I would fly as high as those around me wanted me to fly. Well, over my almost three score and ten years in show business, I've had more than my share of friends who wanted me to soar like an eagle (and a few waiting in the blinds to down me), and you've met many of them in these pages. But it is difficult—no, impossible—to weave into a few hundred pages of one book all the names of all the people who kept cheering me on, and who, therefore, occupy such a fond place in my memory. I'd like to tell you now that I didn't really forget you. You just ended up on the cutting-room floor.

You know who you are. But, for the edification of my readers, I'd like to name you now—even at the risk of forgetting some who belong here.

Oh yes, there's my mother-in-law, Helen Chamberlin, my late father-in-law, John Chamberlin, and my sister-in-law Ronna Riley. My wife Jan's two sons, Chris and Mark Aber. Billy Barty, president of the Little People's Clubs of America. Dan Tabas, Harry Copeland, and Sam Taubman, three wise (business) men from the East, my lawyer friend from Chicago Mel

Weisberg, my lawyer friend from Wyoming Gerry Spence (who there's no beating), and Marvin Davis, the tycoon of Denver.

People from "the business" who are special friends: notably Stanley Kramer, Brandon Tartikoff, Michael King, Marcy Carsey, Alan Landsburg, Len Miller, and Martin Poll. My friends from the world of Broadway: James Nederlander; Hugh Martin, the songwriter; Ernie Flatt, the choreographer; Bill Asher, the producer.

My golfing buddies, Dick Whittinghill, Jack Burke, Jr., the late Jimmy Demaret, Arnold Palmer, Fuzzy Zoeller, and George Von Ell, and my New Jersey golfing partner, Mo Nagiyama.

My Los Angeles Laker connections: Pat Riley, Magic Johnson, and Kareem Abdul-Jabbar. And Hank Stram, who's a helluva good broadcaster but should really be back coaching in the NFL. And another great coach, George Allen, whom the world will miss very much, because he showed us how anybody can win, as long as they're willing to work eighteen hours a day.

My colleagues in the music business: Tony Bennett, Michel Legrand, Henry Mancini, Burt Bacharach, Marty Hamlisch, and Stephen Sondheim.

My friends in the comedy business: Jonathan Winters, Milton Berle, Red Buttons, Buddy Hackett, Syd and Marty Kroft, and Sid Caesar.

My racetrack buddies: a bettor named Walter Matthau (who also happens to be a very fine actor), the trainer Charlie Whittinghill, jockeys Willie Shoemaker, Don Pierce, Eddie Arcaro, Marje Everett, and R. D. Hubbard of Hollywood Park, the entire Strub Family of Santa Anita, and my fellow thoroughbred owners Alfred Gwynne Vanderbilt, Alair DuPont, and Viola Summers.

And I cannot forget some of my writer friends: Monroe Manning, Maurice Schisgall, Neil Simon, Julie Styne, Sid Kuller, Ernie Weidner, Irv Kupcinet and his wife, Effie, and my radio buddy from Chicago's WGN, Wally Phillips, all very good listeners.

And, finally, my TV friends: Johnny Carson, Arsenio Hall, Merv Griffin, and Joe Di Angelo, the president of King Features, who keeps wanting to bring a cartoon character named Jiggs to a new life on TV. That would be a gas because my dad, Joe Yule, played Jiggs in the movies eons ago.

Index